Innovative Presentations

FOR

DUMMIES®

A Wiley Brand

WITHDRAWN

by Ray Anthony and Barbara Boyd

Contents at a Glance

Table of Contents

Introduction

· ·

*S*ooner or later in your professional life, regardless of your profession or position, you'll have to give that really important presentation. Or perhaps giving presentations is your profession and you're looking for new ideas and a razor sharp added edge to boost your already successful career. This book focuses on several distinct and unique aspects of the arc of creating a presentation: topic selection, audience analysis, visual design, and delivery technology and techniques — and imaginative ideas and strategies. This book brings together the latest presentation tactics and technologies to help nascent, casual, and experienced presenters — whichever you might be — develop, write, and give innovative, stimulating presentations, and most important, presentations that give you over the top results — consistently.

About This Book

More than 20 years ago, PowerPoint revolutionized presentations. If you ever used 35-millimeter slides and overhead transparencies to show visuals along with your spoken presentations, you know how drastically PowerPoint changed things: You could do the visuals yourself without sending out files to be developed on slides, you could use as many fonts and colors as your computer allowed, and you could tweak your presentation right up to the few seconds before you gave it.

In the last five years or so, presentation style has evolved once again due to technological developments and research into how people learn and absorb information. If you're using text-heavy bulleted lists and complex charts and graphs, this book introduces you to the new style of presentations that incorporate video, single striking images, few (but very impacting) words, animation, and augmented reality. Rather than listening to one talking head for 45 minutes, speakers and actions change every ten minutes or so to appease the audience's multitasking, easily distracted attention span.

This book shows you how to design and deliver presentations that use the newest technologies and take advantage of what we know about learning to keep the audience's attention. The parts flow in a chronological order, taking you from audience analysis to idea development, to presentation design, and finally how to use the technology, including computers, projectors, tablets, and various presentation apps to deliver your presentation by yourself or with a team. Each chapter, however, is written to stand alone so you can choose a topic that most interests or serves you and start there — you don't have to read cover to cover.

We provide questionnaires, flow charts, and tools to assist you in each step of creating your presentation. Throughout the book we include scenarios that exemplify the techniques we talk about, along with many figures to better illustrate our points. You can adapt these for your own uses or use them as inspiration to create your own innovative presentations.

Within this book, you may note that some web addresses break across two lines of text. If you're reading this book in print and want to visit one of these web pages, simply key in the web address exactly as it's noted in the text, as though the line break doesn't exist. If you're reading this as an e-book, you have it easy — just click the web address to be taken directly to the web page.

Foolish Assumptions

In writing this book, we made a few assumptions about you, dear reader. To make sure that we're on the same page, we assume that

- ✔ You work in a sales, marketing, or entrepreneurial capacity and have some experience talking with other professionals and clients about your product or service.
- ✔ You make presentations to colleagues, peers, potential and existing clients, or investors to train, sell products or services, and close deals.
- ✔ You want to significantly improve the results and audience response you receive when you make a presentation.
- ✔ You've used, or have an idea of how to use, a computer and presentation apps, such as PowerPoint or Keynote, but are frustrated with the ho-hum appearance of your visuals.
- ✔ You have at least a general concept of the phenomenon known as the Web (or, more formally, the World Wide Web).
- ✔ You acknowledge that it's up to you to go on the Web to find updated information about the products described throughout this book.
- ✔ You appreciate — or roll your eyes at — our goofy sense of humor and sometimes exaggerated scenarios.
- ✔ You want to create engaging, compelling, and spectacular presentations that demonstrate your innovative, creative, and problem-solving spirit.
- ✔ You know that your authors' names are Ray and Barbara, so that when you encounter a story that starts out, "When Ray presented to a herd of Tasmanian devils . . ." you wonder about Tasmania and not who Ray is.

Icons Used in This Book

To help emphasize certain information, this book displays different icons in the page margins.

The Tip icon points out useful bits of information that can help you do things more efficiently or explain something helpful that you might not know. Sometimes Tips give you another way of doing a task explained previously.

Remember icons mark the information that's particularly important to consider or that has been mentioned previously. This icon often points out useful information that isn't threatening, like a Warning, but should be factored into your preparation.

This icon highlights interesting information that you don't necessarily need to know but that can help explain why certain things work the way they do or why people behave the way they do. Feel free to skip this information if you're in a hurry, but browse through this information when you have time.

Watch out! This icon highlights something that can damage your presentation or reputation — don't worry, there aren't too many in this book. Make sure that you read any Warning information before following any instructions.

Beyond the Book

If we'd put all the data we had into this book, you'd be holding a thousand-page tome in your hands. We trimmed and edited and pulled out only the most relevant information, however, some innovative items remain that we want to share with you. Go to `http://www.dummies.com` to find the following:

- **Cheat Sheet:** (`www.dummies.com/cheatsheet/innovative presentations`) We put some goodies online for you, including the Innovative Presentation Model, which you can print out, laminate, and hang next to your workspace to refer to while you're planning your presentations. You can also find an audience analysis grid and an itemized evaluation sheet, which guides you and your colleagues to provide feedback to each other when rehearsing team presentations.

- **Dummies.com online articles:** (`www.dummies.com/extras/innovative presentations`) We give you several articles that supplement the information in the book. You can read about boosting your strategic thinking, check out tips for presenting in a different language, and learn a quick trick for improving scientific presentations — plus a couple other surprises.

Where to Go from Here

Like all *For Dummies* books, you can begin reading at page 1 or dive in at page 100, depending on your experience with presentations and your immediate interests.

For example, if you'll be attending a networking event soon, flip to Chapter 22 to learn about composing an *elevator pitch*, which is a very brief description of you, your job, and your company all told in pithy prose from the listener's point of view. If that doesn't pique your interest about that chapter, we don't know what will.

If you find you have a hard time reading people, check out Chapter 4, which guides you through analyzing your audience and quickly identifying personality types and the best way to speak to each, as well as how to work the room when there's more than one type present.

If you want to understand what an innovative presentation is, start with Chapter 2, which introduces the concepts that we explore throughout the rest of the book. And, to find out about using the latest technology for your presentations, Chapters 17, 18, and 19 talk about presentation apps, hardware, and future technologies.

Part I

Getting Started with Innovative Presentations

In this part . . .

- ✔ Learn about the different types of innovative presentations.

- ✔ Create clear, concise messages.

- ✔ Understand key presentation elements.

- ✔ Discover why innovation matters.

- ✔ Find ways innovation transforms traditional presentations.

- ✔ Examine the traits of innovative presenters.

- ✔ Evaluate your presentations with specific performance indicators.

Chapter 1

Winning Traits of Innovative Presentations

In This Chapter

▶ Identifying the type of presentation

▶ Striving for effectiveness and efficiency

▶ Delivering a clear, concise message

▶ Understanding the three key presentation elements

A formal presentation is when you make a speech at a conference or introduce your product or service to a potential client, in each case accompanied by visuals in the form of slides, videos, or props. However, when you hone your presentation skills, you find you can use them when you talk about a project in a staff meeting, when you introduce yourself at a networking event, or when you ask for donations for your favorite charity. In this chapter, we outline the different types of business presentations and introduce you to the concepts that make an innovative presentation, which we cover in depth in other chapters of this book.

Understanding the Different Types of Business Presentations

In business, any structured conversation with a specific goal and strategy can be construed as a presentation, however informal.

For example, when someone asks, "What do you do?" you present yourself in what we refer to as an *elevator pitch* — a brief, 30- to 60-second introduction that prompts the listener to say, "Tell me more." Or, when you want to convince your manager to increase the budget to hire a social networking specialist, even if it's an informal conversation, you must present your idea and the potential return on investment.

The following list defines the most common types of business presentations. The steps to creating the presentations listed here are the same, but the objectives and delivery vary. We made this a comprehensive list; however, you may know of other kinds of presentations, too.

- **Boardroom:** When you come face-to-face with the executive staff of your company or of a (potential) client, you must prepare yourself for acute scrutiny. Your presentation should include high-level information, but you must be ready to provide details if asked. More than in any other type of presentation, you need to be precise and concise when making a boardroom presentation.

- **Conceptual:** When you have an idea that's yet to come to fruition, you present a concept. However, you don't throw out your concept willy-nilly, you need to think about and consider your ideas. A conceptual presentation often includes plenty of time for discussion with the audience, as they usually have questions and feedback, which help you better define your idea.

- **Elevator pitch:** The most succinct, yet in some ways most difficult, presentation lasts not more than about one to two minutes. In that short time, you should be able to clearly describe yourself, your product or service — with wit and aplomb. (We tell you how to compose your elevator pitch in Chapter 21.)

- **Financial/operational:** The challenge with a financial or operational presentation lies in making numbers interesting. Of course, if you're talking about a 400 percent increase in profits, you have it easy, otherwise, you need to incorporate graphs and visuals that keep your audience interested. With these presentations, you generally discuss outcomes, trends, relationships, causes and effects, implications, and likely consequences shown by the numbers.

We recommend Perspective (`http://pixxa.com/perspective`), which turns your numbers into interesting charts and graphs. The app itself is free; you purchase the graphs that you create or purchase a yearly subscription.

- **Formal/informal:** Most presentations fall into one of these two categories, determined by many factors such as the industry, your familiarity with the audience, your presentation goal, and the setting.

Informal doesn't mean sloppy; even in an informal, more conversational and discussion-oriented presentation, you should show up prepared and be polite and professional.

- **Informational:** Most presentations convey information, but in an informational presentation, the objective is to — drum roll, please — share information that an audience needs and wants and will use in some fashion in their job. If you conduct research and then present the results at a professional conference, your aim is to give an unbiased, informational presentation.

- **Motivational:** If you're asked to give a keynote speech at an event, chances are you'll give a motivational presentation. Your presentation will contain several personal anecdotes, examples, and memorable stories that your audience can relate to — probably of how you faced a difficult situation, overcame it, and what you learned from it. You want to convey enthusiasm and passion about your topic and instill inspiration in your audience.

- **Persuasive:** As opposed to the informational presentation, here you build your case — in a methodical, studied manner — and end with a call to action, which may be to persuade a potential client to hire your firm, a venture capitalist to fund your idea, or your manager to promote you to a higher position.

- **Planning:** If you manage a team or committee, planning presentations is a key element of your responsibilities. Although often informal and conducted in a meeting setting rather than a formal presentation setting, you need to be prepared to state the current situation, the situation you want to create, and the steps to get from the first to the second. You need to persuade others to buy in to your plan — or contribute to developing it — and to participate and complete their assigned action items.

- **Progress updates:** When you give a progress update, whether to colleagues or to a client, you give more than a simple state-of-affairs presentation. If you have to report a delay, you want to explain the reasons and provide a solution; likewise, if you're ahead of schedule or under budget, you want to highlight the good news.

- **Solutions:** When you sell a product or service, what you really sell is a solution to a problem the audience, customer, or client is experiencing. Although all presentations should be developed with the audience in mind, that consideration is the foundation of the solutions presentation. We dedicate Chapter 20 to selling solutions.

- **Technical:** Technical presentations can be some of the most interesting to prepare and the most entertaining to watch. Convey enthusiasm about the process or product you discuss and display great visuals that take advantage of the latest technologies available and you'll have the audience on the edge of their seats.

The presentation types aren't mutually exclusive. For example, you can give a conceptual boardroom presentation to venture capitalists.

Rewards of your halo effect

Why the extreme fascination and adulation with famous actors, singers, and other celebrities? Singer Katy Perry has over 50 million followers on Twitter! Many of us tend to put famous people on a pedestal simply because of the roles they play on television, in movies, or on stage. There's something larger than life about seeing a person brilliantly act out a character who conquers fear, does amazing stunts, becomes a heroine, saves the day, or is the romantic swashbuckler who wins the hand of the fair maiden on the big screen.

Yet in real life, these talented folks are generally fairly average, not very educated or too exciting, and in some cases quite shy and insecure. But being an impressive performer gives celebrities a *halo effect,* whereby, because you see them in fictional contrived situations, you attribute all sorts of positive traits to them that aren't necessarily justified. Just because someone plays a brilliant doctor on television doesn't make him smart, but the halo effect of repeatedly seeing him perform brilliant diagnoses and surgical miracles every week means that the perceived characteristic is often attached to him and follows him in real life.

There is also a positive halo effect associated with being a terrific innovative presenter, and it can be a real and justified image. Being an articulate, poised, and polished speaker does wonders for your public image. In many instances, people view you as a competent and passionate leader — a person of action who gets impressive results. Depending on your presentation, they may be impressed with you as a visionary, grand strategist, innovator, technical expert, or problem solver. Because you gave a motivational, inspirational, and entertaining keynote speech, your status and credibility are elevated. If you give an impassioned presentation advocating a noble cause, you may find yourself being featured in numerous newspaper or magazine articles and suddenly being invited to talk on the major broadcast and cable networks.

Becoming that special innovator presenter — a consummate performer who communicates in different and immensely better ways than other speakers — will change your career and life. You'll find people clamoring to get your advice, beckoning you to be involved in new business ventures, and eagerly inviting you to talk at major conferences or social events. There is usually no quicker and surefire way to catapult you up the career ladder of success than to give a blockbuster presentation in front of the senior executives in your company. This book shows you how to outperform all other presenters and light up that warranted halo.

Finding Common Characteristics of Consistently Winning Presentations

Regardless of type, presentations share a similar flow and format, and preparing for them with our proven method results in an innovative, winning presentation every time.

Factoring for effectiveness and efficiency

The recurring message you hear when talking to people is "I'm so busy." With that in mind, when someone gives you the time and respect to attend and listen to your presentation, you owe it to them to be as effective and efficient in your delivery as possible.

In order to be effective, you must leave your ego and needs at the door and consider your audience. Your presentation is not an opportunity to boast about your accomplishments, but an invitation to provide useful information or a solution that makes the audience's life easier.

Your efficiency will be appreciated and remembered. Although people may remember a windbag, they probably won't remember what he said. Keep your statements simple and tell them in a logical order. By all means, tell a story — people remember stories better than charts and bulleted lists — but make sure the story is relevant to and conveys your message.

While developing your presentation, you can make bulleted lists if that's the way you think about things, but then come up with a story or anecdote that relates the same information. If that's not possible, rather than one slide with five bullets, make one visual for each bullet and display a single image that's relevant to the point.

We say it for the first time here, and you'll read it repeatedly throughout this book: rehearse, rehearse, rehearse. With good preparation and consistent practice leading up to the actual presentation, you'll deliver a natural presentation without hesitation and in keeping with the established time limit.

Different types of presentations require different intensity of rehearsal. If you must present your status report at a staff meeting, gathering your notes a day or two before and doing a quick run through is probably enough to make sure you present in a logical order, whereas for a keynote that uses multiple types of technology in front of several hundred people, you may need more than 20 hours of rehearsal. (Chapter 8 explains rehearsal methods.)

Remembering the Five Cs: Being clear, concise, compelling, captivating, and convincing

In addition to being effective and efficient, any presentation you make should pass the Five C's test.

Your presentation should be:

- ✔ **Clear:** Use words and speech your audience understands. Jargon is fine for an industry or staff meeting, but if you have any doubt your audience is familiar with a term, either don't use it or define it immediately upon using it.

  Make your points in a logical order. You can make your introduction, briefly tell your conclusion, and then explain how you get from the beginning to the end — this style sets an expectation and curiosity for the audience, and gets them wondering and paying attention to see how you prove your point.

- ✔ **Concise:** "Brevity is the soul of wit," wrote Shakespeare in *Hamlet,* and his point holds true today. In other words, say what you have to say in as few words as possible. People will love you for that! Preparing an elevator pitch is an excellent exercise in being concise, and we explain how to do that in Chapter 21.

- ✔ **Compelling:** A compelling presentation, by its very definition, is irresistible! Use your words, voice, visuals, and powerful information to demand and deserve total interest. If you show enthusiasm and interest in your subject, your audience will mimic you. Throughout the book we give you specific tactics for vocalization, gesturing, and using creativity and technology that rivets your audience's attention.

- ✔ **Captivating:** A compelling presentation is typically about information that is powerfully convincing, but a captivating speaker holds an audience spellbound with his energy, passion, charisma, and stage presence. As a captivating speaker, you keep the presentation moving forward filled with anticipation, you tell impacting stories and incorporate stunning video, guest speakers, and/or audience activities. The audience can't wait to find out what's going to happen next.

- ✔ **Convincing:** When all is said and done, this last point ultimately determines the success or failure of your presentation. Have you swayed the audience to your point of view? Have you persuaded your audience to buy what you're selling?

For important speeches, one of the best ways to determine whether your presentation meets these criteria is to videotape yourself and do a self-evaluation; even better is to ask someone similar in position or mindset to your audience to listen and give you honest, constructive feedback. Again, even brief, informal presentations, such as those you give at staff meetings, should meet these criteria — even recording yourself with the camera on your computer or smart device can be helpful to see and hear how you appear and sound.

Combining the Message, Messenger, and Medium

Your presentations have three components:

- **Message:** What is said.
- **Messenger:** Who says it.
- **Medium:** How it's said.

A successful presentation combines these three elements seamlessly to create a coherent argument.

Creating the message

Your message — what's often referred to as *content* — can be simple or complex or somewhere in-between, but it should always be relevant to your audience's needs and be structured to satisfy the Five C's mentioned in the previous section (clear, concise, compelling, captivating, convincing). Sometimes, the audience need only know what's going on, other times you want to give them a call to action.

If you were stranded on an island and decide to put a message in a bottle in the hopes of being saved, which message is more effective:

- I'm on an island in the South Pacific.
- I'm stranded on an island in the South Pacific; come find me, please!

When the first message washes up on shore somewhere in Australia, the reader might think, "Oh, how cute, a message in a bottle." Whereas after the second message is read, the Coast Guard will be on their way.

Your message must align with the audience's needs: if they want only information, give that; if they want a solution — which is more likely the case — provide a solution or a call to action that can bring them the solution.

Prepping the messenger

As the presenter, you are the messenger. If you work in sales, your message may have been prepared by someone else, and you must practice and deliver it as if it's part of your DNA. If you create your presentations, you have the advantage of knowing your material, or researching it, while you develop the message and accompanying visuals.

Choosing the medium

The technological options available for how you present your message can be overwhelming, but it pays you to choose carefully. In some circumstances, your voice and posture provide an adequate medium. For example, if you have 30 seconds to introduce yourself, and you pull out a pico projector attached to your smartphone to show a video, your time is up before your video begins. In an informal progress update meeting where you have 15 minutes to talk about the status of a construction site, quickly setting up your pico projector and smartphone to show photos you took on your way to the meeting adds interesting proof to back up your words. Pull out your pico projector and smartphone in front of 300 people in a conference hall, however, and you risk being laughed off the stage.

Not only do you want the right equipment for the presentation, you also have to feel comfortable using it. You can reach a comfort level through practice and rehearsal, but if, for instance, you don't feel ready to command your visuals from a tablet and have remote speakers broadcast into your presentation, choose one option at a time and add them as they become familiar. We talk about technology options in Chapters 18 and 19.

The technology should support and enhance your message; if it distracts or overwhelms your message, don't use it.

Chapter 2

Communicating Innovatively

· ·

· ·

*I*nnovative presentations are *different* and *better*.

How different and how much better depends upon how you oh-so-ingeniously combine and use technology and creativity — along with solid, established presentation techniques — to transform your presentation into a communications work of art. Some innovative presentations use subtle, indirect, and sophisticated methods while other innovative presentations take advantage of special, power-packed speaking techniques, cool resources, and visual dynamite that explodes from the screen with a persuasive shockwave radiating outward to your audience.

The broad spectrum of your innovative presentations can range from being creatively mild-to-wild and make your talk interesting, fascinating, compelling, entertaining, and captivating. And when needed, you can accompany your presentation with deeply warm, heartstring-pulling elements of unforgettable emotion.

Today's technology and software encourage you to create stunning visuals and enable you to translate and communicate your ideas and visions into practical, profitable business. But don't think for a moment that an innovative presentation is simply a jacked-up and dressed-up version of other presentations or that it has more fluff than stuff. On the contrary, from a business perspective, your innovative presentation can be ultra-professional and cold-bloodedly efficient and effective, giving you over-the-top results you've only dreamed of before.

J. Paul Getty, the famous American industrialist who was considered the world's richest private citizen during his time, boldly said, "No one can possibly achieve real or lasting success or get rich in business by becoming a conformist." In this chapter we show you how to break the existing rules, make new ones, and reinvent your presentations.

No amount of creativity and technology can save a poorly designed, organized, or delivered presentation, but they can dramatically improve a presentation that has a solid foundation, content, and strategy.

Changing with the Times

Like the famous Ford Model T car when it came out in 1908, PowerPoint was an exciting breakthrough when it was released in May of 1990. Ford's brilliant assembly line turned out cars that offered affordable travel to nearly every middle-class person, and PowerPoint opened up possibilities for visual presentations by practically everyone. PowerPoint, like the Model T, added new features and got a little bit better with each new generation. Ford, though, refused to come out with a fresh new car when competitors were innovating like crazy. This industrial giant and visionary, who birthed an entire industry, saw no need to change and almost lost his company. It was ultimately his son Edsel and Ford executives who forced Henry Ford to allow the long-overdue creation of a new Model A sedan, which became a top seller. PowerPoint today is the digital equivalent of the Model T, unchanged to a major degree 20 years after its debut.

Modern presentations lie trapped in a black hole of text-heavy slides read by presenters. Although widespread innovations occur just about everywhere else in business and industry, presentations are stuck, stale, and stagnant. Most people design and give cookie-cutter presentations using templates and formats that haven't evolved in decades. Although PowerPoint offers more features than the 35-millimeter slides used by presenters 30 years ago, often presenters use PowerPoint simply as a digital replacement for slides.

What's more, people don't say they're giving a presentation; they announce they are giving a "PowerPoint presentation," which often involves the use of unnecessary animations, transitions, cheesy stock images, silly sounds, and other bells and whistles that only distract and annoy the audience. Even when you use PowerPoint correctly, it limits your creativity because it is about creating a slide presentation, not about making a presentation using slides — or better yet visuals. There's a huge difference between the two.

The future belongs to changing the way you communicate with your audience and to new presentation apps that focus on well-designed visuals, photos, video, and 3-D renderings and animations. These interactive, flexible apps enable you to randomly navigate around your talk easily and seamlessly.

Defining innovation

Many people incorrectly associate innovation exclusively with technology. Although technology is definitely a critical aspect of most types of innovation, including presentations, other factors contribute to a broad definition of innovation.

Innovation is the application, implementation or commercialization of imaginative and visionary ideas, plans, strategies, and concepts.

In addition to innovative technologies, there are also innovative processes, operations, systems, business models, management techniques, strategies, and more. And now there are innovative presentations. For example, with the advances in social media, new web-style advertising, augmented reality, and various other digital outlets, marketing has become ever more innovative compared to old-style print or broadcast media. Virtual selling is becoming more widespread with all the video, meeting, and communications apps that reduce the need to travel and meet face-to-face. People can learn about your products and services just from watching YouTube (www.youtube.com), Vimeo (https://vimeo.com), or other video-laden websites.

Often the terms *creative* and *innovative* are used interchangeably and that's fine, although many people still primarily associate *creative* with somehow being artistic, while the term *innovative* is generally perceived as having a more practical and useful business-related application and benefit. Creativity is really about coming up with novel, original, and useful ideas for anything. But unless you do something with that idea — turn it into a new product, service, business model, or way of giving mind-blowing presentations — it's just that: an idea in your head, or on paper, or in your computer. What innovators do is to take their ideas and as quickly and effectively as they can, turn them into valuable contributions to their business, industry, or area of expertise. Creativity is about imaginative thinking; innovating is about doing and making money from ideas.

What it means to be an innovator

Innovators, by their very nature, crave change that makes a difference. Some are futurists and visionaries. None, though, are blind followers of old, outdated ideas. But, each has either a little bit or a whole lot of being a maverick, a contrarian, a bold and daring nontraditionalist who pushes the boundaries of imagination, limits, and possibilities. Some are proud to call themselves crazy enough and driven enough to do the impossible. Most are never quite satisfied, even with excellence — they are looking for the next transcendent achievement. They echo what Dmitri Shostakovich, the renowned Russian composer and pianist said, "A creative artist works on his next composition because he was not satisfied with his previous one."

Innovators live by the philosophy that there are always better ways to do something, and in this case, an immensely better way to design and deliver presentations.

Monica W., an executive in a leading aviation firm that manufactures business jets and other smaller aircraft, was asked by her friend, a professor in the MBA program of a prestigious West Coast university, to give a presentation about business strategies. Monica decided to use a clever prop she bought online from a company called Laserlyte (www.laserlyte.com), thinking it would add a memorable focus on strategy. At the beginning of her university talk, she discussed both broad strategies and narrow strategies and wanted to imaginatively emphasize that tightly aimed and focused strategies that hit the bull's-eye for customers are the most useful. So, on a table about ten feet away, she set up what looked like six soda cans with a red circle in the middle of each. Monica then pulls out a blue plastic target pistol that fires a red laser beam. She says, "Remember that a targeted strategy aimed directly at your goal will often give you the best results." With that, she rapidly fires the fake pistol and knocks down all six of the cans in a row. (Each can is battery powered with a small piston that comes out of the bottom and causes the can to fall over when the laser hits the circle on the can.) Monica then asks two volunteers to come down from the large classroom to try their luck and both do well, further reinforcing the point of aiming for a precise target. This is just one simple example out of practically limitless ways to add some relevant and fun elements of creativity to your presentations.

Little bits of creativity throughout your presentation give it an innovative flavor.

Why innovation matters to business

An innovative company demands and deserves to give innovative presentations! And a company striving to brand itself as innovative would surely benefit from giving an ultra-creative knock-your-socks-off series of presentations to its customers and the public.

Innovation is hot, even if some journalists defined it as one of 2013's most overused (and perhaps in too many cases, undeserved) words. Just look at the explosion of books on the topic, and the use of the word in advertisements on the web, in papers, and on television. Countries such as China, Korea, Russia, Singapore, Israel, and Japan spend untold billions to build and expand innovative research-and-development centers for materials science, nanotechnology, and other exotic and promising developments that will create new and exciting industries.

Whether touting innovation in their cars and trucks, airplanes, computers, or tablets or announcing advances in the fields of medicine, engineering, science, finance, banking, or education, corporations and organizations proudly hail the innovation of their products, services, and people and boast about how much money and effort they devote to leading-edge research and development. These innovations enable them to better delight their customers while giving the company an impressive competitive edge. Various studies confirm that innovative companies prosper more and get a higher return than their less innovative counterparts.

Describing the Innovative Presentation

Have you ever thought about how you might define and describe the ideal presentation — the innovative type — that gets you spectacular, over-the-top results on a regular basis? First, it's helpful to understand the two primary metrics critical in any innovative presentation — effectiveness and efficiency. Understanding these metrics enables you to better appreciate the dynamic power and raw impact of giving an innovative presentation to any audience on any topic. We also discuss some characteristics of an innovative presentation so that you can determine how your presentation stacks up.

Effectiveness is the most critical factor about innovative presentations. Effectiveness means getting the best results from your presentations, results far superior to those you got from your former presentations and better than any of your competitors. It's about reaching or exceeding your goals and objectives. Who cares if your innovative presentation is more clever, enjoyable, interesting, fascinating, or captivating? Sure, that's desirable in itself, but a highly effective presentation is about unrivaled success for you and your audience.

Picture being able to close 10, 20, 30 percent or more sales as a result of giving a competitive wrecking ball of a presentation. Imagine closing more huge deals, especially with customers you've never previously had any success with — customers that formerly eluded you and your company? If you're a professional or aspiring speaker, wouldn't it be grand to get more goose bumps creating standing ovations because you not just did a superb job informing, inspiring, and motivating, but you also marvelously entertained the crowd?

If you're a corporate trainer, can you see how imaginative ideas can add to your presentations, activities, case studies, learning games, and participant exercises? And, if you're a political, community, non-profit, or association leader, envision how your creatively unique, exciting speech will get your audiences marching to your requests or toward your plan. The primary goal of developing and delivering those innovative talks is to radically improve the effectiveness of your presentations to give you more and immensely better results. It's as simple as that.

Efficiency generally means achieving maximum effectiveness with minimum effort, time, or resources. As comedian Dennis Miller notes, "The average American attention span is that of a ferret on a double espresso." The fact is, whether you're giving a presentation, lecture, or sermon, the longer it lasts, the more audience attention fades. So, if you can get your major points across in 30 minutes instead of an hour, you stand a greater chance of keeping interest high and achieving your goals.

Technology, such as the wireless interactive presentation gateway devices from wePresent (www.wepresentus.com), will dramatically boost both presentation effectiveness and efficiency, especially when giving interactive presentations in meetings or in training situations. (See Chapter 18 to learn more about innovative hardware.)

Showing and reading text slides is the least efficient way of communicating business, financial, technical, engineering or scientific ideas, designs, plans, proposed solutions, or strategies. Creative use of great examples, profound metaphors, and relevant stories enables you to simplify complex topics and do so more efficiently.

But the real way to boost efficiency in your innovative presentations is through proper use of photos, illustrations, diagrams, video, 3-D animations, virtual walkthroughs, and, now, augmented reality. Digital technology enables you to vastly improve both effectiveness and efficiency of communication. For example, if you see a photo-realistic 3-D animation of a machine, process, or chemical reaction, you can understand it immensely better and quicker than someone simply describing it with words on a slide or even a static illustration. These are visual digital jackhammers that can shatter any confusion, lack of understanding, or ambiguity about certain topics. 3-D rendering and animation software programs such as SolidWorks, Autodesk, Bryce, Maya, and LightWave are incredible visual tools to bring abstract concepts and designs to life in such realistic ways that were never possible before 3-D computer graphics, rendering, and animation were available. Google "3D architectural virtual tours" or "3D walkthrough animation presentations" to understand how incredibly efficient 3-D can be for communicating building, landscape, decorating, and interior designs for residential or commercial buildings. (Go to www.icreate3d.com to see incredible examples of what we mean.)

Then there are the commercial 3-D printers that can print multiple materials such as metal, plastic, rubber, concrete, plaster, and more to create real prototype products. Instead of showing photos or even impressive 3-D renderings of new design sunglasses to potential buyers in your presentation, for example, you can give them several attractive pairs you printed out the day before. Now, people can touch them, put them on to see how they fit and look so they can judge whether they like them enough to order those styles.

Innovative presentations, mostly using digital technology, enable you to present in an ultra-efficient way to communicate a lot, and a lot better, in a minimum period of time. You can't do that with text slides or words alone. Being creatively efficient enables people in your audience to clearly and precisely understand your ideas, main points and key messages in ways that enable them to make more informed and faster decisions.

Using the innovation process

How do you go about reimagining, reinventing, and remaking your presentation? Figure 2-1 shows you the four basic steps to do it. These steps outline the innovation process and are followed by several examples.

Innovative Presentations Model & Process

Creativity + Technology to Develop Superior Communication Effectiveness, Efficiency, and Quality

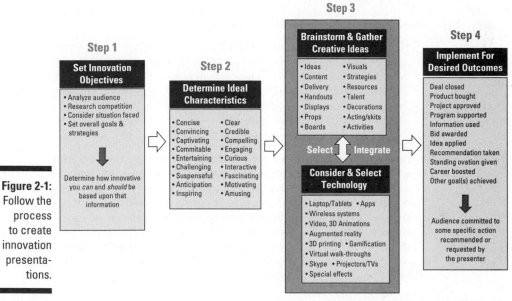

Figure 2-1: Follow the process to create innovation presentations.

Illustration courtesy of Ray Anthony and Barbara Boyd

1. Set innovative objectives.

Every presentation should involve the basics of analyzing your audience, the situation you're dealing with, the likely competition you're facing, and the goals you set for getting your intended results. After you do that, you can figure out just how innovative your presentation needs to be to reach your goals. Innovative presentations often take more time and resources to be effective. Why use a sledgehammer when a light tap will do? If you stand little initial chance of winning your audience over, you have nothing to lose if you engineer a bold and daringly different presentation.

2. **Determine the ideal characteristics of your presentation.**

   Take a look at the various combinations of characteristics you need to reach your goals. Essentially all good presentations should be clear, concise, and convincing, right? But, what if you're giving a sales presentation for an important deal, for example, and you're going against two brutal competitors who have an edge to win the deal? That's when you also have to communicate in a captivating, compelling, and ultra-credible fashion to make your presentation blow away your competitors. If you're giving a motivational talk, you may have to ramp up the inspiring, amusing, and entertaining characteristics to engage your audience and get them committed to your advice.

3. **Mix creative ideas with technology.**

   Here is where you brainstorm what creative ideas, tools, strategies, and approaches you can use with what technology. If you determine that your technical topic (to a non-technical group) needs to be simplified and clear, understandable, and captivating, you may want to use 3-D animations to show the audience how your topic unfolds, clever metaphors to give your topic a common ground of reference, and perhaps 3-D printed props or models that show people what your topic is about.

   Say, for example, that you're leading an important team presentation located in your company's meeting room to close a big deal with a client involving building a planned community. You may decide to decorate your room with customized signs and presentation boards to impress your prospective buyer. In terms of talent, you may ask one of your company's most senior executives to give a five-minute talk on your company's commitment to the prospect. And you may want to create customized videos and virtual flyovers and walkthroughs to show your company's impressive design for the planned community.

   Each innovative presentation involves integrating a mix of creative ideas and approaches with different technologies. Some have more creativity and less technology, others have more technology and less creativity depending upon how you perform Steps 1 and 2.

4. **Design and deliver for desired outcomes.**

   This is where you actually develop, put together, and then deliver your presentation for specific results. You combine content, visuals, handouts, and resources from your creative ideas and the technology you chose to use to meet the goals you developed in Step 1. Your planning and execution of it pays off in this final step.

The following example shows one dramatic way to implement Step 3: Selecting and integrating creativity and technology:

The founder and CEO of a fast-growing company that develops advanced nanotechnology manufacturing processes held a special two-day session at a large hotel for 300 managers, scientists, and engineers to discuss critical strategic changes she and her executive board decided were vital at that point in the company's growth. But she wanted to stress that the decision was not easy and that she went back and forth evaluating the pros and cons of moving the company in a new direction.

She wanted to recreate her thought process for her managers, but didn't want to give a typical PowerPoint presentation with just the bulleted facts. The CEO wanted her staff to experience her emotional difficulty and angst in making a decision that affects everyone in the company — hopefully for the better. Being a creative and caring person, she took some acting lessons and worked with a presentation coach to fine-tune this very important part of her presentation. She had herself videotaped with an ultra HD (high definition) (4K) video camera against a black background so her image was highlighted. During one session, she wore a darker color outfit and videotaped herself as arguing against changing the company's focus. The next day, she was videotaped with a different, lighter colored outfit talking about moving forward with the proposed company changes.

As she began her talk to her anxious managers, she set the stage, "As you know, there have been rumors about where our company is heading. I want to reassure you that I labored over this decision. I went back and forth on what to do. Sure, I had advice from the executive committee and board, but as CEO and major stockholder, the buck stops with me. It is ultimately my decision. I'm not going to tell you right away what I decided, but, because I so care for every single employee in our corporation, in about five minutes I'm going to put you right smack inside my head and heart, so you can go through a representative sample of what I went through so you can understand how and why I made that decision on whether to stay on course or move our company to another path."

In the large hotel ballroom on the elevated stage, she gave her managers a five-minute break to go outside and get some refreshments. During that time, stage hands vertically positioned two 80-inch ultra HD televisions on the stage. Special spotlights were set up to focus on the CEO while keeping the televisions and rest of the stage totally dark. As people came back and sat down, the CEO started talking as the stage lights slowly illuminated her in a dramatic way. She said, "Now I want to put you in my shoes as I was going through making this decision." Standing between the television sets, she used her iPad to bring up a life-size image of herself on each screen. On her right was the high-resolution video of her playing advocate against changing course. On her left was the video of her playing advocate for moving the company in a new direction.

Over a period of about seven minutes, she used her iPad to activate the videos to show what appeared to be a natural (obviously well-rehearsed) conversation with her pro and con video selves.

Finally, the compelling reasons to move in a new and exciting direction came forth as the audience was transfixed on a presentation the likes of which they had never seen before. With the entire stage darkened and the spotlights on her, because her videos were filmed against a black background, her stunning life-sized videos filmed in ultra HD format seemed to float as if they were real duplicates of the CEO!

She could have taken the easy route and just done a quick summary of the sterile, analytical pros and cons, but she rehearsed this innovative presentation and the empathic, psychological effect on her managers and professionals was not just incredibly persuasive, but empathically spell-binding. As a result, she galvanized her people and showed what a sensitive, thoughtful, and creatively articulate leader she truly was, which dramatically helped to garner the commitment and support of her people for the major transformation.

Re-imaging, reinventing, and remaking your presentations

Following are a few fictional examples of how innovative communicators can transform their presentations.

Using traditional PowerPoint talks are out of the question in these examples. Instead, the presenters add large doses of smart, entertaining creativity to transform their presentations into communication works of art, leading to exceptional results. (We discuss alternatives to PowerPoint presentations in Chapter 17.)

Welcome to the world of imaginative and innovative presentations where nothing is out of bounds as long as it is professional and mildly-to-wildly different and better!

Example 1: Power presentation

Trade show exhibitors are always looking for attention-getting gimmicks to draw people in and hopefully get lots of leads and close some deals. A power- and hand-tool manufacturer wants an innovative presentation unlike any other. Next to their exhibit, the company sets up a uniquely and beautifully decorated tent that can seat about 50 people inside. Outside the tent a hired magician does amazing tricks such as the "disappearing nail through the hand" trick and using a magical electric stapler to create works of art with staples to draw people into the tent to watch a 30-minute performance.

The show starts with music. As the lights dim, out comes a five-foot tall robot on wheels dressed in a shop apron with a tool belt holding a wrench in one hand and a cordless drill in the other. The robot greets the group, "Hi, my name is HandiBot, and I welcome you to our session today. In the next 30 minutes, you will see a radically new era of advanced tool design that will, you guessed it, radically change the way you use tools. You'll do your work faster, better, and with more precision than ever before. Get ready to be amazed." Fireworks explode on the screen behind HandiBot with accompanying loud audio.

As the robot moves around the front of the room and gestures with its arms and hands, the video camera in its head captures people in the audience and wirelessly projects them on the screen, much to their delight. HandiBot turns around, points to the side and said, "Now I'd like to introduce you to Ms. Charlotte W., our distinguished vice president of design and engineering." HandiBot exits stage left through the tent's side opening as the presenter comes to stage front to begin speaking.

Charlotte avoids the dreaded PowerPoint slides, and instead shows exploded 3-D views of the design of her new tools and 3-D animations and captivating videos of her tools in impressive action, illustrating the dramatic difference her tools make in construction, manufacturing, and home improvement. With this exclusive focus on visually compelling information, people could understand, and most importantly, appreciate the superior value and performance her tools create. Halfway through her talk, there was a surprise visit by her company's CEO who used Skype to personally address each audience and take questions and comments from them.

As a real treat for the attendees, Charlotte explains that she would let them handle and operate exciting prototype tools still being refined. She had her department use a 3-D printer to create ultra-realistic, full-color prototypes that audience members could feel, handle, and in some cases, actually operate.

Charlotte explains that the available printed handouts use the latest visual technology — augmented reality (AR). Listed on the handout is information on a free downloadable AR app for smartphones and tablets that people could use to see extra photos, detailed product specifications, videos, animations, and testimonials — all from an eight-page brochure!

At the conclusion of the presentation, HandiBot comes out again and says, "Anyone wanting photos with me, follow me outside the tent and we'll shoot some pics that we will post on our website for you to download."

Now that was an awesome innovative performance!

Example 2: Some presentations are just going to the dogs!

Angelina G. was a top engineering salesperson for a new 3-D printing company that came out with a quantum-leap breakthrough in 3-D printing capabilities at significantly reduced prices. She was giving a presentation in her company's facility to a variety of potential clients who she hoped would order several hundred (or more) machines. She emphasized how easy her 3-D printers were to set up and operate. She said, "I know some of you are concerned that you need highly trained people to begin using our 3-D printers for custom fabrication of your product parts or to develop prototypes. I'm going to have a team member come out and demonstrate the operating procedure (she used the term *team member* purposely as a setup for the audience) for our advanced machines. His name is Riley."

With that, Angelina opened the door and a beautiful golden retriever came out. Angelina said, "Riley, are you ready to demonstrate?" The pooch enthusiastically barked in readiness, as Angelina prompted, "Go ahead, begin the complex procedure." As Angelina smiled mischievously, Riley jumped up to the table (that held the 3-D printer), and hit the large start button with his paw. The machine began functioning immediately. That was the procedure! "Thanks, Riley," Angelina said as the happy pup barked goodbye to the group and walked out the door! The audience laughed, then actually stood up and applauded in awe and appreciation.

How creative can you get to make a point that the printer is that ridiculously simple to start up? And what a terrifically fun, surprising, and unconventional way to make that point!

Angelina was an experienced amateur dog trainer and used her own pup, but if she wasn't, she could have hired a talent dog that could be trained to do such an easy trick. As one member of the group facetiously said after Angelina ended her talk, "Doggone it, we have to buy your machines!" Other heads in the group nodded in agreement. That innovative presentation helped garner huge orders.

Example 3: A small business doing large business

Clever entrepreneurs can take an entrenched, traditional business and add a niche *value proposition* to it — those unique and special benefits and terms that help differentiate a company and its products and services from others. For example, Ladonna T. developed a special process to ensure the bathrooms her cleaning service works on in business buildings are as clean, neat, and germ-free as possible. During her innovative presentation to potential customers, she never uses any text on her visuals, she simply shows videos of her sanitary engineers using proprietary solutions and specially designed equipment to keep bathrooms sparkling clean and free of germs.

In between the well-done informational videos showing her people in action are one-minute testimonials from satisfied customers, each of whom verifies a specific aspect of Ladonna's value proposition. Every attendee receives a realistic-looking roll of toilet paper. Around it is printed paper that acts as a handout to explain her company's unique benefits! Throughout Ladonna's 30-minute presentation, she stops at strategic points to ask potential customers to unroll their handout to read information Ladonna then explains and highlights.

She gives away a gift to every potential client — a battery-powered plastic toilet (see Figure 2-2) that makes a flushing sound when its small lever is pushed down. With her creativity in presentations, let's say she's wiping out competitors!

Figure 2-2: Tongue-in-cheek props make for a memorable, innovative presentation.

Photograph courtesy of Ray Anthony

Choosing evolutionary or revolutionary

After reading some of the somewhat far out examples in the preceding section, you're likely saying, "Those are great, but that level and type of creativity is either inappropriate for my serious business presentations, or I don't have the resources to do the really cool stuff." Think of an innovative presentation along a continuum that ranges from mild-to-moderate creativity to revolutionary creative elements. In some situations and for some buttoned-up audiences, you need to stay at the more traditional, less creative end of the scale, but for other presentation circumstances, you may need something flat-out revolutionary and daring. You can move the needle over to the imaginatively bold, original, wild side of the spectrum in order to achieve those difficult-to-reach goals you can't reach by conventional means. The results will be light-years and a quantum leap ahead of what you've done before, even if you've had relatively good success with your presentations.

The entire reason and purpose of transforming your presentations from good ones to innovative ones is to significantly improve your results. What you're doing is re-imagining, reinventing, and remaking your presentations so that when people first experience your talks, they will be in utter amazement and wonder how you've done it . . . and why other, even accomplished, presenters never thought of doing it your special way.

There is no standard, one-size-fits-all type of innovative presentation. Imaginative ideas from mild to wild combined with the latest technology can skyrocket your presentations from incrementally better to monumentally better, depending upon the time you invest, the stretch goals you want to achieve, the intent of your presentation, and your personal appetite for being bold and daring. Compared to your old PowerPoint and ways of speaking, with innovation, you can now become a presentation master with a seventh degree black tongue in the martial arts of communication.

Deciding when to be innovative

Practically all presenters and audiences benefit from some degree of innovation in presentations because the speakers achieve superior results and the audiences better understand and buy into what the presenter is advocating. And, who wouldn't appreciate attending interesting, relevant, enjoyable, and entertaining talks at work? Innovative presentations, desirable for all types of business and technical talks and speeches, should go all-out and have their greatest returns on the following:

- **TED talks:** Speakers at these events are always encouraged to give insightful, unique, and captivating presentations with fresh originality and panache.

- **Motivational speeches:** Professional speakers or aspiring ones use ingenious props, weave creative tales, show riveting videos, use magic, and often devise emotional approaches to the needs and drives of the audience to entertain, amuse, and inspire. There is no limit to the imaginative, but always professional ways, you can perform.

- **Training sessions:** Sessions that last for days can get tiring and boring unless the trainer uses all kinds of engaging and stimulating games, exercises, and challenges along with props and killer presentation visuals to keep the group alert, focused, and participating.

- **Trade shows:** The sky's the limit here for innovative presentations. Trade show professionals are always looking for something radically new and entertaining to draw crowds to their area and to make their presentations produce solid orders.

- **Public seminars and workshops:** If you're an independent trainer, consultant, or author, you can have free rein with innovations to become more well-known by using the latest technology and creativity to present in immensely better and more striking ways compared to other seminar leaders.

- **Professional and industry association speeches and presentations:** Beat the PowerPoint crowd of other speakers with your stunning presentation that people will rave about long afterwards.

- **Sales conferences:** Salespeople who attend these off-site meetings love and expect dynamic presentations from the speakers — the more creative, the better. You can serve as a role model and use your innovative presentation to show ideas and techniques they can use with their prospects.

- **Conventions:** Attendees don't just want to discover new things at these events, they crave entertaining and novel presentations that give them new outlooks on a topic.

- ✔ **Videos:** Like most presentations, most videos are dry and dull. Creative ideas to use purposeful special effects, graphic designs, and interesting stories make your video stand out from others and just may cause it to go viral.

- ✔ **Award ceremonies:** If you're the host or a presenter at an awards show (live or taped), you can show amusing photos and customized cartoons and use imaginative humor to both honor the nominees and entertain the audience.

- ✔ **Product and service demonstrations:** There is great opportunity here to make your demonstrations more theatrical, entertaining, and sharply relevant. You can use props, get attendees involved, add curiosity and suspense and use other over-the-top imaginative ways to dramatically show the superior capabilities of your product or service.

- ✔ **Teachers, lecturers, professors:** Who doesn't appreciate a teacher who makes her subject come alive with video, props, displays, dioramas, eye-opening examples, stories, and metaphors?

- ✔ **Film producers:** Screenwriters and directors can create stunning, brief excerpts of innovative presentations to hold viewers spellbound.

- ✔ **Elevator pitches:** Imagine using an iPad or other tablet combined with all sorts of creative approaches to give an impromptu brief but exciting presentation that generates a lot of initial interest? We discuss elevator pitches in depth in Chapter 21.

- ✔ **Political speeches:** Politicians can communicate concepts and proposed solutions to problems and use technology, 3-D rendering software, augmented reality, props, metaphors, and models to make their visions come alive with compelling and rich realism.

- ✔ **Actors, entertainers, comedians:** If these talented people want to become part-time professional speakers while earning lots of extra money and having fun, learning the tricks of combining creative ideas with the latest technology can put them at the front of the pack.

Applying innovation to business presentations

Entrepreneurial companies love having internal presentations that are interesting, lively, and creative rather than sleep-inducing and boring. Advertising and marketing companies embrace as much relevant and focused creativity in their presentations to clients as possible. After all, it's expected of them! Architects can use subtle innovative touches to highlight and differentiate their firm's special characteristics and successes. Sales professionals are the ideal ones to run with ingenious presentations that show overwhelming superior value propositions and a business case for doing long-term business with their company. Innovative sales presenters dispatch even their fiercest competitors quicker than a prospect can say, "You have a deal!"

Engineers, technical professionals, and scientists can use 3-D animations, 3-D printed prototypes, augmented reality, holograms, 3-D virtual flyovers and walkthroughs, and props along with mind-opening analogies to brilliantly interpret complex and abstract information into fully understandable topics, quickly enlightening their technical and non-technical audiences with unique perspectives on their topics. Boardroom (really Bored Room) presenters are notorious for wildly wielding their laser pointers like light sabers at information-packed slide after slide of their PowerPoint deck. This is where a brilliantly concise, yet complete, clear, and convincing presentation would be so valued and appreciated because the bigwigs in the room would be much better able to make an informed decision quickly. Small business owners can use the power of imaginative communication and presentation excellence to win contracts that were unavailable to them before.

So, everyone who gives presentations can make them more interesting, more vital, and more effective by using various types and degrees of innovation through clever mixes of creativity and technology. As authors, we use words and pictures to get our ideas across. A fiction writer was once asked, "How do you write such fascinating books?" to which she amusingly replied, "I take 26 letters of the alphabet and arrange them in various and often unusual and surprising combinations." That's the key to being creative!

Passion is in all people and is necessary to all creative endeavors.

Mixing low tech and high creativity for sales

Our broad definition of an *innovative presentation* is one where creative ideas are applied. Here's an example of that: An enterprising energy salesperson, Rashida C., attended Ray's course on "Selling Creatively For Results" that he did for a major energy company in Texas several years ago. A week after the course, Rashida called on a new prospect who was a major food manufacturer of tortillas near the southern Texas/Mexico border. Rashida walked in with two attractive boxes bearing the name and logo of her energy company. She gave each prospect a box and told them to open it up as her presentation was inside. On a dish in the box were five tortillas rolled up with a ribbon around each. Rashida said to unroll the tortilla labeled Tortilla #1 and that would begin her sales presentation.

On each thin flatbread, Rashida printed part of her sales proposal on bright colored paper that she then cut into a round piece and glued to each tortilla. The marketing slogan for buying gas and electricity from her company was "Simple, Easy, Quick." As she mentioned the slogan and said to the prospects, "We try to make your buying gas and electric from us as easy and simple as my presentation to you." The prospects were amused, pleased, and impressed, and the nice personal touch endeared her to the prospects.

Rashida's proposal to buy from her energy company was crafted in such a simple, concise, but compelling way on those five tortillas, that she closed a big deal in her first call on that prospect! No PowerPoint, no laptop, no multimedia, but a big sale nevertheless. Would this creative approach have worked with most potential customers? Probably not. But Rashida, after having two phone conversations with the prospects prior to meeting them in person, gauged that they would be the types to appreciate this unconventional approach. She analyzed her audience, took a bit of risk, and had it pay off. It took some nerve and daring to do something that unique and different. But that sense of calculated, smart boldness is the very thing that makes such presentations successful. Was that an innovative presentation? Absolutely, because by our definition of innovative Rashida took a creative idea and applied it to a finished presentation.

Latching onto ideas and examples

While reading our book, you may be saying to yourself, "Where do people come up with these incredible ideas?" You may be thinking that you're not creative enough to develop a stunning presentation packed with riveting content and clever use of technology. If so, let us frankly tell you that you can be much more creative in a relatively short period of time by looking for ideas in novel places such as:

- ✔ **SlideShare (www.slideshare.net):** This sites has some terrific presentations you can learn from in terms of how people communicate with visuals, charts, diagrams, photos, and other design elements. Don't just search for slides about presentations. Look for other topics where people have demonstrated their creative approach to a subject.

- ✔ **TED talks (www.ted.com):** The slogan is "Ideas worth spreading" and that certainly applies to getting creative ideas from excellent TED talks. You can see some outstanding speakers cleverly using props, gadgets, backgrounds, excellent visuals, videos, and superb presentation techniques. Check out some of the best speakers and most popular topics. Diverse content will tug at your heartstrings, not just fire up your cerebral neurons. TED started out in 1984 as a conference bringing together people from three disciplines: Technology, Entertainment, Design, although the TED Talks (which can last no longer than 18 minutes) include a wide variety of captivating topics.

✔ **Professional speakers:** Go to the websites of professional speakers to see their demo reels for ideas. You can search for "speakers bureaus" using any browser and get results showing thousands of people who give keynotes and motivational talks for a living. You can get lots of ideas on how the pros develop creative content using vivid examples, metaphors, fascinating facts, and, most importantly, memorable stories that touch the heart. See how the pros use their voices and bodies as instruments of communication and dynamism.

You may someday decide to become a full- or part-time professional speaker. Entry level professional speakers starting their career typically charge $1,500 to about $2,500, and more experienced pros charge fees ranging from around $6,000 to $20,000. Well-known authors and sports, television, movie, and political celebrities have fee structures anywhere from $30,000 to over $250,000! But, don't be fooled. Just because someone is famous and gets lots of bucks doesn't necessarily mean that she's a masterful or innovative speaker. We recommend viewing the videos of motivational, entertaining, and inspiring presenters. Then look at those who focus on technology, sales, and other business topics.

You can glean much from TED speakers and professionals and get general ideas to build your own. But, never steal or borrow their content or style, which they have spent years developing as their brand.

Chapter 3

Coming Across as a Consummate Presenter

*M*en and women who drive themselves to success and aim for *self-actualization* — the pursuit of inner talent, creativity, meaning, personal and professional potential, and fulfillment (from psychologist Abraham Maslow's highest hierarchy of needs) — hate being considered just one of the crowd. Because you bought this book, you likely are one of those special people who want to stand out and above the crowd. You have no tolerance for a performance that's average, adequate, or acceptable. Those are not the A's you yearn for and strive to achieve. You love originality, change, and doing something different — not just to be different, but to be vastly better. And that's what innovation is about.

If you want to be that exceptional innovative presenter, you embrace Ralph Waldo Emerson's advice, "Do not go where the path may lead. Go instead where there is no path and leave a trail." You want to make a difference, not just a presentation that wows.

This chapter gives you insights and a collection of vital core competencies that take your presentation skills from good or very good to great. Transforming into an innovative presenter is a surefire way to get quickly noticed, respected, and admired. When seen by those in power and influence, your presentation skills can help catapult you to the top. If your audience thinks they've seen and heard it all, prove them wrong!

Being the Messenger and Message

A great presentation alone doesn't ensure success. Even a sterling innovative one does not guarantee it. Why? Because in so many important ways, you — the presenter — are the message. An audience accepts and buys you before they buy into your ideas, recommendations, or messages. They want to know what you stand for. Your professionalism, demeanor, fine-tuned speaking skills, personality, experience, knowledge, integrity — and more — greatly count.

We've watched strong, talented keynote speakers and business presenters unintentionally come across as arrogant, slick, opinionated, rigid, or self-aggrandizing. These characteristics kept the audience from liking, respecting, or trusting them.

Your way of thinking, the content in your presentation, the language you use, how you respond to questions or comments, and your subtle body language all paint the picture that others see of you. The chapters in Part II help you identify and refine your presentation style.

Identifying the qualities of a consummate presenter

Fresh out of graduate school, Ray got a job with a leading international computer company and attended a public seminar given by his principle competitor on their latest small computer. The presenter gave a polished, professional presentation, and Ray was awed by her poised demeanor, articulate skills, and commanding presence. Yet, something very important seemed to be missing. She came across as cold and impersonal with little if any warmth or friendly tone in her voice. She seemed surprised, almost annoyed, when people asked detailed questions. And, she projected a somewhat intimidating and haughty attitude that caused her likeability and approachability to take a nose dive. Although her speaking skills were admirable, and she was, in many respects, professional, Ray wondered if people would enjoy working with her. He knew he wouldn't.

Your image, behavior, and personality are all part of the formula for being the ultimate presenter. When people like, respect, and trust you, you enter the realm of the transcendent performer — one who far surpasses the ordinary.

A great presenter is more than a talented speaker: he is a full package that people are drawn to. To better understand how you are the message, look at the various characteristics listed in Table 3-1 and think about how you are likely to be seen by others during your presentation. Besides having the technically good speaking skills that we describe in Chapter 7, we recommend you assess your entire image. After each of your presentations, ask yourself how many of those traits you exhibited. Better yet, have others give you objective feedback, too.

Table 3-1	Positive Traits and Behaviors that Move Audiences	
adaptable	convinced	methodical
approachable	cordial	motivating
articulate	decisive	natural
charismatic	dedicated	open-minded
commanding	dependable	passionate
compelling	empathic	personable
competent	enthusiastic	practical
composed	flexible	professional
confident	genuine	trustworthy
considerate	inspiring	witty

We're certainly not suggesting that master presenters possess all the traits in Table 3-1, which would practically qualify them for sainthood or super hero status. Displaying a number of positive personal traits combined with good voice and body language skills and interesting and meaningful content makes for a successful talk.

Advancing your skills

As an innovative presenter, you often reimagine, reinvent, and remake your presentations with creativity and technology in the most focused, goal-oriented ways to give more dimension, depth, and perspective to your topic. Look at the characteristics in Table 3-2 and, again, ask yourself which combinations of those describe you from an audience's viewpoint. Keep in mind, we don't suggest a major demarcation between an excellent presenter and an innovative one as many of the qualities can belong in both Tables 3-1 and 3-2.

Notice the differences between the descriptors in both tables. Innovative presenters experiment and try new — sometimes bold and daring — things on the audience — always, though, within the sphere of professionalism. As a result, people in your audience know they're having a remarkable experience because of your special use of creativity and technology to communicate in such clear, concise, compelling, and convincing ways. You give a whole new perspective, dimension, and rich depth to your topics. As a result, audiences are inclined to support, commit, embrace, and act upon your recommendations and requests. And, they can't wait to attend your next talk, meeting, or event.

Table 3-2	Innovative Traits and Behaviors that Move Audiences	
advanced	farsighted	resourceful
audacious	fun	spellbinding
brilliant	imaginative	stimulating
captivating	mesmerizing	symbolic
courageous	metaphoric	unconventional
daring	nontraditional	unexpected
engaging	optimistic	unforgettable
entertaining	original	unique
exceptional	playful	venturesome
exciting	profound	visionary

Seasoned keynote speaker Bill Lampton found that becoming highly mobile during his presentations conveyed his topic mastery and his control of the situation. "Years ago," he says, "I started asking my host to provide me with a wireless microphone, giving me freedom to roam the room. In fact, during the first five minutes of my keynotes, I walk to the back of the room and say to those on the last row (as I grin widely), 'You may have thought you'd get away from me in this location, but here I am.' Invariably, this fosters a chuckle, and illustrates the bold and daring step Ray Anthony wisely advocates."

Projecting Your Desired Image

How often have you thought of how people might categorize you, in a good way, when giving a speech or presentation? Being a great public speaker or presenter often has a halo effect. Many people attach positive attributes to you when you give a terrific talk and develop rapport with your group. The audience sees you as knowledgeable, insightful, smart, cultured, seasoned, sharp, and highly professional simply because you gave an impressive performance. Of course, if you give a commanding performance, you are all those things. Depending upon your objectives for an important presentation, consider how you want to brand yourself.

Think about how you might craft and deliver your presentation differently to convey these various images:

- ✔ Visionary
- ✔ Problem solver
- ✔ Strategic thinker and planner
- ✔ Action- and results-focused professional
- ✔ Politically savvy
- ✔ Organizational change driver
- ✔ Team builder
- ✔ Technical expert
- ✔ Financial wizard
- ✔ Productive and efficient manager

Your focus, language, content, and presentation style help shape the image you want to convey. In coaching thousands of executives and professionals, Ray emphasizes that projecting the image you want to develop doesn't mean pretending to be something you're not. An image should reflect reality and consistency. People are born with flexibility and adaptability. These are skills you often lose as you grow up. However, you can develop them again, becoming a chameleon who can naturally and genuinely change colors to adapt to the situation as needed. You can be serious or humorous, self-deprecating, soft-spoken, and gentle or roar like a lion when needed.

Acting classes can help you develop the skill of seamlessly adjusting your personality and behavior.

Pursuing the ideal image

A stunning presentation creates a buzz about how impressive you are that circulates through your audiences. However, to garner more responsibility, prestige, and acclaim, you must be seen as a *transformation leader,* a person of decisiveness, swift action, and consistent results who knows how to work well with all kinds of people. A transformation leader improves the organization by making it more effective, productive, efficient, and competitive. He embraces creative ideas, offers fresh thinking, uses the latest technology and unconventional approaches, takes smart, calculated risks for big gains, and knows how to excite, energize, and activate followers. A true transformation leader combines branding, vision, strategic thinking, problem solving, and team building. Truly great people are humble, often believing the greatness is not in them, but through them.

Even if you don't have a leadership role, you can portray leadership qualities during your presentation by doing the following:

- ✔ Be fully prepared, ready, and complete in the presentation.

- ✔ Show relaxed confidence and poise.

- ✔ Be decisive and sure with your answers, especially to tough questions, in an articulate and convincing way.

- ✔ Show that your plan, program, or project is extremely well thought out in every aspect. As is said, "Leaders know the way and show the way."

- ✔ Use imaginative ideas to solve problems or show how to take quick and full advantage of possibilities and opportunities.

- ✔ Come across as seeing and understanding the implications and workings of the complex situation as a whole.

- ✔ Use will-do, action-oriented language, such as: "I will take care of that right away" and "This needs to be done right and I will assemble a highly competent team to do it" or "I'll take immediate responsibility to get those results you want."

- ✔ Own the stage. Command the audience without intimidation. Don't hesitate, waver, or contradict yourself.

- ✔ Demonstrate enthusiasm, energy, and passion about your subject. It shows stamina, drive, and dedication — characteristics of a good leader.

- ✔ Be honest, direct, and straightforward. Show integrity, and don't mislead or put a clever spin on information.

- ✔ Embrace bold and daring ideas by communicating prudent, calculated risks with great thought to contingencies and options. Real leaders are innovators.

Good leaders who know how to motivate and inspire people to be their best while supporting a goal are so rare in any organization that when a potential leader is spotted, opportunities open up and blossom for that person.

To grow as a superb speaker, you must go beyond your comfort zone while maintaining the essence of who you are.

Incorporating Innovative Competencies

In this section, we translate the qualities from Tables 3-1 and 3-2 into specific, actionable competencies and performance indicators to guide you and enable you to critique yourself as you head toward speaking excellence.

Don't be intimidated by this checklist: Throughout the chapters that follow, we give you details on how to achieve these seemingly daunting performance metrics. We provide the goals up front to give you a frame of reference for the tasks to come. If you reach proficiency in only 10 of those 25, you're likely 50 percent better than the majority of presenters. With diligence and practice, you may ace most of them!

❑ Start with a riveting, creative introduction that immediately grabs the interest of the audience and whets their appetite for more.

❑ Use elements of the unusual, suspense, surprise, and anticipation to tease and tantalize the group and keep them constantly wondering what's next.

❑ Master your topic as well as the audience's business; don't use slides to recall detailed information.

❑ Develop rapport with the audience by interacting with and engaging them in an appropriate, even playful, way.

❑ End the presentation with a well-structured, imaginative, rousing, and — most importantly — memorable conclusion.

❑ Use occasional and mild self-deprecating humor to show humility while endearing yourself to the group.

❑ Never use slides with bullet points; use minimum text with a focus on compelling visuals. The images may be photos, illustrations, relevant cartoons, attractive charts, diagrams, graphics, video, 3-D photorealistic renderings, and animation.

❑ Use meaningful, interesting props and prototypes that support, further explain, and highlight key points.

❑ Apply targeted, purposeful humor that solicits brief laughter, but is remembered weeks afterwards because of its profound insight and validity.

❑ Create a well thought out and executed presentation plan and strategy designed to ensure presentation goals are met and results are achieved.

❑ Conduct a thorough audience analysis.

❑ Tell stories and anecdotes that have deep meaning and impact the audience intellectually and emotionally.

❑ Use the latest technology, for example gesturing systems, augmented reality, ultra-high definition (4K) video, wireless systems for multiple projection screens or virtual walkthroughs, in unique and creative ways.

❑ Pass the "Five Big Cs" presentation test: Make sure your presentation is: Clear, Concise, Compelling, Captivating, and Convincing. (Chapter 9 talks more about the Cs.)

❑ Create a flexible structure that lets you adapt the presentation to the changing needs and requests of the audience.

❑ Demonstrate creativity and showmanship throughout.

❑ Use voice (volume, rate, pace, pause) and body language (posture, gestures, eye contact, movement) to keep the audience focused and engaged and to reinforce the spoken word. (We talk more about these techniques in Chapter 7.)

❑ Tailor, customize, and personalize the presentation to the specific group.

❑ Remain calm, cool, and collected in the face of interruptions, hostile audience members, or unexpected difficult situations. (Go to Chapter 13 for tips on dealing with questions.)

❑ Radiate an impressive, yet subtle, commanding presence without being authoritative, domineering, or intimidating.

❑ Tap into the secret reveries and emotional pockets of the audience to give them hope, comfort, assurance, and optimism to reach their dreams, assuage their fears and anxieties, lift their spirits, and cheer them onward.

❑ Watch and actively listen to the audience to detect confusion, feelings of being overwhelmed, bored, or concerned and modify the presentation accordingly, for example, slowing down, giving further explanations or examples, or moving ahead more quickly.

❑ Highlight and repeat main points, key messages, and critical pieces of information.

❑ Generate audience interaction by using meeting and presentation apps on smart devices.

❑ Use powerful, imaginative content and visuals to give a 360-degree perspective of the topic: mix facts, examples, quotations, statistics, descriptions, stories, definitions, case studies, news articles, research studies, demonstrations, metaphors/analogies, comparisons/contrasts, videos, and animations.

❑ Use clear language suited to and known by the audience; incorporate their terminology, acronyms, jargon, and industry terms.

Return to this list frequently to ensure you meet as many of the criteria as possible. This is one of the most valuable parts of the book!

Part II
The Secrets of Presentation Success

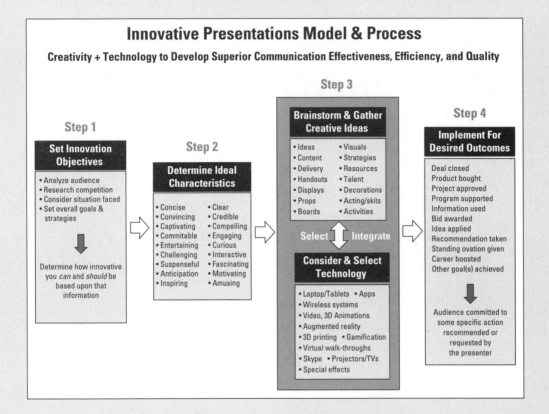

Innovative Presentations Model & Process

Creativity + Technology to Develop Superior Communication Effectiveness, Efficiency, and Quality

Step 1

Set Innovation Objectives

- Analyze audience
- Research competition
- Consider situation faced
- Set overall goals & strategies

Determine how innovative you *can* and *should* be based upon that information

Step 2

Determine Ideal Characteristics

- Concise
- Convincing
- Captivating
- Commitable
- Entertaining
- Challenging
- Suspenseful
- Anticipation
- Inspiring
- Clear
- Credible
- Compelling
- Engaging
- Curious
- Interactive
- Fascinating
- Motivating
- Amusing

Step 3

Brainstorm & Gather Creative Ideas

- Ideas
- Content
- Delivery
- Handouts
- Displays
- Props
- Boards
- Visuals
- Strategies
- Resources
- Talent
- Decorations
- Acting/skits
- Activities

Select ⇅ **Integrate**

Consider & Select Technology

- Laptop/Tablets • Apps
- Wireless systems
- Video, 3D Animations
- Augmented reality
- 3D printing • Gamification
- Virtual walk-throughs
- Skype • Projectors/TVs
- Special effects

Step 4

Implement For Desired Outcomes

Deal closed
Product bought
Project approved
Program supported
Information used
Bid awarded
Idea applied
Recommendation taken
Standing ovation given
Career boosted
Other goal(s) achieved

Audience committed to some specific action recommended or requested by the presenter

Visit www.dummies.com/extras/innovativepresentations for help refining your strategies when preparing a presentation.

In this part . . .

- ✔ Get a handle on your audience.
- ✔ Spot the four personality types.
- ✔ Make a strategic presentation plan.
- ✔ Prepare for unexpected, last-minute changes.
- ✔ Create interesting content.
- ✔ Examine ways to add variety to your presentation.
- ✔ Sharpen your speaking and gesturing skills.
- ✔ Choose the appropriate projection and sound equipment.
- ✔ Rehearse your lines.

Chapter 4

Analyzing and Focusing on Your Audience

Surely you've met and, unfortunately, experienced these people many times: The monologue super-talkers who seldom, if ever, listen. They know very little about you, your life, and situation, but they flood you with information about themselves as if the world revolved around them — and as if you truly cared to listen to everything they had to say. They give you all sorts of unsolicited advice, little of which is useful or appreciated by you, and they have an opinion about everything that they expect you to be interested in and agree with. They don't care to hear your thoughts or feelings or ask questions to get to know you better, even though you have shown interest in learning about them. They talk *at* you, not *with* you. There's no connection or relationship with them. You know the people we're describing.

Some presenters act the same way. They give canned presentations or speeches that have little real value to an audience because they haven't invested time to understand what that group wants and needs to hear. It's like taking aim — while wearing a blindfold — and believing you'll hit the bull's-eye.

A successful presenter doesn't wear a blindfold, instead she targets the audience by learning as much about them as possible and then tailoring, customizing, and personalizing her presentation. However, our experience shows this analysis and focus on a particular audience does not happen to the extent it should with most presenters and, as a result, their presentations miss the mark resulting in lost sales or otherwise missed opportunities to get the support or action needed from the group.

In this chapter, we give you insights into what you should know about your audience and how to concentrate on them, not on yourself, your company, or anything else. Your presentation and your focus should be all about your audience. For example, movie producers strive to make films that target and appeal to specific audiences. They know that age, education, race, cultural backgrounds, and other potential audience characteristics determine who wants to see an action feature, horror movie, love story, or science fiction flick.

We can't say it enough — giving a canned, one-size-fits-all presentation to various and diverse groups leads to sub-par results, and at times, total failure.

Like movie producers, presenters need to know how to cater to each unique audience. The more important your presentation, the more critical it is to thoroughly and accurately understand your audience so you can precisely tailor your pitch to their unique makeup and needs. After you profile your audience, you can:

- Create the best content.
- Pinpoint the most effective approach and strategy.
- Craft appropriate language (vocabulary and technical, financial, or scientific terms).
- Identify the focus areas.
- Find the balance between logical and emotional appeals.
- Determine the degree of interaction you want with your audience.
- Plan to deal with situations that may prevent you from reaching your presentation objectives.

Doing Your Research

You establish credibility when you communicate directly from your audience's perspective, priorities, and positions regarding your topic. These analysis factors enable you to customize and tailor your presentation in ways that increase your chances of success. After you answer the following questions about your audience, you can begin to build a profile of the people your presentation caters to:

- **Group size:** Find out how many people will be in attendance. This determines the resources you need, such as the number of handouts and sound reinforcement or other equipment, and what size meeting room best fits your needs and theirs. Larger groups make individual engagement difficult. Smaller groups lend themselves to informal, casual interaction. You need to display more energy and typically have more attention-grabbing tactics to hold the interest of bigger audiences and to tone down the high-energy factor with small groups.

✔ **Knowledge and experience with your topic:** What does the audience already know about your topic and how much do they know? If you talk over their heads, you'll lose them. If your content is too basic, your group will quickly become bored, annoyed, and possibly insulted. Your audience's level of understanding of your topic also dictates the terminology you use, specifically whether you can employ technical or other specialized terms or acronyms. If your ideas or proposed solutions are new to your audience, you have to spend time building up to your main points so they understand the big picture and all the connecting points.

✔ **Opinions, feelings, and attitudes toward your topic:** When your goal is to influence, motivate, or persuade people to do something, it's critical that you discover what your audience's likely stance toward your topic is and why. Where do they stand intellectually and emotionally regarding your topic? Are people generally favorable, neutral, or do they lean toward a negative consensus? Can you discover the underlying reasons for why they feel skeptical, cynical, or cautious? With a friendly or neutral group, you can be more direct in advocating some course of action, but you have to be more subtle and indirect with a group somewhat hostile to your topic.

✔ **Needs, wants, and expectations:** What does your group most need and want from your presentation in terms of specific type of information and at what level of detail? What assurances, commitments, or guarantees do they expect from you and your organization? Overall, what does your audience hope to get from you and your presentation? What would they likely see happening as a result of your talk?

✔ **Priorities and pain points:** What are the two or three highest priority areas of information your group needs most to make the decision you want? What are the primary interests and concerns (some call them *hot buttons*) your information should address? What can you say that would likely prompt them to make a commitment? What do they least want or need to hear about regarding your topic? What important pain points are they experiencing that your presentation's solution would help them overcome? What fear or worry can you alleviate? These are vital questions to get answers to in your audience analysis.

✔ **Decision makers:** Who attending your presentation can — and likely will — sign the check? Which people may be key advisors, recommenders, and influencers of decisions to be made as a result of your presentation? If you can, find out how your group makes its decision — their specific process — and how they'll make one regarding your presentation. What criteria (in priority order) do they use to make that decision? Understanding these issues helps you come up with a persuasion strategy for all the parties involved in the decision.

- ✔ **Position levels and professions:** Do most of the people attending hold C-level, executive, and senior vice president positions or are they middle managers? What fields do they specialize in — sales, marketing, research and development, distribution, operations or other? Obviously, with senior leaders you need to focus on the big picture with bottom-line results. With technical professionals, you need to get into greater detail and provide information relevant to their particular set of occupational needs.

- ✔ **Audience makeup:** Other group characteristics that are helpful to know include the gender mix, education levels, average age, socio-economic level, and perhaps ethnic background and political leaning. These factors dictate the examples you use, the stories you tell, your vocabulary mix, the facts you provide, and the persuasive strategy you need to apply. For example, with older, conservative audiences, you need to rein in on your energetic speaking style and creativity, but with younger audiences (Generations X and Y, for example), you can be bolder, have higher energy, and be more imaginative in your showmanship.

- ✔ **Potential problems from the audience:** How might the audience react unfavorably to your talk or your call to action? What might they disagree with or be cynical or skeptical about? What could make them feel uneasy and unsure? With what objections or tough questions might they ask to challenge you? Determine what possible misinformation, unrealistic expectations, and faulty perceptions or assumptions need to be dealt with and how. What other forms of direct or silent resistance might affect reaching your planned results? Can you identify those likely to oppose your plan or solution? How can you best deal with these threats to your presentation goals?

- ✔ **Mood and condition of group:** The emotional, mental, and physical state of your audience can dramatically affect their receptivity, decision making, and participation. If your presentation is scheduled for 3 p.m. on Friday after the group has sat through four other presentations that day, you may have a challenge on your hands, compared to speaking to them on a Tuesday morning when they're fresh and alert.

The condition of your audience dictates the energy level you have to display, key points you need to strongly emphasize to make sure they get them, and whether you should perhaps cut your presentation short in ways they will appreciate. Their mood may be negative if the company is in flux — for example had layoffs, poor financial results, or something else that affects their optimism or desire to get involved with your proposal.

Understanding Your Audience

Today, extensive online information can — usually — provide everything you need to know about your audience. With the names of the key people attending in hand, start with the following searches:

- ✔ **Company website:** Read the biographies of any executives or managers you'll be presenting to and study the company history.

- ✔ **LinkedIn, Facebook, Google Plus, and other social and business networks:** Get to know key audience members' backgrounds and expertise and find colleagues you may have in common.

- ✔ **Google/Bing/Yahoo! search engines:** A simple name search often brings up trade, business, or consumer articles that talk about the company, management, or personnel.

Think of other databases that can give you deeper insights into either the entire group or specific individuals you'll address. Contact several of the attendees before your presentation to find out what they need, want, and expect. Most people appreciate being asked about their preferences, and you can use their answers to ensure that you provide the information they require and prefer. Chatting with people who have presented to them in the past, although not always possible, can provide great insight about what drives, or irritates, the audience. When giving a speech to an association or at a convention, peruse the association website and check with the meeting planner or the program chairman to learn about the group.

Contact the public relations or corporate relations department, which can provide annual reports and executive bios, if you run into difficulty finding online information.

Targeting the four dominant personality types

Suppose you and your team work on a very important presentation for weeks. The presentation means a bonanza for your company and a huge boost up the career ladder for you and your cohorts. You want to give a game-changing presentation, but you have to prepare for the audience first. You create impressive content and Hollywood-style visuals that build an undeniably powerful business case and value proposition for your clients, but unless you communicate your ideas effectively from a psychological, strategy-based standpoint, all your hard work may not be perceived as you desire.

To win over the hearts and minds of people at your presentation, you need to wear the hat of a streetwise psychologist who understands how each of the four dominant personality profiles think, feel, perceive situations, and process information. We define these personality types as Director, Energizer, Affable, and Thinker. You need to know what motivates, influences, and persuades each personality type to make decisions that lead to actions based upon your presentation objectives.

Later in this chapter, we describe each of the four personality types so you can identify them in the audience. We then tell you exactly how and what to say when you are presenting to one or more individuals or groups. This section of the chapter gives invaluable insights on how to precisely target your information and messages, and how to adapt your presentation style to the four major personality types.

Building credibility and trust

When you think like a psychologist, you can psyche out your audience in your presentation for effect. This method employs neither manipulation nor head games. Instead, it enables you to understand how various personality types think and act and what will motivate and propel them to commit to your proposed ideas, recommendations, or solutions. It's not just your content that people evaluate. It's you, the messenger. You are the message.

A well-known sales maxim says that to get a sale, you must get a prospective customer or client to like, respect, and trust you. This is great advice for leaders and speakers. The challenge lies in achieving all three with all the people in your audience. Aim for 100 percent success, but be satisfied upon reaching two out of three of those factors. Garner two of the three to achieve a firm commitment from the group and the third will follow with time. Your credibility determines your success rate.

Trust and respect are the cornerstones of credibility. You may really like a certain presenter, but if you feel she doesn't have the experience, knowledge, or drive to meet your goals, then you will not go along with what she proposes. Likewise, you can be drawn to the warm, engaging, and perhaps charming persona of a speaker but hesitate to do business with her because she comes across a bit too rehearsed, a bit too slick for your liking. Therefore respect and trust (with believability and integrity as the anchors) are the two most important elements of presenter credibility for the four personality types we cover later in this chapter.

If you can develop a rapport with the audience by building up your likeability factor, all the better. Competence and confidence, displaying leadership and initiative, having a reputation for responsibility and reliability and a successful track record in the field gain respect from the audience. Trust develops from demonstrated consistency, openness, honesty, and frankness in communications along with sincerity without pretense or hidden agendas.

The Greek philosopher Aristotle developed the art of persuasion by focusing on the three primary elements of *ethos*, *pathos*, and *logos* — ethical appearance, logical reasoning, and emotional appeal. The four primary personality types we cover next in this chapter put a different focus on each of these. Of course, everyone in an audience wants to feel that the presenter they're listening to or working with possesses ethos — good intentions, upright character, and trustworthiness.

Certain of the personality types that we describe put a greater focus on the logical side of reasoning — logos — where verifiable facts, statistics, and other forms of empirical proof and evidence are paramount to making an informed decision. Other personality types may be swayed more by a passionate presenter who targets and appeals to their emotions through heart-wrenching, heart-pounding, or heartstring-pulling stories or videos that evoke the intended positive or negative emotions.

Getting to Know the Four Personality Types

Personality types have been defined and researched for centuries. See the sidebar "A brief history of personality types" for a quick summary. We developed our own basic composite of many of the commonly used personality profiles. We use the terms *Director, Energizer, Affable,* and *Thinker* to indicate the dominant personality types. We want to make several general points about these personality profiles before we get into details about each one:

- You typically have a dominant (strongest) personality type that shows in the way you view things, communicate, make decisions, approach situations, relate to others, and behave.

- You have a mixture (or blending) of each of the four personality types, including your weakest personality component. For example, you may be a very strong Director and somewhat strong Thinker (second), with a weaker Energizer side, and an almost non-existent Affable side to your personality.

- You may be one of the lucky human chameleons gifted with the genuine, natural ability to adapt your behavior style — or emphasize the necessary quadrant — to fit the situation at hand. For example, a highly social type (Energizer) takes firm command of a situation and acts like a tough, get-it-done now Director. Or, a strong, analytical, but generally introverted Thinker type behaves more like a social Energizer in a sales situation when called for because of a genuine (not forced or contrived) ability to adapt.

A brief history of personality types

The Greek physician Hippocrates (460-370 BC) developed what is commonly called the *Temperament Theory*. The Father of Western Medicine as he is known held the unusual belief that four bodily fluids — blood, yellow bile, black bile, and phlegm — create certain moods and emotional behaviors in people. According to Hippocrates, the four temperaments are

- ✔ **Choleric:** Ambitious and leader-like
- ✔ **Sanguine:** Sociable and pleasure-seeking
- ✔ **Melancholic:** Thoughtful and introverted
- ✔ **Phlegmatic:** Relaxed and quiet

In the millennium after Hippocrates, others in the Western world modified and expanded his theory to include more emotional and mental aspects, moral attitudes, and other behaviors related to the temperaments. Hippocrates's thesis, though, still forms the modern psychological underpinnings (minus the bodily fluids, of course) of the four basic personality types that every successful salesperson, leader, and presenter has used to her advantage.

In the early 20th century, the famous Swiss psychologist and psychiatrist Carl Jung developed concepts of extrovert and introvert archetypes that divide people into thinking, feeling, sensation, and intuition personality types that define the fundamental ways people perceive and interpret reality and respond to it. If you have ever taken a Myers-Briggs Type Indicator Assessment (MBTI) and been amazed at how accurate the description of your personality is, thank Jung, as it is based upon his work.

This tool focuses on four dichotomies:

- ✔ Extroversion/Introversion (E or I)
- ✔ Sensing/Intuition (S or N)
- ✔ Thinking/Feeling (T or F)
- ✔ Judging/Perceiving (J or P)

Although very useful in a number of situations at work or home, the complexity of MBTI, with its 16 possible psychological types, makes it impractical to use for presentation purposes in quickly identifying how people would likely think, feel, and react to a presenter.

Director personality

The most-likely-to-succeed candidates grow up to be the Big Cheeses, VIPs, Top Dogs, or Head Honchos — as nicknames for the boss go. Most business chief executives (CEO, COO, CIO, or CFO) and others in positions of power in government, military, or academia likely have this strong-willed, hard-charging, tenacious personality type. They are the Cholerics as described by Hippocrates's temperament theory (see the sidebar "A brief history of personality types"). Quintessential strong, steel-willed leaders exemplify Directors, who tend to be left-brain dominant people. Some think of these successful people as Type A personalities.

The Director displays strength in different ways: General George S. Patton represents the iconic, tough-as-nails Director personality who barked orders and pushed his troops to always be on the aggressive offensive; Hillary

Clinton exhibits a steel-spined, strong, and bulletproof Director type; and actor Denzel Washington exudes confidence and poise but in the direct, regal, subtle manner of a Director. Read the typical characteristics, traits, attitudes, and behaviors that define this take-charge personality and think about who you know who fits the Director quadrant — it may be you:

- Focuses on goals, results, action, and achievement
- Highly competitive — loves tough challenges to overcome
- Forceful, authoritative, commanding (large and in charge)
- Wants it all yesterday
- Demanding and impatient
- Decisive and direct — blunt and opinionated in communication
- Exerts control — of self and others
- Seeks power, status, prestige
- Big (often fragile) ego requiring feeding
- Independent and self-sustaining — takes quick initiative
- Does not allow himself to show vulnerable emotions or any sign of weakness
- Opportunist — a smart risk-taker and methodical innovator

Directors make decisions more quickly than any other personality type — if you present the right type of information to them. People in positions in power are likely to be Directors. High-powered individuals have to make lots of decisions in their job. They cannot afford to overanalyze, procrastinate, or delay things. They want to see results and to move ahead quickly and purposefully. Sure, they take prudent, calculated risks, but if they see something they view as beneficial to them, they jump on it.

At the extreme end of this profile, Directors can be Attila the Hun types — ruthless, tyrannical, control-freak bullies who ride rough-shod over people with their domineering personalities, gruff style, and cold-hearted obsession to gain power and riches by exploiting others. They see people as simply a means to an end. At their best, Directors are superb visionaries and commanding, well-intentioned leaders who take care of their people and bring impressive, positive change to an organization or country. They can be prolific producers with major accomplishments. Their take-charge abilities and cool-under-fire demeanor are invaluable in an urgent or crisis situation.

How to identify a Director within a minute

A Director's body language, voice, and behavior typically show the following traits:

- ✔ Direct
- ✔ Fast-talking
- ✔ Loud voice
- ✔ Formal
- ✔ Reserved, even closed
- ✔ Unemotional
- ✔ Down to business

How to best present to Directors

Directors respect presenters with high credibility who show self-assurance and competence and exhibit good leadership qualities while presenting. Directors expect you to thoroughly and accurately do your homework and cover the critical, priority information (without extraneous details) they need to make a good decision. You must be clear, concise, direct, and specific about how your recommendation fits and improves the vision, mission, and goals of the Director's organization.

Open your presentation with a crisp, sharply focused executive summary of the projected results. Directors' interests lie in improving productivity, efficiency, quality, and innovation to generate higher profits and an attractive return on investment for their organization.

Plan your presentation thoroughly and meticulously. Be organized and fully prepared to have reserve information available if the Director needs it. Stick to business and get right to the point without being abrupt. Be personable, but reserved and professional at all times. Build a rock-solid, attractive business case using provable facts, statistics, and other empirical information.

Directors respect presenters who are composed, poised, and relaxed, but who can also show their steely resolve, conviction, and firmness when needed.

Communicate viable options and choices with realistic pros and cons and have key information for Directors to compare to aid them in deciding. Focus on strategic (high-level) issues and minimize the tactical (detailed, lower-level) information.

Avoid the following behaviors when presenting to Directors:

- ✔ Don't ramble, be vague or elusive, or give unprepared extemporaneous answers to questions.
- ✔ Don't become emotional or make emotional appeals.
- ✔ Don't get personal or be cute, witty, or clever with these all-business types.
- ✔ Don't exhibit fear and don't hesitate or vacillate when challenged.
- ✔ Don't leave gaps or loose ends in your presentation.

Directors like appropriate, purposeful creativity in your presentation as opposed to window dressing or entertaining creativity. If your imaginative approach or creatively designed visual media can better highlight key information, spotlight important comparisons, or otherwise aid in their decision-making process, bring it on.

Thinker personality

If you're in the peanut-butter section of the grocery store with an exaggerated form of this personality, get ready for a long stay — you may just die there. The Thinker reads every label of every jar for intricate comparison of ingredients, nutritional data, cross-checking of prices, while using her smartphone to go online to get even more information and consumer reviews and otherwise fret about what others would consider an easy, on-the-spot purchase. Thinkers echo what human behavioral psychologist Ivan Pavlov said:

> Don't become a mere recorder of facts, but try to penetrate the mystery of their origin.

Thinker types frequent the fields of finance, law, engineering, science, and technology. After Directors, competent and successful Thinkers often occupy the C-suite, running major businesses and organizations. They are the Melancholics described by Hippocrates's temperament theory (see the sidebar "A brief history of personality types"). The extreme left-brain human computer, Mr. Spock from *Star Trek,* is the oft-mentioned epitome of the hyper-cerebral, but detached and impersonal archetype Thinker. Billionaire Bill Gates is, indeed, a full-blooded Thinker personality. Socially awkward, introspective geeks are another variation of quirky, sometimes neurotic Thinkers. Actor and director Woody Allen fits that description nicely.

Here are the characteristics, traits, attitudes, and behaviors that define this extraordinarily logical, precise, and deliberate personality:

- Objective, rational, methodical, and orderly
- Cautious, skeptical, prove-it-to-me cynic
- Traditional, conventional, slow to change, and risk-averse
- Needs abundant, precise, and accurate empirical, hard-core proof
- Slow and methodical in decision making — meticulous researcher and fact-checker
- Serious, stoical, reserved, conservative — hides reactions and feelings (but can suddenly erupt with wacky or goofy humor or behavior when unguarded)
- Craves discovering and solving complex, challenging problems
- Can be inflexible and tends to see issues as black or white — no gray areas
- Follows rules, methods, procedures, and protocols with little to no deviation
- Prefers incremental changes to radical (game-changing) innovations

Thinkers pride themselves on being extremely smart, well-informed, and systematic ponderers who reach the crux of problems in a highly effective way. At their worst, Thinkers can be smug, self-righteous, rigid, and defensive people who obsessively nitpick the tiniest, insignificant details at the expense of the big picture. Extreme Thinker types can come across as ice-cold robots who cannot feel or envision the emotional or irrational human side of issues. Although they try to hide it, they still possess human DNA, and even half-human Spock has a certain propensity for feelings, sentimentality, and compassion.

Thinkers can be snail-slow and ponderous in their evaluation of a problem or opportunity and unbelievably frustrating with their paralysis of analysis to those who want decisions, results, and actions quickly. On the positive side, Thinkers are conscientious, responsible, and diligent in their attention to those complex details that others dismiss or miss, and indispensably important in implementing solutions. Thinkers excel at research, compiling data, and planning and, when working alongside other personality types, bring to successful completion visions, goals, and innovations of all kinds.

How to identify Thinkers within a minute

Thinkers' body language, voice, and behavior typically show the following:

- Subtle
- Tendency to talk at a slow pace with a soft, often monotone voice
- Reserved

- ✔ Formal
- ✔ Unemotional
- ✔ Unexpressive
- ✔ Unassertive
- ✔ Questioning

How to best present to Thinkers

Thinkers respect and appreciate prepared, precise presenters who provide detailed information. They want objective, impartial data communicated in a sequential, logical, and methodical way that leads to a rational and justified conclusion. They want to understand the relationships, trends, and cause-and-effects brought about by useful, practical data.

You have to convince Thinkers of the outright feasibility and validity of your ideas, recommendations, or solutions with hardcore evidence. Thinkers require proof — and lots of it — from numerous, verifiable sources. Be quantitative in listing and explaining the benefits of your product offering or solution and describe the process or model that's the basis of your recommendations or position. Be sure to outline tangible consequences of a problem or situation in measurable terms and carefully calculate probabilities (remember Spock?). Stress the proven track record of programs or projects like yours, which validate your cause.

Always be prepared to answer questions in a detailed and concrete (not abstract or vague) fashion. During your presentation, avoid giving your (subjective) opinions, suppositions, attitudes, feelings — or worse yet — unsubstantiated speculation or assumptions on your topic. Instead, come across as strictly objective, impartial, unbiased, and open-minded — especially to feedback or counterclaims. Stick to the facts and your credibility will remain intact with Thinkers.

Also, Thinkers feel comfortable with a presenter who is non-assertive and open to being engaged. High-energy, in-your-face, fast-talking sales and motivational types are not welcome or respected by these personalities. Finally, remember that you often have to build an airtight case — like a lawyer in front of a jury — to convince Thinker types.

During a presentation to Thinkers:

- ✔ Don't rush them or pressure them to make a decision.
- ✔ Don't come across as flippant, cavalier, or jocular.
- ✔ Don't use personal or emotional appeals; such appeals seem weak and irrelevant to Thinkers.
- ✔ Don't make them defensive by directly challenging them or their expertise.
- ✔ Don't exaggerate, pontificate, or over-promise on anything.

When it comes to being creative during your presentation, some Thinkers will really enjoy it (finding it intellectually pleasing), while others might see it as detracting and distracting from the serious nature of the data. Most Thinkers, though, like ingenious and imaginative ways of viewing a situation from a new and valid perspective. So if your media (such as compelling, unique visuals or video) helps clarify and solidify your points, Thinkers will welcome that form of creativity. Don't expect kudos and compliments from most of them, even though you labored over your presentation. Be ready for them to nit pick about some detail you failed to mention, even though the other personality types in your audience might be drooling over the awesome job you did. It's just the Thinker's style — nothing personal!

Energizer personality

Ultra-extroverted, multi-talented comedian and actor Robin Williams could be the poster child for the high-end, fast-talking Energizer. Walt Disney was an endlessly passionate, idealistic, and inspirational shining example for a prolific creator — the ultimate imagineer — who exemplifies this type as well. Former U.S. President Bill Clinton has great flexibility in his personality style. His dominant type is Energizer. He will go out of his way to smile, shake hands, and enthusiastically talk with anyone he comes in contact with. His flexibility enables him to naturally and effortlessly take on characteristics of a Director, Thinker, and even Affable when situations call for it.

These optimistic personalities love an imaginative presentation because they adore novelty and innovations of all sorts. Energizers are fun-loving, highly sociable, and sometimes flamboyant personalities who can be the life of the party. Journalist and bubbly television personality Katie Couric and the supremely entrepreneurial and charismatic benefactor Oprah Winfrey are typical Energizers, throwing off positive energy in all directions.

Energizers are the Sanguines as described by Hippocrates's temperament theory (see the sidebar "A brief history of personality types"). These mostly right-brain dominant people become sales and marketing professionals, entrepreneurs, motivational speakers, media celebrities, and politicians. *Communicative, motivational, entertaining,* and *visionary* describe Energizer personality types.

The characteristics, traits, attitudes, and behaviors that define this most outgoing, confident, and creative personality type are

- ✔ Imaginative, innovative, intuitive, and daring risk-taker
- ✔ Dreamer, visionary, idealist who loves big and bold ideas
- ✔ Impulsive, intuitive, spontaneous, and emotional
- ✔ Great at synthesizing ideas, concepts, and theories

✔ Can be unconventional and unorthodox in solutions

✔ Mercurial — enjoys exciting, meaningful change

✔ Thrives on admiration, recognition, and applause

✔ Dislikes rigid rules, regulations, or tradition — can be a maverick

✔ Easily distracted and bored — changes direction and focus frequently

✔ Excellent communicator who takes pride in influencing people and events

If you want sharp-witted visionaries, innovators, and passionate business evangelists, Energizers are the best personality types to fill the bill. Their brilliance and frequently fearless risk-taking combines with large does of creativity at work. They come up with amazing and impressive ideas almost on cue. On the negative side, Energizers become bored easily if situations stagnate. They scatter their energies on too many projects, thus diluting their effectiveness. They over-promise and under-deliver because of their unrealistic optimism and may be unreliable with deadlines, which they often see as tentative in nature and importance. Their unabashed, lofty idealism comes across as naïve to other personality types. Energizers can fall short by being too emotionally truthful — wearing their hearts on their sleeves. Their verbal and behavioral impulsiveness can damage their professional credibility.

How to identify Energizers within a minute

An Energizer's body language, voice, and behavior typically show the following:

✔ Outgoing

✔ Fast talker

✔ Loud voice

✔ Animated, informal, friendly

✔ Emotional, expressive

✔ Relaxed

✔ Open, social

How to best present to Energizers

Giving a presentation to Energizers is almost always a pleasant, uplifting experience. As you present to a group, you see these personality types looking at you, smiling, and maybe even giving you a subtle thumbs-up. They pay attention to fast-paced, interesting, creative, and entertaining presentations; they languish in those filled with volumes of extraneous data and slow-talking, passive, or solemn presenters who seem to drone on with no energy and enthusiasm.

When presenting to Energizers, focus on the unique, new, and innovative aspects of your program, project, or product/service. Show your passion in your presentation without overdoing it. Not only should you exhibit warmth and friendliness, but you can be playful, witty, and humorous with these informal, fun personalities who enjoy bantering with you.

Use lots of relevant graphics, diagrams, visuals, animations, or videos that vividly illustrate your ideas or messages as opposed to a splattering of dull, text-and-numbers-saturated slides. Keep your presentation concise and moving quickly for these somewhat attention-deficit personalities. Let them know who else has successfully implemented your solution, program, or recommendation; what the positive impact was on the people, operation, and financials; and how exciting it was for those involved.

While you're at it, give Energizers lots of personal attention and recognition, and engage them by eliciting frequent feedback. Pose relevant, thought-provoking questions that move them toward a conclusion or decision to act upon your recommendation. Talk about fresh and daring ideas, adventuresome opportunities, worthwhile changes, and enticing possibilities. Energizers tend to procrastinate with decisions, so provide an attractive, compelling plan with assurances and incentives to get them to commit.

Some Energizers pride themselves on being well-intentioned, good-hearted mavericks, contrarians, and non-traditionalists in their organization. If you suspect that to be so, aim your presentation to spotlight the unconventional, but highly effective, results-oriented nature of your project, program, or product/service offering that will make a positive difference for the Energizer and her organization and show the stuffed shirts how it should be done.

These are things you don't want to do during your presentation with Energizers:

- ✔ Don't come across as formal, impersonal, cool, or detached.
- ✔ Don't neglect to get them involved in enhancing your creative ideas and solutions.
- ✔ Don't be rigid and come across as a close-minded know-it-all.
- ✔ Don't let them leave important decisions dangling — subtly redirect them to closure.
- ✔ Don't come across as dismissive of their ideas and recommendations.

Energizers love it when you imaginatively communicate in a dynamic, interactive, and entertaining fashion. When it comes to being creative in your presentation, open up the floodgates for this personality. Think of ways to inform them with fascinating visuals, photos, anecdotes, stories, metaphors, videos, physical props, storyboards, and stunning executive summary handouts. This personality type thrives on *infotainment* (information + entertainment) or *edutainment* (education + entertainment) presentations.

Affable personality

Ever meet someone who is always volunteering for some worthwhile cause and always doing something for others? Then, you've met the Affable personality type. These sociable, nurturing, and agreeable personalities value interpersonal relationships more than the other three major personality types. They are the Phlegmatics as described by Hippocrates's temperament theory (see the sidebar "A brief history of personality types"). These emotionally-driven, right brain-dominant people are unselfish and care for others even at their own expense! Many share the famous psychologist and psychiatrist Carl Jung's philosophy that "the sole purpose of human existence is to kindle a light in the darkness of mere being."

Because they cherish helping others and doing good, you find many Affables in the healthcare industry, counseling, social services, human resources, and customer service — places where they use their personal warmth, kind words, and patience to connect with others and serve them. South African Bishop Desmond Tutu, with his warm, beautiful, and glowing smile, and beloved actress Betty White are Affables. In addition, mild-mannered, sensitive actor Sarah Jessica Parker fits this type as well.

The characteristics, attitudes, and behaviors that define this most people-oriented, congenial, and accommodating personality type are

- ✔ Hates and shuns conflict, controversy, or debate
- ✔ Highly sensitive to their own feelings and those of others
- ✔ Has difficulty rejecting other's ideas and requests — can't say no
- ✔ Supportive team player who always offers to help out
- ✔ Indecisive, tentative, and afraid to commit (especially quickly)
- ✔ Needs approval, validation, and lots of genuine affection from others
- ✔ Good listener and reader of others' body language and vocal tones
- ✔ Dependable, loyal, easygoing, and sincere (does not play games)
- ✔ Dislikes dealing with dry details and impersonal, cold, hard facts
- ✔ Can appear weak and wishy-washy, especially in demanding situations

Affables at their best are wonderful people-persons with an affinity to connect with and belong to groups. They generously share fame and glory in exchange for friendship and affiliation. They are protective and loyal people who go out of their way to make others feel special and cherished. The negative side of some Affables is that they are commitment-phobic, painstakingly slow at making decisions, and unduly afraid of disappointing others or hurting their feelings. They cling to the status quo and thus find change and the slightest loss of security insufferable. Overly sensitive, they can withdraw and psychologically cower.

Affables can be the most risk-averse and dependent personality of the four major types. Because they find it difficult to reject someone's recommendation or purchase of a product, for example, they may unintentionally string people along. Usually they are the least likely people to be in positions of power, especially where political prowess and Machiavellian moves are required.

How to identify Affables within a minute

An Affable person typically shows the following in her body language, voice, and behavior:

- ✔ Calm
- ✔ Indirect
- ✔ Talk at a slow pace with a soft voice
- ✔ Casual
- ✔ Friendly (smile a lot)
- ✔ Low-key
- ✔ Openly express their feelings, but not as directly or strongly as Energizers
- ✔ Unassertive
- ✔ Ask, rather than tell

How to best present to Affables

Affables enjoy presenters who are warm, genuine, and caring with a personal and soft touch. Develop rapport with Affables and let them get to know you while you show sincere personal interest in them before, during, and after your presentation. During your talk, focus on how your solution, program, or product/service can make a positive difference in the work (and even personal) lives of people. If you are selling a product or service, for example, stress how your support team and company will put great emphasis on a close-working, harmonious relationship with them and their co-workers.

Affables lean toward subjective decision-making based on values, harmony, emotions, and their intuition. Therefore, your presentation should focus on assured, tried-and-true outcomes, effective ways to deal with unknowns, and strategies to minimize risk to their lowest level to make them feel comfortable that you are doing right by them in every way possible. Demonstrate sensitivity to their opinions, feelings, and concerns while showing your intention of being highly cooperative.

If you advocate change, show the Affable how your step-by-step (hand-holding) support plan will create meaningful change in a non-painful, non-anxiety-producing way acceptable to these personalities.

Things you don't want to do during your presentation with Affables:

- ✔ Don't communicate using only sterile, cold, hard facts.

- ✔ Don't be assertive or act formal, reserved, serious, or overly professional.

- ✔ Don't begin abruptly with business talk — warm up to them with social interaction first.

- ✔ Don't offer options that will cause them to over-think, hesitate, and procrastinate in taking action.

- ✔ Don't become impatient or rush them because of their slow decision-making pace.

Affables feel comfortable with a personal presentation, where instead of showing lots of visuals filled with text and data, you make frequent eye contact and have direct interaction — talking through key points, smiling frequently, asking them questions to get feedback, and showing deference to their emotional needs, sensitivities, and inclinations. Affables are receptive to a creative presentation with photos or videos that link business goals with a personal sense of satisfaction and worthwhile contributions to the lives of those impacted at work. Always try to include aspects of the warm and fuzzy type among business-related criteria and information.

Presenting to a Mixed Group of Personality Types

Let's face it; it's relatively easy presenting to just one type of personality because you can develop a straightforward strategy to effectively customize your communication. But what if you have to give a business or technical presentation to an audience comprised of all four personality types?

This section helps you devise an all-inclusive presentation using a sample scenario: Suppose your boss asks you to give a presentation (within the next two days) to tell a potential customer about a new, radically advanced robotic assembly tool the customer is interested in buying from your company. The only thing you know is that there will be several department heads and their staff from the customer's human resources, purchasing, operations, and engineering groups. Unfortunately, time doesn't permit a thorough audience analysis. You have given detailed aspects of this presentation before to other prospects, but you only have 30 minutes now to present a high-level overview to get them excited and motivated to learn more about how the robot can improve their manufacturing metrics.

Scoping out the crowd

With your laptop or tablet connected to an LCD projector, you show up early, test the equipment, grab some coffee, and return to the room before your scheduled presentation to observe the following people:

- A serious-looking woman walking in. With a very upright posture, she's talking on the phone, speaking directly, decisively, and giving directions to someone on the other end. She looks at her watch, sits down at the end of the table, and begins reviewing some paperwork she brought with her. You determine she is likely a Director personality and is probably the head person and decision maker in the group.

- Sitting on the sides of the table are three people working diligently on their iPads, not looking up or talking to anyone. Next to them are marketing brochures and technical flyers about your robotic product. You believe these are Thinkers.

- Standing up and engaged in a lively conversation are a man and two women who smile and gesture enthusiastically as they converse. Two are laughing about something the other said. These are Energizers, you feel.

- Lastly, you notice a woman reading a business magazine published by a major consulting company. The cover story says, "Nurturing Your Engineering Teams on the Job." That's likely a dead giveaway that she is an Affable type.

Warming up the room

Over the next 30 minutes, your strategy and actions appeal to all four diverse types of personalities: Prior to beginning, you go around the meeting room to establish rapport and personally introduce yourself to everyone, starting with the Director female. With a firm handshake, a confident tone, and direct eye contact, you mention to her that you will be talking about the impressive financial and operational results that your robots will deliver for her company.

You meet the two Thinkers and say, pointing to the brochures about your robot, "Impressive. Looks as though you have already done some effective research and homework about our machines. I look forward to answering any detailed technical or operational questions you have about them. I appreciate your reading up about our systems already!"

You greet the cheery Energizers, give them a big smile, thank them for their attendance, and say, "Your company prides itself on being innovative. I'm sure you'll be interested in hearing about the four ultra-advanced features of the robot that put it light-years ahead of any other types out there. Glad to have all of you here today and please jump in with your ideas and comments during my talk!"

Finally, you display a big smile at the Affable and welcome her with a similarly friendly approach. After initial chit-chat, you state how much easier and more pleasant working conditions will be when the robot makes obsolete the dull, repetitive, and difficult fabrication work currently done by people and frees them up to do more creative work in building better products for their company.

Appealing to the entire crowd in your presentation

You have set the stage by warming up the group with some conversation and ever so briefly hitting the likely hot buttons of the group. Now you're primed to rock-and-roll.

During your presentation, you:

- ✔ Start with a compelling, crisply communicated three-minute executive summary of the most important points of your product's value proposition, including results, technical highlights, operational benefits, and financial returns on investment.

- ✔ Mention that you are available afterwards to discuss in-depth, detailed technical information and to answer other questions about your product. You add that you have brought more comprehensive write-ups as handouts for those wanting to analyze and evaluate them in more detail.

- ✔ Give an excellent overview of your product and show operational and financial comparisons (focusing on important contrasts) to not only the machines currently used by this prospect, but in relation to two of your strongest competitors. The group is very impressed when you use your laptop or tablet to show videos and animations of your robot in real operations (similar to what this group does) with an emphasis on impressive gains made in productivity, efficiency, quality, and reductions in waste materials. Throughout the 30-minute presentation, you point out and highlight the exclusive innovations of your robot.

- ✔ Tell the group how your company prioritizes its relationships with customers and that you have the best support program and team in place to make installation relatively easy, painless, satisfying, and rewarding to those who will be the assembly robot operators. You highlight why success is guaranteed and why risk is negligible. You show three psychologically compelling one-minute video testimonials from satisfied customers who back up every claim you've made.

- ✔ Wrap up with a concise, clear, and convincing summary of why your robotic systems will give your prospective customer the proven, impressive benefits that will give their company a significant competitive edge and boost in market share.

This type of presentation should appeal to all four personality profiles.

You don't have to be Dr. Phil to put on the hat of a psychologist to better understand how to customize your presentation and your speaking style to the various personality types of people you communicate with. You can become quite effective at quickly gauging the dominant personality style of the person or group you're presenting to.

Practice observing people based upon the descriptors we provide in this chapter. It will also be a lot of fun. Your overall audience analysis — using the criteria we provide — will make a huge difference in how successful you will be in reaching your innovative presentation goals. It's an investment that will definitely pay off handsomely.

Chapter 5

Planning Your Winning Strategy

．．．．．．．．．．．．．．．．．．．．．．．．．．．．．．．．．．．．．．

In This Chapter

▶ Making a plan

▶ Setting goals

▶ Strategizing for success

▶ Testing the strategic plan

．．．．．．．．．．．．．．．．．．．．．．．．．．．．．．．．．．．．．．

*A*German proverb says, "What's the use of running if you are not on the right road?" Likewise, what's the use of presenting unless you know what you want to achieve — goals — and how you can best get those results — strategy? Your investment in meticulous planning and preparation helps you win before you even step in front of your audience.

No company can be successful in the long term without innovative strategies for product development, sales and marketing, engineering, research and development, and financial management and investment. And it when it comes to dealing with competitors, strategy is king. *Strategy* is a smart game plan — a roadmap — to guide people to achieve goals and strengthen performance. *Tactics* are detailed and specific steps that support a strategy. When you have a goal, a mission, or an objective, strategy then answers the vital question, "How do we best achieve it as quickly, effectively, inexpensively, and as easily as possible?" Strategy in a presentation is an integrated set of ideas, approaches, actions, resources, behaviors, and information, that, when linked together, move you straight toward achieving your goals and ensuring best results.

Our experience training and coaching thousands of presenters tells us that perhaps only five percent of people focus on developing a communication, business, and psychological strategy for important presentations. Instead, they concentrate solely on content. They ask, "What should we talk about and focus upon?" and "What slides should we use?" Although those questions are a part of strategy, presenters miss enormous opportunities to transform and leverage creative ideas into strategies to achieve aggressive presentation goals. Even with important presentations, far too many presenters rush to create content before setting a firm goal, let alone doing a thorough audience and situation analysis and creating an effective strategy.

In this chapter, we explain this most important, yet oft neglected, factor in determining a winning talk. We give you specific steps to set your goals and create a strategy for reaching them. At the end, we describe the steps in action.

Planning for Success

The following steps detail the overall planning process for an innovative presentation.

1. **Identify your desired goal.**

   This is a goal(s) you want to achieve, but don't yet know whether it's reasonably possible. First, you must find out more about your audience and the situation you face regarding the topic and other aspects of your presentation. You can call it your hypothetical goal at this point.

2. **Analyze your audience.**

   Research and discover as much as possible about your audience — their needs, wants, priorities, concerns, current focus — a process we cover in detail in Chapter 4. Gather information about the situation as well: Who is your competition? What obstacles, risks. or constraints for your audience pose problems for you? What factors beyond the situation could impact your presentation?

   For example, is the solution (idea, program, capital expenditure) you propose aligned with the plan and priorities of the organization you're pitching to? What policies, values, strategic directions, and long-term priorities of the organization dictate your goals and strategies? You may have a great solution to the wrong problem. Analyzing the situation gives you a critical edge in your talk.

3. **Confirm or modify your goals.**

   After considering the audience and situation, you can confirm your hypothetical goal stated in Step 1, if it's still realistic and achievable or modify your goal based on information you learned about the group that makes your hypothetical goal unattainable.

   For example, your hypothetical goal may be "sell a project to the group." You discover that the group isn't ready to make a decision, so you change your goal to "generate interest in the project and schedule a follow-up presentation when they're ready to decide."

4. **Create a strategy.**

   After establishing a goal that meets the needs of the audience and situation (based on your research and analysis), you can create a solutions-focused strategy that encompasses aspects of persuasion, communication, psychology, finance, and other factors. Because you are an innovative presenter, you consider creative strategies that are bold, daring, exciting, and interesting — perhaps with elements of surprise, anticipation, suspense, and a bit of tease to them. Think of all the ways you can reach your goals and objectives, and then develop the one you feel has a chance of getting the best results.

5. **Develop content and visuals.**

   Research, select, and develop your content and visuals to support your strategy.

   The content should transition from general to specific during the course of your innovative presentation. Using real facts and examples, it should focus on the needs, wants, and priorities of the audience while explaining and supporting your main points in a relevant, insightful, and motivating way. See Chapter 6 for more information about creating compelling content.

   Your strategy may require targeting people in your group who are both right and left-brained, so you want the content on your visuals to appeal to both intellect and emotion. Create visuals that effectively and efficiently describe, define, explain, prove, and justify your most important messages and claims.

6. **Rehearse and fine-tune.**

   Doing several rehearsals (and videotaping them, if possible) helps you evaluate your presentation. You may decide to modify (add, delete, enhance) your strategy, content, and/or visuals. Ask for feedback from colleagues attending your rehearsal, and use their input to polish and sharpen your presentation. Chapter 8 contains ideas and guidelines for an effective rehearsal session.

Setting goals: What do you want to achieve?

When you give a presentation, do you always know precisely what you want to accomplish and how to best do it with that particular audience? "Of course I do!" you respond. But too many speakers have a somewhat hazy view of the exact results they want to get after they present to a group. Many are just concerned with selecting the slides in current PowerPoint decks instead of thinking of and applying effective strategies to attain their desired results.

After doing your audience and situation analysis, you need to set clearly defined goals that give you and your audience a directional compass. Do this for every presentation or speech. The better you can describe the specific outcomes you want from your presentation, the more precisely you can focus your strategy and resources to reach it. The typical reasons — goals — for giving your presentation or speech are to:

- Show the group how to solve problems or reach a desired goal.
- Get approval for a recommended proposal, project, or program.

✔ Entertain, amuse, or award someone.

✔ Inspire, motivate, and challenge a group to do something.

✔ Sell a product or service (or a vision, idea, or plan).

✔ Showcase a new concept or approach for further discussion and consideration.

✔ Inform, teach, or train a topic or specific set of skills.

✔ Provoke and incite people to take action (as in a political speech or fundraising event).

Creating objectives for your strategy to fulfill

Creating objectives, which are parts of goals, further fine-tunes the planning for your innovative presentation and increases your chances of success because you know with complete accuracy what you want from your audience in terms of a response. With that in mind, you can craft a better strategy, which improves your odds of success.

Consider writing down your specific combination of objectives, and sharing them with your team if you are presenting with others, as in the following example:

As a result of my presentation (or speech), my audience will . . .

✔ Know _____ and be able to use that information in the following ways: _____

✔ Believe and be strongly convinced that _____.

✔ Be able to _____.

✔ Fully feel that _____.

✔ Agree with and support me on _____.

✔ Change their mind and attitude about _____.

✔ Set the stage for the group to think (or brainstorm) with me about _____.

✔ Authorize and make a commitment to _____.

✔ Join with me and my team to _____.

Crafting a Winning Strategy

When your goals and objectives are complete, it's time to do some strategic thinking. Developing a presentation strategy becomes absolutely vital when the stakes are high, when your presentation is fiercely competing with others, and when your audience is likely to push back on your ideas, proposed solutions, or requests.

Your strategy answers the critical question, "How exactly do I get this particular group to buy into (commit, support, approve, act upon) and let me achieve my goals and objectives given the situation they and I are facing?"

An effective strategy is designed to:

✔ Sell your ideas or proposal.

✔ Eliminate doubt, resistance, apathy, cynicism, and other barriers to reaching your goals.

✔ Get your audience to quickly decide to support your plan or project.

Presentation strategies take into consideration the timing of your presentation, obtaining support (from advocates, supporters, and champions) before your presentation, using clever approaches, ultra-compelling content, new technology (that helps the audience better grasp and accept the value of your information and points), and innovative presentation boards, aids, and handouts — all of which lead to smashing success.

You become a communication strategist by pondering all possibilities, opportunities, and options and thinking through every aspect of your presentation and asking, "Do I need to say or do this?" and "Can I say it or show it in a more meaningful, captivating, and compelling way?" and finally, "How do I best capture the imagination, interest, and commitment of this audience to quickly and eagerly act upon my recommendations?"

Preparing for the worst

Another important aspect of your strategy is coming up with contingency actions by asking hypothetical questions such as:

✔ What if the decision maker in the group tells me he's behind schedule, and I have to cut my presentation in half — 30 minutes instead of an hour?

✔ What if people disagree with what I believe is overwhelmingly convincing evidence?

✔ What if an emotional exchange occurs between two audience members while I am presenting?

✔ What if several people in the group strongly want to deviate from my planned topics?

✔ What if the equipment, handouts, or resources I depend on don't arrive or suddenly cause problems that interfere with my presentation?

By carefully thinking through potential (though unlikely) situations and scenarios that would jeopardize your presentation, you're in a better position to eliminate or compensate for them, and your planning will impress your audience greatly and add to your professional stature.

Innovative presenters put extra attention in their strategy by asking how they can add large doses of creativity to make even a technical, scientific, or financial presentation more interesting, fascinating, captivating, enjoyable, fun, amusing, entertaining, playful, and, most importantly, meaningful and valuable.

Learning by example

Fictional WunderVille Consulting is a small, highly imaginative four-person firm that focuses on helping organizations be more creative. WunderVille developed a new process around an exciting game called the Fast Forward Course. Think of it as a mini-amusement park where Sam H., the founder, and his team set up a huge obstacle course in a large hotel boardroom with tape marking roads. The competitive game pits teams of six against each other. Each team drives a remote-controlled truck through brick (paper) walls, runs over dinosaurs, and maneuvers through obstacles and over bridges at the same time other team members operate giant trains to haul robots and get cargo from motorized cranes. It's a comprehensive game with many elements and roles in which teams get scored for how well they symbolically drive change through a course that represents a typical organization.

Sam H.'s company is too small to market this incredibly cool and fun learning event, which teaches the fundamentals of organizational innovation and change, so he found a medium-sized, aggressive consulting company that focuses on change management for clients, Xcelsior Squared, which he wants to partner with to promote and co-run his Fast Forward Course in a revenue-sharing mode. He sets up a presentation with Sara G., the executive vice president (EVP) of planning and marketing and Marcia S., director of change management programs.

Desired presentation goal

Sam's goal is to generate enough interest that the two people attending become willing to quickly negotiate a contract to team together to market and run the Fast Forward Course.

Audience analysis

Sam discovered that Sara, the EVP, loves innovation and creativity, and is a prudent risk-taker and opportunist who wants to expand into new, cutting-edge programs for Xcelsior Squared to boost their market penetration and revenues and garner more prestige in the industry for herself and her firm. However, she depends very heavily upon Marcia, her director of services, in her decision making and won't approve any project or program without Marcia's strong endorsement.

Sam found out that Marcia is very cautious and conservative in her approach and does not rush when making a decision. She thinks her current change programs are sufficient to meet the firm's goals, but she is being asked to attend your presentation by Sara. Marcia sees herself as a leading, respected expert in organizational change management.

Situation analysis

Doing web searches and other research, Sam found out that Xcelsior Squared has some bold plans to expand and grow their client base. They tout their culture as being visionary and innovative. The firm had two bad experiences, however, trying to do a strategic alliance with two potential partners. Marcia led these efforts.

Modified presentation goal

Based upon Sam's audience and situation analysis, he must modify his intended goal. The new one involves generating enough interest for Sara and Marcia to attend an upcoming Fast Forward Course event to see for themselves what it is like and how valuable it would be to do a pilot together before considering negotiating a long-term contract.

Specific objectives

Sam's specific objectives and intentions for his presentation are as follows:

As a result of my presentation, Sara and Marcia will . . .

- ✔ Believe and be strongly convinced that my proposed opportunity needs to be explored with more serious consideration.
- ✔ Be able to understand and appreciate the benefits of my program for Xcelsior Squared.
- ✔ Feel that I and my company are reliable, dependable, and trustworthy.
- ✔ Begin to change their minds and soften their attitudes about having a strategic alliance with WunderVille Consulting.
- ✔ Begin thinking about a contract that mitigates risk of a strategic alliance, but that builds in factors and assurances for long-term success.

✔ Make a commitment to attend my upcoming Fast Forward Event to see a client in action and talk with him about what his department is getting out of participating in the event.

Strategy

Based upon his analysis and his modified presentation goals and objectives, Sam creates the following presentation strategy:

✔ Open with a four-minute video collage of several Fast Forward Courses that emphasize how attendees learn while having fun. Explain the powerful and unique instructional methodology behind the course, which is the only one of its kind in the world right now.

✔ Show empathy and touch Marcia's emotional interest by sharing a disappointing experience similar to that Marcia had with past strategic alliances. Provide assurance that everything possible will be done to avoid another pitfall.

✔ Show three one-minute video testimonials of clients from a small company, a medium-sized one, and a Fortune 50 company who give specific examples and rave about the course.

✔ Explain and justify why the course is perfectly positioned to help Xcelsior Squared grow and prosper with new clients and align with its values and culture of innovation.

✔ Share the overall concept of a rock-solid strategic alliance guaranteed to work extremely well for both parties and prevent the mistakes made in the two previous disappointing ventures.

✔ Provide names and contact information of four organizations WunderVille has had close strategic alliances with so Marcia can verify the integrity, dependability, and excellent cooperation and performance of the WunderVille Consulting team.

✔ Show Sara articles that showcase the course in magazines, newspapers, and websites and mention that Sara would be featured in future promotions as a visionary who took advantage of this opportunity to work together.

✔ Tell Marcia that you understand her experience and expertise are invaluable in making a strategic alliance work and that you would strongly encourage her ideas and input to make the course even better.

✔ Describe how actually seeing this course in person is invaluable to understand the numerous unique and exceptional benefits derived from it and ask for their commitment to attend the next two-hour session.

Chapter 6

Creating Compelling Content

ontent gives substance to your presentation. When it comes to innovative presentations, content creates a vivid picture for your audience. Throughout our book (and in this chapter's title), we use the term *compelling* numerous times. It's a strong, descriptive word meaning to arouse interest in a powerfully, irresistible way or urgently requiring attention. Truly compelling information holds your audience in awe of your presentation.

The best type of compelling content impacts people intellectually and emotionally from various perspectives. Metaphorically, if a standard presentation gives black-and-white, two-dimensional information, a compelling presentation comes across in rich color 3-D. Great presenters don't just inform, they enlighten; they don't just motivate, they move audiences to action.

The guidelines and information in this chapter help you create irresistible content. We show you how to select and use content that consistently compels your audiences to do what you want them to. We focus on the creative aspects of content, but we include some important tips for organizing and outlining your content, too.

Most people jump into content before, or without, going through the essential process of analyzing and planning and don't get the results they expected or hoped for. Worse yet are people who give slide presentations rather than presentations using slides. Using visuals, rather than text, broadens your choices dramatically. For example, some presenters look through an existing slide deck and simply remove the slides they don't need for their upcoming presentation, when truth be told, most presentations — and especially important presentations — need customized, personalized visuals tailored to the audience.

In Chapter 4 we present the four main personality types so you can determine how to present your information to meet the needs of your audience. In Chapter 5, we talk about the presentation planning process and how to use audience analysis to determine the critical strategy that best meets your objectives.

Getting Your Content Up to Par

Compare your presentation content to a well-written article or script that grabs your attention with the opening or introduction, makes information interesting with descriptive narrative, and solicits an emotional reaction. Content can inform, arouse, stimulate, captivate, persuade, rivet, and illuminate. Compelling content — delivered sincerely, with passion and conviction — can change minds and hearts. Content presented creatively alongside unique images and video gives people a new, enriched perspective on a situation and adds dimension to a topic, thus helping people to commit to and act upon your request or recommendation.

Determining your content's purpose

Use your strategy to guide content development. What specifically do you want to accomplish? Think of the effect you want to achieve intellectually and emotionally, such as:

- **Educate:** Enlighten and inform people about a topic they aren't familiar with.

- **Emphasize:** Highlight, spotlight, or focus on something so your audience easily remembers and appreciates its importance.

- **Prove:** Give evidence of something and fully convince people of your claims or points.

- **Reverse:** Change the audience's perceptions or assumptions about something in your topic.

- **Explain:** Make crystal clear why your claims or perspective on a topic are valid and perhaps the best.

- **Justify:** Give valid reasons for doing what you propose.

- **Motivate:** Inspire or urge people to act to improve something.

- **Entertain:** Stimulate and amuse to make your information interesting and fascinating.

When it comes to your content, determine three to five main points you want to make with your audience. Finally, think how to condense and encapsulate your content and message into just one or two sentences for your audience.

Covering your points in priority order

Some movies and television shows pride themselves on clever, unexpected endings that leave the best for last. Likewise, many presenters think surprising their audience with the most important benefit, message, idea or negotiating point in their conclusion creates the most impact. Instead, we recommend that you cover your topics and information in priority order:

1. **Introduce the most critical and valuable areas of interest to your group first.**

2. **Discuss the details of those topics you know your audience values.**

3. **Present extra, potentially valuable but less important information.**

When you use this priority hierarchy, you cover the most vital areas first when you have the highest attention of your group. If, for some reason, several decision makers or technical experts (who are evaluators and recommenders) have to leave your presentation early, they have heard the most essential and valuable information. If people ask more questions and want more discussion on the priority information, you can choose to not present the least important information or topics and devote more time to what matters most to your group.

You still want to repeat and highlight the priority information throughout your talk and especially during your conclusion.

Navigating content

If you're giving a presentation to a large group at an association meeting, convention, or trade show, your presentation can be sequential and tightly structured. However, if you give a presentation where you expect a lot of questions or requests for more specific information, such as in a sales situation, your content and visuals need a flexible organization so you can quickly and smoothly respond to changing conditions.

What would you do if you find out just a few minutes before beginning an important presentation that instead of having the scheduled 45 minutes, you now have just 15 minutes? In that kind of situation, you must re-engineer your presentation. With some careful planning ahead of time, you can quickly adjust. By preparing the following three levels of information, the more time you have, the deeper you go, whereas if your time is cut short, you cover the first level and pick and choose appropriate information from the other two.

✔ **Level 1: Summary:** Communicate your main points and critical highlights. This is the distilled essence of your presentation and can stand alone as a presentation if necessary.

✔ **Level 2: Planned:** This level contains the talk you originally planned for your allotted time with content at the appropriate level of detail to fill the allotted time. With less time, choose the most salient points to add to Level 1.

✔ **Level 3: Extra:** Prepare more detailed or tangential content and visuals that you use to answer specific questions from the audience.

Most presentation apps let you create *hyperlinks,* which can be graphics or text that you click to jump to other, non-sequential, visual content in your presentation. Hyperlinks make your presentation impressively interactive because you can swiftly go right to the information or visual you need rather than click through slide after slide until you get to it.

Don't let extra information go to waste: Consider preparing handouts or publishing the information on your website.

Adding Variety and Impact

You can be a marvelously creative presenter with riveting voice and body language skills, but if your content lacks substance, focus, and relevance, your presentation will miss its mark. In addition to making sure your content fulfills your presentation strategy, you want to present it in creative, interesting, and enjoyable ways. In this section, we describe different types of content and various ways of communicating it.

Think about action movies that keep you on the edge of your seat. Film editors take input from dozens of cameras from different angles and elevations to give variety to a scene. Editors also change entire scenes quickly so as not to let your attention flag for a moment. You seldom see a shot last more than ten seconds! Movie scenes and angles typically change every three to six seconds.

Now think about your presentation. What if your presentation has facts and statistics throughout communicated from a single perspective? Bo-o-o-o-ring. Instead, you want to mix interesting examples, fascinating stories, good video, humorous illustrations, eye-opening comparisons, and metaphors that encapsulate your message in one sentence. Move your presentation along with a rich combination of important information shown from different angles and perspectives to enable people to better understand and appreciate your points.

You won't want to use all of the content types in one presentation. Strive to create the ideal mix that best supports your presentation strategy and goals.

Using facts

Facts are those indisputable things like names, dates, dimensions, specifications, operating characteristics, number of employees and customers, and so on that are accepted or can be easily verified. When a salesperson says, "Our product has been used in over 170 countries for the last 40 years" and can back that up, that's a plain fact, not a claim or guesstimate. Lawyers build their cases exclusively on solid evidence from a body of facts and information, never opinions, speculation, or assumptions. Think about what specific set of facts are important to use in your presentation.

Present the most important facts and make the supporting ones available in a handout or on your website; using too many facts in your presentation leads to audience confusion and boredom.

Giving examples

Great examples clarify your points, reducing any misconceptions or misunderstandings. They add interest and variety to your information, as well as extra meaning, which amplifies the effect of the conveyed information. Throughout our book, as you may notice, we use more than 100 examples to help you fully understand both meaning and context. Using specific cases and situations illustrate potentially abstract or general concepts.

Use brief, realistic, relevant, and complete examples that interest your audience. Consider prefacing your examples with phrases like, "For example" or "An example of that would be." Here are just a couple instances when presenters used examples:

✔ When a politician talks about government waste in spending, she cites several specific, blatant, and shocking examples of money that was foolishly squandered.

✔ The president of a big metropolitan photography club explains the rules for the new members who want to enter the novice photos category to win a prize. She shows 25 photos from different categories that won recognition in the last three competitions and explains why the judges chose each one. Now, the new photographers have a critical base of reference (ideas and evaluation criteria) to go by.

Citing references

Reference written pieces that support or confirm information you present. Search the web for white papers and government reports that provide detailed information about your topic. Respected publications such as *The Wall Street Journal*, *Forbes*, *Fortune*, *Fast Company*, *The Economist*, and *Scientific American* provide excellent sources for quotes. Consult specialized trade or industry publications and journals for the latest research and trends. Companies including IBM, Booz & Company, Capgemini, McKinsey & Company, The Boston Consulting Group, Accenture, and many others conduct research and make the results available to the public.

When quoting from these types of publications:

✔ Mention the name, issue, and date, the title of the article or report, and the author(s).

✔ Use concise excerpts when possible, but if called for, discuss more detailed information such as reading a half-page of the publication.

✔ Always relate the key information in the article to the point you stress.

✔ Consider using the cover or article page as a visual in your presentation.

Here's a (fictional) example:

> According to the June 2015 issue of *Aviation Technology News* in an article titled "Are Light Aircraft Ready for Electric Motors," radically lightweight motor designs made of new materials combined with exotic batteries with ten times the energy density of current ones will usher in an era of inexpensive single-engine planes. Let me quote from the article, "Dr. L.W. Chou said his university has established six critical quantum-leap breakthroughs in integrated electric propulsion over the last three years. The entire package is only six months away from commercialization." With the other information I discuss, this article builds yet a stronger case of a growing trend that can open opportunities for us in. . . .

Telling stories

The best speakers in the world agree on the extraordinary power of storytelling in business or even technical presentations because you can include all kinds of content (facts, statistics, examples, explanations) within the format. Stories have a bottom-line moral along with key messages and learning(s) that reveal purpose. Stories effectively and efficiently convey novel ideas. They illustrate how to solve problems, reach for opportunities, and deal with setbacks, challenges, and outright failures as well as how to pick yourself up to reach new heights of success. Captivating stories inform, motivate, inspire, and enlighten by triggering an emotional response. Peter Guber, the former

Chairman and CEO of Sony Pictures, aptly said, "Move listeners' hearts and their feet and wallets will follow." You can weave a creative tale and use technology, voice, and body language to mesmerize audiences.

When crafting your stories, keep the following tips in mind:

- A good story involves transformation. First the protagonist faces a conflict, and then finds a cure. As the plot progresses, something important changes for the main characters.

- Your story fits your audience — their needs, wants, and interests — and has a key point or moral they'll appreciate.

- People relate to and value your story because it envelops them intellectually and emotionally. Your story must address the situation and issues confronting your group.

- The characters in your story come alive. You explain their pain, fear, concern, hopes, and desires along with their decision making, their struggles, and their ultimate victory or personal and professional change as a result of the conflict or challenge facing them.

You can find many superb storytellers when you search online for both motivational and also TED speakers; let the ways they masterfully use stories in their presentations inspire you. Browse the library at TED talks at www.ted. com/talks/browse. You can also type "speakers bureaus" in to a browser for a list of agencies that represent motivational speakers who specialize in telling great stories. Go to the speakers' websites to view their video demo tapes and see the power of storytelling!

Going by the numbers

Although many presenters know the meaning and relative importance of the numbers they throw at audiences, numbers can be abstract unless you supply a point of reference and bring statistics to life.

Several years ago a U.S. politician sounded the alarm bell that a foreign nation had created the world's fastest supercomputer and that the United States could lose its critical technological edge. He gave the numbers: speed was 2.5 petaflops (one quadrillion floating point operations per second) or 2.5 followed by 15 zeroes; it had over 7,000 GPUs (graphics processing units); and over 14,000 CPUs (central processing units — the computers). He went on to say it cost almost $90 million and required a little over 4 megawatts to power up. Even though he correctly rounded the numbers off, the non-technical audience might have been glassy-eyed until he put it in clearer context and perspective. He said this new computer was 29 million times more powerful than the first Cray supercomputer in 1976!

Make sure the numbers relate to the point you want to make, that they are necessary and add validity to your other information. Be prepared to give the source of your statistics, if asked. Unless exact numbers are critical to make comparisons to baseline numbers, round them off. Consider breaking numbers into more recognizable and meaningful units and terms such as per person, average, median, and ranges (minimum to maximum), ratios, or percentages.

Use the old rule of thumb to simplify numbers: Instead of saying 84.7 percent, say 5 out of 6; instead of 12.5 percent, use 1 out of 8.

Quoting experts

Quotations not only add interest to your talk, but give relevance and support to the points you want to highlight. Use a combination of serious and humorous quotations to add a fresh new look to things your audience values.

Use quotations that directly connect with your points from well-respected, established authorities in their fields from your own country. Keep in mind the old faithful standbys of famous Greek and Roman philosophers, Winston Churchill, Abraham Lincoln, Mahatma Gandhi, Albert Einstein, and humorists like Will Rogers and Mark Twain. Make use of statements by current business experts, famous authors, celebrities, comedians, and other popular icons in your culture.

Innovative presenters try to find those creative, interesting quotations that add punch and pizzazz to their messages. As with any other type of content, you can use several quotations throughout your talk without overdoing it.

Contrasting and comparing

Contrasts show striking differences between two things. A presenter at a software design conference speaks about advances in 3-D gaming animation where the facial hair, skin, and other physical features of animated characters are almost indistinguishable from photographs of actual people. To illustrate the advances made in this software, he shows a game created 15 years ago compared to today's latest being played on Microsoft Xbox and Sony's PS4 PlayStation. The difference is shocking in terms of the past technology's lower resolution, lack of realism, lighting, and shading aspects, among other characteristics, capabilities, and performance. This comparison visually communicates the stark differences between old and new. An author and keynote speaker uses contrast to discuss and describe the vast differences between how an open-minded company with an innovative culture operates, grows, and prospers versus a closed company that shuns creativity and innovation and instead embraces the status quo that leads to mediocre operational and financial results.

A comparison, on the other hand, evaluates the qualities of being similar, yet different. For example, presenters use comparison when discussing options available to their audiences. Say, for example, a presenter wants to show her internal group of executives that she came up with three program designs to help her organization go through a major change process. She discusses how each specific program, although having the same goals and objectives, has different strategies, resources, and activities with their own mix of pros and cons. She compares the three by describing their attributes and then recommends program number two and explains why she believes this is the optimum one based upon the stated needs and criteria from the executive board. The well-done comparison aides the audience in their decision making.

Find circumstances in your presentation where stark, eye-opening contrasts and detailed comparisons help to describe, explain, and emphasize your points.

Giving demonstrations

"Seeing is believing," as the saying goes. Demonstrations, when performed properly during a presentation, lend proof to your claims, especially with skeptics or cynics. If you work in sales, marketing, or in a technical capacity, product demonstrations back up and verify your claims about your product being the fastest, most durable, most flexible, easiest to use, lightest, most quiet, or whatever the outstanding capacity places your product or service above the competition. Demonstrations add dynamism, drama, and interest to your talk. They create three-dimensional realism that appeals to several senses. Numerous research studies confirm the obvious fact that the more a person's senses (sight, sound, touch, smell, taste) are involved in an evaluation process, the easier and faster they can be persuaded. Just look at infomercials and the creativity they use to demonstrate their slicer-dicers, vacuums, or exercise equipment, and you'll understand why they're so successful. (We analyze infomercials' effectiveness in Chapter 20.)

Oftentimes the more dramatic the demonstration, the more impressive. At the annual Paris Air Show, the world's oldest and largest commercial air show, major manufacturers (such as Boeing, Lockheed, BAE, and Sukhoi) demonstrate the capabilities of their military and civilian aircraft to potential customers. You see the best pilots doing what look like impossible maneuvers — straight up take-offs, hairpin turns, stalls, and steep landings — to prove their machines are the best of the lot.

Demonstrators use a traditional demonstration technique called FAB (Feature, Advantage, Benefit). Say that at a trade show for construction and remodeling companies, your company features an industrial-quality cordless drill. You talk about its brushless motors and say, "One key *feature* of our drill is the industry's most advanced brushless motors. The *advantage* is they are more powerful, durable, and have greater efficiency. The *benefit* to your construction professionals is greater productivity and reliability, which enables them to do more in less time. And that translates into more profits for your company."

When you include a demonstration in your presentation, practice ahead of time so it comes across as realistic and is done smoothly and professionally.

Any time you can, invite people from the audience to actually use your product or service as you guide them through the demonstration. Experiencing your claims firsthand removes any doubt an audience member may have.

Defining terms

Definitions ensure understanding of your information. Unless you specifically define terms that may be ambiguous, unknown, or leave space for multiple interpretations, your audience may misunderstand your meaning. For example, an aeronautical engineer says, "This potentially quantum leap wing design is *bleeding edge,* not just leading edge." She goes on to say, "Let me define what I mean by bleeding edge. . ."

Obviously, you need to know your audience and their level of knowledge before you start defining terms that may be totally known to them. But, if unsure, you can subtly build in definitions without insulting the audience's knowledge or experience, as in this example, "Our R&D department is expanding our studies into new forms of *nanotechnology,* which, as you know, is the manipulation of matter on an atomic and molecular level for the fabrication of novel new products with a vast range of applications. Let me give you several jaw-dropping examples of what we're doing." As you develop your content, think of all the terms you may need to define for your audience.

Rehearse your presentation in front of someone who has a knowledge level similar to your prospective audience and ask her to identify terms that may be confusing.

Answering rhetorical questions

Although more of a technique to enhance content instead of a type of content, rhetorical questions create anticipation, curiosity, and suspense for what follows. A *rhetorical question* poses a query without expecting an answer. It creates curiosity, anticipation, or even suspense and gets your audience thinking about the question you just asked.

Say you have skeptics in your audience who don't believe using your company's new manufacturing and assembly process is a good idea because of disruptions in the changeover due to training time, halted production, and poor return on investment. In this example, after your introduction, but before you get into the brief process overview, set the stage with several rhetorical questions that have a touch of devil's advocate in them to get people thinking:

> Your current process has been very successful for so long. That's a great testimony to your accomplishments! But nothing stands still for long. Your competitors are biting at your heels to knock you out of the lead position in your industry by implementing significant innovations to make their operations more productive, more efficient, more accurate, and higher quality.
>
> Can you afford to let them do that at your expense? Of course not!
>
> Why change right away and go with our comprehensive fabrication and assembly process when others are less costly and take less time to install and start operating?
>
> Aren't you going to get hassles and disruptions in changing over to our new integrated system with the complexities you perceive it having?
>
> How can you know for sure you'll get rapid payback and a return on investment that you'll be proud of?
>
> In the next 45 minutes, let's explore solid answers to those questions, which anyone in your position would naturally have. I say this with a sense of confidence and assuredness: You will be surprised and, I believe, quite pleased with what you hear during our presentation!"

Asking those tough rhetorical questions without expecting answers will pique the audience's curiosity as to how you'll answer them, which means you will have their full attention and can then earn their interest and acceptance.

Explaining yourself

Explanations help your group understand, and perhaps better value, what you discuss. If a description involves answering *what,* then an explanation answers *why* and *how.* While reviewing your content, look at where explanations are needed to describe the *why* and *how* of your information.

You may use explanations to:

✔ Explain the cause of and reasons why a problem developed before you discuss your proposed solution, as in, "Let me explain exactly why the problem surfaced and how it affected that organization before I tell you about our carefully engineered solution to eliminate that problem and keep it from occurring again."

✔ Explain why a product or service was designed a certain way or why it operates the way it does. For example, "There's a reason we made the structure out of titanium instead of high-strength steel. Let me explain the purpose and benefit of it for you."

✔ Interpret anything your audience didn't fully understand by saying something like, "I guess I didn't cover that area as much as I need to. Let me explain with more clarity and detail how we arrived at those return on investment and net present value estimates."

Making assumptions

Surely you've been cautioned to never assume anything but in discussing your program, project, or proposed solution, you sometimes have to make and communicate reasonable and likely assumptions when solid facts and data aren't available, especially when you're forecasting future situations. You want to tell your audience your necessary assumptions and why you're making them. It's a way of saying, "Assuming this happens, then that will occur."

Explain your assumptions and communicate them only if needed when concrete information isn't available. Make sure to create realistic and probable assumptions. Consider this example of an effective assumption:

> The financial returns on your investment with our advanced systems is predicated on several likely assumptions or expectations. One: Interest rates will not change or will change very little. According to the Federal Reserve, interest rates will not vary more that one half of a percent over the next year. Two: Your production levels will increase by about an average of 15 percent over the next three years, according to the estimates you gave to me. Three: You'll receive an increase in productivity of about 35 percent if you follow our procedures strictly. Although this improvement isn't a commitment, it is a solid and realistic projection based on the fact that over 90 percent of our 76 customers experienced productivity increases between 30 and 40 percent over the last two years.

Use assumptions when unknowns or unpredictable situations only allow you to guess at future projections or forecasts. Use assumptions sparingly and consider calling them *expectations* or *likelihoods* if the term *assumption* might hurt your credibility.

Showing testimonials

Testimonials help close business deals with new customers and get approval for internal projects, programs, or strategic changes. It's one thing when you say that your training business can get stellar results, it's another when four sincerely satisfied clients brag about what you delivered and describe your team's stellar performance in very specific ways. Video testimonials are a powerful way to highlight your product's features and address concerns, doubts, skepticism, or fears people might have. Several, brief (one minute) testimonials from a diverse group of articulate people in jobs and positions that have meaning for your audiences can be a terrific tool to help you convince your group.

Well-done testimonials are really short stories that present a problem the testifiers faced, their decision-making process (including some hesitations), what critical factors made them buy into your product or program, and the results that made it worthwhile. Although a testimonial should give some important specifics on the virtue of what you advocate, a winning one helps people in the audience relate to the decision-making process others went through and the criteria others used, which can help provide context for your group's upcoming decision.

Include scanned photos of testimonial letters with the key parts highlighted or show comments from satisfied customers on your website in your presentation. Some innovative presenters use a live telephone or Skype call to provide a testimonial from one or more customers or experts who endorse your presentation messages and even let the audience ask questions. If you have such a willing and able person, prepare her carefully by describing your audience, your presentation objectives, strategy, and content along with likely questions (include possible tough ones) from your audience. Skype calls can be risky because of unknowns, but they are *very* powerful if all goes well! And, you really want your customer to be frank and truthful, even if some answers disappoint you, otherwise, it seems like a setup.

Making analogies

French novelist and poet Victor Hugo, who wrote *Les Misérables*, waxed metaphorical with, "Laughter is the sun that drives winter from the human face." Deep, isn't it? Aristotle said ". . . it (a metaphor) is the mark of genius, for to make good metaphors implies an eye for resemblance."

Professional speakers use lots of good metaphors such as: "Your past should be a springboard, not a hammock," and "A mind is designed to be a storehouse (of ideas), not a wastebasket." One motivational speaker, who cautioned his audience to learn from the past and to never dwell in it, but move on, quoted a poignantly profound metaphor from Richard Kadrey's book, *Kill the Dead,* "Memories are bullets. Some whiz by and only spook you. Others tear you open and leave you in pieces." Memories take on new meaning and perspective.

An *analogy* is a perceived likeness between two things. The only real difference between a metaphor and analogy is the addition of the word "like" to "is." Shakespeare used his famous metaphor, "All the world's a stage." If he'd used an analogy, it would have been, "All the world's like a stage." Comedian Joey Adams used to say, "A bikini is like a barbed-wire fence. It protects the property without disturbing the view." Innovative presenters look for the right humorous analogy to perfectly illuminate and encapsulate many points into one strong and memorable one.

Chevy's "Like a rock" campaign is an example of an innovative business analogy, not to mention one of the most successful, long-running (1991 to 2004) television commercials of all time. Accompanied by the Pete Seeger song, *Like a Rock*, scenarios show Chevy trucks taking incredibly brutal punishment and handling it . . . like a rock. The gobs of emotion and Americana jammed into a captivating, 30-second commercial produced record sales for Chevrolet.

Steve Jobs said, "When you touch someone's heart, that's limitless." If your metaphor or analogy evokes or awakens feelings in your audience, you can count on a making a lasting impact.

Look for every opportunity to translate your important information and messages into those clever, colorful, and compelling metaphors and analogies that will be appreciated and long remembered.

Chapter 7

Honing Your Platform Skills

. . . .

. . . .

Richard Burton, one of Britain's premier actors, had a supremely magnetic and charismatic stage presence along with an incomparably rich and resonant voice. It was said that Burton could read names out of a phone book and make it sound like a dramatic Shakespearean performance. James Earl Jones, Morgan Freeman, Ben Kingsley, Elizabeth Taylor, Orson Wells, and Meryl Streep are just a few of many other actors who brilliantly use(d) their voices to enchant, scare (Jones was the voice of Darth Vader in the first *Star Wars* movies), tease, express remorse, taunt, show affection or passion, punctuate, surprise, add urgency, and, with consummate skill, project every emotion that human beings can feel and show. Former U. S. president Ronald Reagan used his professional acting skills — body movements and broadcast-quality voice — to look and act the part of the confident world leader, giving speeches that touched the hearts of millions.

Every innovative presentation requires not just excellent technical speaking skills, but personal and imaginative ways to connect with and fascinate, enthrall, motivate, inspire, enlighten, and compel the audience to take action. If you have ever experienced a superb motivational speaker who mesmerized you with captivating stories that evoked belly laughs, tears, and an outpouring of inspiration, then you appreciate how masterfully good speakers use their bodies through facial expressions, gestures, movement, and posture, and their voices through rate, tone, pitch, volume, and pauses. They play their nonverbal and vocal skills like fine musical instruments to make their words sparkle, and you remember their messages long after they leave the stage. When they tell an electrifying story, they make it burst alive with the most reliable audio-visual equipment at their command — their words, voice, and body — which gives them exceptional platform presence and command of their topic and audience.

The finest speakers know that subtle changes in volume, voice tone, and pitch, along with articulated body movement, arm gestures, and facial expressions, can convey important emotion cues that powerfully and psychologically reinforce the spoken word, adding greater meaning and substance to their persuasive messages. Finely honed presentation delivery skills rivet your audience's interest and set you far apart from the crowd of ordinary presenters who give just an average or good performance.

This chapter covers the special delivery secrets for your presentation, speech, or video taping. You learn creative ways to use your voice and body for impressive effect and superior results.

Using Your Voice to Command Attention

Today's busy, multitasking business audiences quickly tune out a monotone, passive speaker who drones on like sleep-inducing white noise. Whether in front of thousands in a stadium or a dozen in the boardroom, a great speaker owns the stage with his confidence, self-assurance, and convicted way of presenting information with passion. This secret of performance success revolves around not only being a great public speaker and presenter, but also letting your natural, sincere personality shine through while talking. Enthusiasm and speaking dynamics can have many variations and degrees of effect. This doesn't require bouncing off the walls like the late comedian Chris Farley's hysterical *Saturday Night Live* skit playing the over-caffeinated, boisterous motivational speaker Matt Foley who "lives in a van down by the river."

In this section, we present three rules for using your voice and additional speaking tips.

To professionally hone your delivery skills — one of the seven secrets of performance success — join a speaking club such as Toastmasters and consider taking an acting or presentation skills class and working with a voice coach.

Rule 1: Speak out loud

Volume is the loudness or softness of your voice. It's the amount of energy, intensity, and force you use to emit sounds. Good speaking volume is critical because if you can't be heard, nothing else matters. If people can't hear, they become frustrated, restless, and annoyed. If they have to strain to listen, they tune you out or get up and leave if they can.

Leaders — actual or aspiring — leverage their voice and body language to project a strong image of competence, confidence, and conviction. A strong, dynamic, and resonant voice shows that you're confident, that you believe what you're saying, and that you're enthusiastic about your topic. It may also convey a sense of urgency and commitment. As simple as it sounds, a sufficiently powerful voice gives people the impression that you have the vigor, energy, and even leadership to get the job (you're proposing) done.

Consistently using a low speaking volume, especially if combined with poor eye contact, monotone, and a stiff or defensive posture, is likely to give people the impression that you lack confidence, feel uncomfortable speaking in public, or are nervous or overly meek (or weak).

Talk loudly enough to be easily heard by everyone, including those farthest away from you at the extreme corners of the room.

Showing emotions

Great presenters and speakers can display intended emotions for effect. The combination of your words and voice and body language in presentations and speeches can convey a gamut of expressive, rich emotions, including:

Affection

Aggression

Agitation

Alarm

Amusement

Anger

Annoyance

Anxiety

Boredom

Calm

Compassion

Concern

Confidence

Contempt

Conviction

Curiosity

Defeatism

Delight

Desire

Disappointment

Dismay

Distress

Empathy

Enthusiasm

Exasperation

Excitement

Ferocity

Frustration

Fury

Gloom

Guilt

Hurt

Interest

Irritation

Joy

Longing

Optimism

Pain

Passion

Playfulness

Poise

Regret

Remorse

Revulsion

Sadness

Scorn

Shock

Surprise

Triumph

Urgency

Rule 2: Project your voice — without shouting

If the first rule is to raise your volume so that your listeners can hear you (especially in the face of background noise in the room or around the area in which you are presenting such as at a trade show), then the second rule is to *project* your voice instead of shouting. Speaking loud by shouting comes across as strained, empty, and unnatural. It may also appear overbearing, harsh, or irritating.

Did you ever wonder how orators in antiquity could be heard by thousands of people without the benefit of amplifying speakers? And, how is it that a small dog can bark so loudly and an infant cry with such surprising lung power for so long? These three examples all involve projecting voices using *diaphragmatic breathing* (also called *deep breathing* or *belly breathing*) which is used by yoga practitioners, martial artists, and singers, as well as professional speakers.

Your *diaphragm* is a thin sheet of dome-shaped muscle that separates your lungs from your stomach. In deep breathing, as you slowly and deeply breathe in air through your nose, your abdomen expands (rather than your chest) along with your diaphragm, thus sucking in large volumes of air that fill your lungs. As you exhale slowly, your diaphragm contracts upward pushing air from your lungs. Visualize the air filling your lungs from your collarbone to the bottom of all of your ribs and then that same space emptying from the bottom of your ribs to your clavicle as your exhale. Make your inhalation as long as your exhalation. Do this deep breathing exercise ten times in a row several times a day, ideally while standing or lying flat on your back, or at least sitting up straight with your shoulders pulled back. Work up to a count of ten on both the inhalation and exhalation, After you develop a routine like this, you won't even know you are doing it while speaking, and you'll be amazed at how much better your voice sounds. Good, rich voice projection facilitated by breathing deeply and naturally does not sound like shouting in the least.

You can compare deep breathing to the woofer of a speaker system that visually moves in and out pushing larger quantities of air than smaller mid-range speakers or a tiny tweeter. Just like the woofer, diaphragmatic breathing enables your lungs to push out greater volumes of air, which produces deeper and richer speaking tones along with a louder volume without straining your throat or sounding harsh. The increased oxygen in your bloodstream relaxes you as well, reducing speaking jitters.

Deep breathing exercises performed throughout each day provide health and relaxation benefits and serve you well when speaking.

Rule 3: Vary your volume

Although you must speak loudly enough for everyone to hear you, you should vary your volume to match your intention. Variety of volume as well as speech rate, tone, and pitch, is key to making your presentation easy and enjoyable to listen to.

Even if you possess a room-filling, bone-rattling baritone voice, without variation, it becomes monotonous and monotone. By changing your volume throughout your presentation, you come across as conversational.

Aim to maintain the volume level that projects your voice to the back of the room and then vary between three and six different voice levels — from a whisper to a shout. As a theatrical style technique, many motivational speakers and some highly skilled business presenters selectively speak low enough to whisper. You'd be amazed how — at the right time, in the right way, for the right reasons — that whisper suddenly grabs hold of an audience's attention because they are intensely curious and straining to hear what the whisper might be about. (We talk more about this in the next section, "Speaking softly.")

Use volume to emphasize and highlight certain words or terms. When you suddenly increase or decrease your volume, it shocks or alerts your audience to a change that jolts their attention. The rise and fall of your voice indirectly signals differences between major ideas and information and subordinate details that support them.

Raise your volume when you come to important parts of your presentation such as:

- ✔ Benefits of the product, service, program, or project you're proposing.
- ✔ Key points, main messages, critical facts, statistics, or other information the audience must understand to appreciate the value of your proposal.
- ✔ Recommendations, suggestions, requests, and solutions you offer to the group.
- ✔ Quotations, metaphors, examples, comparisons, and contrasts that support your main points.
- ✔ Specific aspects of a visual, video, or animated part of the presentation.

Speaking softly

Speaking for a time at one volume level and then suddenly lowering your voice and saying important words or numbers softly (and even repeating them) can separate and spotlight them as much as raising your voice. Combine lower volume with a slower speech rate and a pause to command rapt attention.

Determine where in your presentation a whisper would create a dramatic effect that arouses curiosity, suspense, or otherwise builds anticipation to hear more. Your choice of raising or lowering your voice depends upon the type of audience, their mood, your presentation goals, and the effect you want to produce.

Varying your volume, rate, pitch, and tone makes you sound more natural and more interesting.

Adjusting your rate

Rate of speech is how fast you talk in words per minute (wpm) and is also called *speed, pace, tempo,* and *rhythm.* The typical or average speech rate is about 125 wpm, and we recommend that you speak between 110 to 180 wpm, although not consistently.

How can you tell if you speak within the 110 to 180 words-per-minute guideline? Read one or two pages of a prepared (scripted) speech or presentation out loud and time yourself for a minute. Count the words you read and divide it by 60 to get your average wpm.

A constant rate of speech almost always accompanies a dull, monotone speaking voice. Using an unvarying speed and pitch works great for a hypnotist ("you are getting very sleepy . . . "), but it's not so effective for a presenter. Like a fine passage of music, which alternates between speeding up and slowing down, your voice should vary in rate throughout your talk. Changing your pace sounds more natural and makes your delivery come across more animated and conversational.

Fast talking at higher speeds can confuse an audience, make it difficult for them to concentrate, or just plain annoy them. Other than your attempts at vocal showmanship, speaking quickly during your presentation suggests nervousness, lack of confidence, irritability, or being rushed — the audience may get the impression you have somewhere else to be! This feeling is magnified when you accompany fast talking with poor eye contact, stiff posture, and lack of gestures. Worse, with certain glib personality types, fast talking can be perceived as slick or smarmy. However, when combined with sincere smiling, meaningful gestures, and effective eye contact, a somewhat faster pace indicates enthusiasm, excitement, and enjoyment.

The term *fast* is relative: Trisha Paytas, a model and actress from Los Angeles, has a black belt in fast talking. She set a world record by speaking (if you call it that) 710 words in only 54 seconds! It sounds like gibberish until you slow down the recording and find her articulation is nearly flawless!

Don't pack your presentation with overflowing information if you have a limited amount of time. That forces you to rush through your presentation by talking fast and furiously.

Varying your speaking rate in a presentation is like shifting gears in a car — you use each speed for a purpose as the situation and needs dictate: starting out, going up hill, straightaway cruising, speeding up to pass, or coming to a stop.

The following sections offer tips to help you use the appropriate rate of speech.

When to slow down

A slower pace can help in these situations:

- ✔ At the beginning of your presentation. Rather than rushing into your presentation, start slowly. If you have some stage fright, speaking slowly helps, and it makes you come across poised, calm, and composed.

- ✔ When your audience isn't familiar with your material. Especially if the information you're presenting is technical, complex, statistical in nature, or has abstract concepts, going slowly helps your audience keep up with you. A slower pace helps with words and complicated terms you're introducing for the first time and those that may be hard to pronounce.

  For example, a presenter may want to speak more slowly while discussing an acronym: "Great strides have been made in the last two years with laser technology for medicine, science, construction, and other applications. As you may know, *laser* is an acronym that stands for light . . . amplification by . . . stimulated . . . emission of . . . radiation." (Speaking the acronym slowly lets the meaning and definition sink in.)

- ✔ To add vocal punch when you want to highlight key ideas, main messages, or vital pieces of information. Slowing down lets significant points sink in for your group. To add weight, use a louder volume and a two-to-three second pause before and after those points. Then, speed your rate up as you add details and filler information to illustrate, give examples, or otherwise describe the essential parts of your presentation.

- ✔ When declaring your call to action. When you're requesting donations from the audience, asking to close a sale, or seeing specific support or commitment, you don't want to appear rushed, nervous, or hesitant, which a sudden burst of faster talking may imply.

When to accelerate

Picking up the pace is appropriate at these points:

- ✔ To show extra enthusiasm, excitement, or emotion or as a suspenseful buildup to a secret.

- ✔ When you go over necessary but familiar background material, provide additional details, or do several quick summaries throughout your presentation.

- ✔ To change transitions in your content, as a segue to a quicker pace of talking.

> ✔ During certain parts of an interesting story you tell to make a point. A good storyteller, like a stage performer, uses the ebbs and tides of vocal variety to guide the energy flow of the tale up and down to make stories captivating and impacting.

Even though you vary your speech rate between slower and faster, avoid speaking hiccups (abrupt stops and starts).

Adding a solid punch to a statement

You can use a vocal trick to emphasize something by exaggerating your rate slowdown, while increasing your voice volume and energy. Here's an example of how it works: Say you want to gloss over something. So in an almost trivial, matter-of-fact way (with no tonal energy or variation) you say, "With the total U.S. debt at 20 trillion dollars, we have a major problem." Then follow that statement by saying, "Health insurance costs are also an economic hardship. The average deductible for people is an incredible F-I-F-T-E-E-N T-H-O-U-S-A-N-D D-O-L-L-A-R-S!" See the difference? By using voice tricks, you can de-emphasize the titanic dollar figure — $20 trillion dollars — while pumping up the (relatively) less critical $15,000 amount. It's a psychologically powerful tool.

We're not suggesting that you be devious, we're simply illustrating how, by dramatically slowing your rate down and methodically drawing out each work with a pumped-up volume and passionate expression, you can direct your audience's attention where you want.

Pausing eloquently

The English poet, writer, and novelist Rudyard Kipling aptly said, "By your silence, ye shall speak." And as classical pianist Artur Schnabel profoundly noted, "I don't think I handle the notes much differently from other pianists. But the pauses between the notes — ah, there is where the artistry lies!" Using pauses effectively and dramatically in your presentations reflects your speaking artistry and eloquence.

The main reasons to use pauses are for variety, understanding, and emphasis. A pause is a form of oral punctuation that can help your audience reflect on what you just said. In a way, sudden silence (especially if you've been using a quickened rate of speech) has the same effect as a sudden loud noise. It alerts your audience and makes them attentive to what you say next. When using a pause for emphasis, you want to focus audience attention on your most important pieces of information.

Pauses regulate the rhythm of your speech like that of a natural conversation. They also help you collect your thoughts before moving onto the next piece of information.

Determine when and how long a pause should be to enhance your presentation. Typical pauses last one to two seconds; dramatic, extended pauses last as long as four to six seconds.

Although these commonly termed *pregnant pauses* may seem unnatural for you and uncomfortable for your audience, the longer theatrical-style pauses — done at strategic times in your presentation — can have a very strong impact. They are often used to give people time to consider the paramount consequences of your statement.

Keep in mind that too many long pauses or too many pauses in general can make your presentation choppy.

Consider using a pause either before or after the following types of content:

- ✔ Key points and critical messages
- ✔ Vital facts, statistics, or other shocking information
- ✔ Important quotations
- ✔ A rhetorical or thought-provoking question
- ✔ Key names, dates, events, or titles
- ✔ Essential benefits of your product, service, proposal, plan, or program
- ✔ During the buildup of suspenseful parts of your story
- ✔ Impact and consequences of problems or situations your audience is facing

Proper use of pauses can prevent *sentence run-on,* which is going from sentence to sentence without stopping. An attendee in our training session called it "a motor mouth without a brake."

If you enumerate points, using a pause in between can help an audience absorb each one. When you use pauses, make sure that you apply them deliberately and cleanly. You don't want to give your audience the impression that you're repeatedly groping for words or hesitating, which can come across as being nervous or unprepared. You want to be articulate, but don't be too deliberate in terms of pausing frequently between words, so that your pace, combined with a slow, even rate of speech, becomes either frustrating or sleep-inducing.

To add extra punch to your pause, slow down your speech rate and increase your speech volume just before you pause. While you are pausing for several seconds, use good eye contact around the room to reinforce what you said. You can use pause and repetition of your point for a dramatic effect. Raise your volume in steps as you repeat each point for increasing emphasis.

The acclaimed British Shakespearean stage actor Ralph Richardson had this insight, "The most precious things in speech are pauses." Consummate presenters, those who have learned the power of perfectly timed silence, know the value and truth of that. As you watch good movies, television dramas, and plays, for example, see how the seasoned professionals use pauses. You'll be impressed and you can adopt some of those refined techniques.

Avoid using fillers like *uh, okay, uhm,* and *you know* instead of intended pauses. Practice and concentrate on finishing each sentence without a filler, and you'll soon rid yourself of that bad speaking habit.

Captivating Audiences with Your Eyes

Whether in a romantic novel or a spy thriller, much has been written about the mystique of a person's eyes and the effect they can have on people. It's been said that the face is a picture of what lies in the mind and heart with the eyes as the interpreter. You have, of course, heard that the eyes are the mirrors of the soul and the expression "They were seeing eye to eye." These sayings reinforce the major role that eye contact plays in human relations, including speeches and business presentations.

The majority of presentation trainers and coaches consider eye contact to be the most important of the nonverbal speaking skills. It is so important that without effective eye contact, you cannot reach your objectives. The numerous benefits of great eye contact include:

- ✔ Establishing and maintaining rapport with your audience
- ✔ Setting a positive tone for your presentation
- ✔ Subtly controlling your audience, while holding their attention
- ✔ Reinforcing and emphasizing your key points and ideas
- ✔ Getting immediate feedback on people's reaction to your talk
- ✔ Giving you an enhanced image of credibility, confidence, and charisma

Eye contact is a personal thing. It shows that you want to connect and that you care.

Understanding the importance of eye contact

Do you trust someone who talks to you but doesn't look you in the eye? Does that make you feel uncomfortable? Well, the same applies to people in your audience. If you don't engage them with eye contact, it not only takes away the personal touch and hurts rapport, but people in your audience will form a negative impression of you — that you're nervous, feel uncomfortable with your topic, are hiding something, or are afraid of the reaction to your talk. But if you make good eye contact, your audience members sense you're enjoying your presentation, that you like being with them, and that you're confident in your topic and speaking ability.

An audience mimics your behavior, so if you display enthusiasm about your topic, they will too.

What's interesting is how you can psychologically keep the interest of people — influence their reactions — by looking directly at them. Next time you give a presentation notice this: As you look at people, in almost 100 percent of the cases, they look back at you.

On the one hand, looking directly into someone's eyes pressures them to look back at you. On the other hand, if you look at the walls in the room or stare at the projection screen, people may feel free to look at their smartphone or tablet or otherwise redirect their attention away from you. Even with large audiences, systematically making eye contact with different sections of the room will keep people looking back at you.

Flexibility and adaptability characterize innovative presenters. While maintaining eye contact with as many people as possible, you constantly analyze and gauge how the group is reacting to your talk. The audience's body language, whether positive (sitting on the edge of their seats, nodding in agreement, and smiling) or negative (yawning, looking at watches, fidgeting, frowning), tell you whether they're eagerly listening, anxious to hear more, positively receptive to the information, or bored, restless, frustrated, confused, or irritated. Because you continuously look at people, you can judge whether you need to speed things up, move onto the next area in your presentation, slow down and give more explanations, examples, and details, engage people in discussions, or ask them questions to determine whether they're bothered or are having difficulty understanding something.

Use your eyes for emphasis. When you come to your main points, maintain strong eye contact with your group. To add dramatic effect, you can walk to the center of the meeting room (or stage) to get closer to your audience right before you communicate your critical point, add more voice volume, and pause while you look around the room with direct eye contact. This combination of voice and body movement adds powerful emphasis when needed.

Speaking with your eyes

Tarjei Vesaas, a Norwegian novelist and poet aptly quipped, "Almost nothing need be said when you have eyes." Obviously, eyes alone, without talking and visuals, won't cut it for your typical business presentation, but your eyes do communicate, so here are some tips for effective eye-speak:

- ✔ When you begin your talk, let your eyes sweep through the audience.

- ✔ Look directly into the eyes of others. Don't look over their heads or anywhere else.

✔ Maintain random eye contact around the room — don't make it look contrived by mechanically swinging your head side-to-side and doing eye contact in a predictable, systematic way. As you speak, ask yourself, "Who haven't I looked at yet?

✔ Look at each person for about three to six seconds as if talking to just that individual. If you look for less time, say a second, that's glancing, and if you look longer, people feel uncomfortable — as if they're being singled out.

Avoid the following eye-contact no-nos:

✔ Staring at your notes, the projection screen, the floor, or anywhere else except your group.

✔ Looking only at friendly, supportive people who are nodding, smiling, and otherwise giving you positive feedback; spread your eye contact around the room.

✔ Overdoing eye contact with specific people such as the senior managers, prominent and influential people, or the top decision makers. However, when you come to important parts of your presentation, look at the key people to emphasize your point and gauge their reactions.

✔ Shifting your eyes; move your head and even your entire body to look around.

Keeping eye contact with a large audience

In our training or presentation coaching programs, people often ask, "How can we really do effective eye contact with an audience of 500 to 2,000 or even more?" The closer you are to someone, for example to your immediate front or close left and right sides, the more that person can detect if you are looking directly at him. The farther away you are from someone, the less he can see if you are looking at him eye-to-eye.

When you select one individual in the front row to look at, only a few people think you're looking at them. The trick is to focus on giving individual eye contact to more of the folks in front of you. But don't forget to look at the extremes of the room — right and left, very back, and balcony if there is one.

Look at the very back of a large room and select one person to gaze at. People in a large radius (perhaps 20 to 40 feet in size) around that person feel that you're looking at them.

Finding the Right Posture

Posture has been deemed a personal display of self-confidence and bearing. It creates a definite impression on listeners. Good posture (along with overall appearance) is important because it's one of the first things the audience notices and judges about you.

The ideal posture to have throughout your presentation is stand erect but relaxed, as if ready for action. Not only does the right posture promote a positive image of yourself, it helps your speech mechanism (throat and lungs) produce strong, resonant sounds.

Giving a bad impression with the wrong posture

Before we suggest some tips on posture and body movement in the next sections, check out some types of posture to avoid.

Timid

This posture is characterized by a stooped, slouched, or otherwise listless demeanor that suggests a lack of confidence, energy, or drive. You'll never see dynamic leaders with the posture shown in Figure 7-1.

Figure 7-1:
Stand up, don't be shy.

Photograph courtesy of Ray Anthony

Too casual

When you have both hands in your pockets, hunch over the lectern, sit on the edge of the table with one foot on the ground, or otherwise appear too relaxed, you risk projecting an image of conceit, indifference, or overfamiliarity with the audience. With your hands in your pockets you seem passive, and what's more, you can't gesture. Holding your hands in a steepled position as shown in Figure 7-2 can convey overconfidence or a feeling of superiority.

Figure 7-2:
Steepled hands can be misinterpreted for overconfidence or superiority.

*Photograph courtesy of
Ray Anthony*

Stiff, uncomfortable, or defensive

When you tightly press your legs together or cross them, hang your hands at your side or cup them in front of you, hold your body very rigidly, and have a serious facial expression as shown in Figure 7-3, the audience senses that you're ill at ease, frightened, or possibly inflexible. Likewise, taking a military stance makes you seem as though you're waiting for orders rather than ready to command an audience. When you cross your arms over your chest with a stern look, most people interpret this as being defensive or closed.

Clasping your hands together in a plea or prayer position (you may be doing that for real) or the meek fig leaf position as shown in Figure 7-4, imply vulnerability and great discomfort and should be avoided.

Figure 7-3:
A tense, closed stance can indicate a rigid, closed mind.

Photograph courtesy
of Ray Anthony

Figure 7-4:
Avoid this position as it indicates discomfort or vulnerability.

Photograph courtesy
of Ray Anthony

Aggressive

Although you don't want to look meek or uncomfortable, standing rigidly with both hands on your hips, your legs far apart, your chin thrust up, and a taut expression on your face makes you appear to be a drill sergeant or an angry parent ready to scold rather than give a presentation. A stance like the one in Figure 7-5 communicates a domineering, overbearing, and opinionated personality.

Figure 7-5:
The scolding parent stance quickly alienates the audience.

Photograph courtesy of Ray Anthony

Standing tall

Good posture shows the audience you're comfortable, relaxed, and professional. You always want to appear confident and in charge without giving even a hint of being authoritative.

Overall, your posture when you stand — or sit — should be erect and poised but not stiffly upright or strained. Your shoulders should show that you're relaxed — they should be squared and not hunched. Your body should look alive and stand tall, regardless of your height. Figures 7-6 and 7-7 show presenters standing and looking ready and relaxed.

Figure 7-6:
Find a comfortable standing position with shoulders pulled back and relaxed.

Photograph courtesy of Ray Anthony

Figure 7-7:
You can look
assertive
and relaxed.

*Photograph courtesy of Ray
Anthony*

To position your body, do the following:

1. **Place your feet 6 to 12 inches apart with one slightly in front of the other.**

   Keep your knees loose, not locked.

   Don't cross your legs as this is unstable, not to mention ungainly.

2. **Do a partial shoulder rotation, lifting your shoulders to your ears then pushing them back and down.**

   Your chest will then be open and lifted, which helps with the deep breathing you've been practicing.

3. **Shift your weight to the heels of your feet.**

   Resting on your heels alleviates lower back pain that's common after hours of standing.

4. **Imagine an invisible, taut thread running from the crown of your head to the base of your spine.**

   Leave your arms free to gesture or operate the remote control or laser pointer.

Rocking and rolling

Moving your body during your presentation makes you more animated, more interesting, and can help reinforce some of your key messages. Your movements should be purposeful without distracting body gyrations.

Whether you have a bit of speaking anxiety or are positively excited to be talking to a group, the increased adrenalin can make you move around more, even unconsciously. Comedian Chris Rock walks briskly back and forth on the stage throughout his performance. Walking helps siphon off some of the adrenalin surge anyone speaking in public feels. Perhaps you remember your college professors moving around as they spoke.

As a presenter, you want to eliminate the following counterproductive — and distracting — movements:

- ✔ **Swaying** from side to side (often called the *speaker's rumba*) or constantly rocking or stepping forward and backward

- ✔ **Shifting** your weight by repeatedly bending your knees, first one leg, then to the other

- ✔ **Teetering** by raising your body up and down by lifting and lowering your heels or standing on tip-toe

- ✔ **Pacing** around the room in a random way

- ✔ **Swinging** or slapping your arms

- ✔ **Turning** your back to the group for more than a few moments

Moving gracefully and purposefully

Standing in one spot for your entire presentation would be boring and quite difficult to do. Animated movement captivates audiences. Instead of staying stuck behind a lectern, move around the stage or to the front of the room to get close to your audience. If possible, move into and around the group to build rapport and create a more personal tone to your presentation.

To stress a major point, move to the center of the room, closer to the audience, pause, and then raise your volume while making your key point. The act of moving front and center psychologically implies that you want to share an important piece of information with your group.

A beneficial movement technique is what we call *move and bolt*. With this technique, you slowly and deliberately walk around the room facing your audience, and then stop as if your feet are bolted to the floor. You remain there without shifting, rocking, or moving for some time before you move again to another area of the room, facing a different part of your audience with your feet again bolted to the floor. This provides animated movement with confidence and purpose and shows your poise in front of your group.

Making the Right Facial Expressions

Facial expressions include movements of your eyes, mouth, eyebrows, forehead, chin, and other parts in any combination that can add meaning to the spoken word. Facial expressions are usually an accurate barometer of how a person is feeling. Smiles, grins, smirks, frowns, grimaces, winks, and raised eyebrows are just a few of the more than one hundred subtle facial expressions that project the attitude and emotional state of a person. By looking at your face, people can tell, for example, if you are:

- ✔ Alert
- ✔ Apprehensive
- ✔ Confident
- ✔ Convinced
- ✔ Doubtful
- ✔ Elated
- ✔ Fearful
- ✔ Frustrated
- ✔ Happy
- ✔ Puzzled
- ✔ Relaxed
- ✔ Surprised
- ✔ Tired
- ✔ Worried

As your speaking ability improves, you can tailor your facial expressions to match and reinforce your spoken words.

Always be aware of how your face communicates. Although it's difficult to control spontaneous facial reactions and hide your feelings, try not to display an unintended negative feeling.

Political and motivational speakers make their faces reflect what they're saying, whether they're telling an amusing anecdote, getting to the sad part of a story, or conveying righteous indignation about some topic. The best facial expression you can use for most business presentations is a smile. As you begin your talk, and periodically throughout it, use a warm, open, and sincere full smile (showing your teeth) to cement a bond with your audience and show that you're relaxed and enjoy being before them.

In some cultures, particularly Asian, body postures and facial expressions have different interpretations than in North America. If you present to an international audience at home or abroad, do a little homework before your scheduled talk to make sure your presentation is respectful and not inadvertently and unintentionally offensive.

Gesturing Creatively

Gestures are primarily arm and hand movements, sometimes along with body movements such as cocking or nodding your head and moving your eyebrows. The correct gestures enhance the tone and meaning of your words and make your presentation dynamic. Studies show that when you use more gestures than you normally would, your voice becomes more lively, varied, and animated. Gestures, more than other type of body language, help you convey and reinforce a spoken message. They give immediacy and conviction and add intensity and emotional impact to what you're saying.

Watch the 2011 Academy Award-winning silent film, *The Artist,* to understand how much you understand from gestures and facial expressions. Or, try muting the volume of your television while watching a movie or television show (particularly a drama, mystery, or comedy show). Look at the facial expressions and gestures the performers use and guess what they're communicating. See how, without hearing words, gestures speak a powerful language of their own. Combined with words and visuals, the synergy of communication is awesome!

Exploring gesture types

You may be wondering, "What do I do with my hands?" Rest assured, with some imagination, there are practically unlimited gestures you can use in a significant way. Generally, gestures fall into the four categories we describe in the next sections.

Size, shape, or dimension

Visualize how using gestures could add to the message in the following two statements:

> "Our new quantum computer is the most powerful of its kind in the world, yet small." (Use gestures to show its height, depth, and width.)

> "Graphene is a miracle material, and we're close to manufacturing it in large quantity. It is a honeycomb lattice made of carbon atoms — only one atom thick. This nanotechnology substance is incredibly strong, light, nearly transparent, and an excellent conductor of electricity and heat. A billion layers of it are only this thin." (Use your thumb and forefinger to show the small thickness.)

Direction

Gestures can show that something is up, down, right, left, sideways, slanted, curved, swerving, spiraling, or wavy — for a few examples. Think about how you might use gestures to show something increasing, decreasing, or standing still, such as the following:

> "We have a choice. We can choose to grow slowly by playing it extra safe (the presenter extends his entire arm out at a small angle like a bent graph line), or we can innovate, make some mistakes, quickly learn from them, and grow like this." (He now extends his arm out with a much steeper angle upwards like a trend line of accelerated growth.)

> "Our company's strategy has been disjointed. First we go in this direction (presenter walks to the left). Then we decide to go here (presenter turns and walks in a different direction). If that isn't working, we transition this way (he now walks in the opposite direction). What are we doing experimenting when we should be implementing something that does not look like this (he is now waving his arms in different directions). Here's what we need to do." (The presenter points straight ahead and walks perfectly straight in that direction.)

Motion, movement, or activity

Picture yourself describing and showing people how to play golf, tennis, bowling, or some other sport or training someone how to use a tool or product. You use your entire body with a focus on your arms and hands to illustrate an activity. These gestures make you much more interesting, regardless of your topic. Think about how, in your presentation, adding these movements and motions might better reinforce your points:

- ✔ Back and forth
- ✔ Grabbing
- ✔ Holding
- ✔ Lifting
- ✔ Pulling, pushing
- ✔ Round and round
- ✔ Spiraling
- ✔ Stopping
- ✔ Turning, screwing, twisting
- ✔ Zigzagging

Notice how a particular motion can add meaning to these types of examples:

"In a moment, I will show you a video of how our new 3-D printer creates complex designs using our new technology and mechanism. Current printers do this. (The presenter uses an up-and-down and side-to-side motion to demonstrate how a nozzle prints material.) But our system does this. (He now uses both hands in a back and forth way as if he were moving a sheet of metal.) We have a metal plate with over 100 nozzles, each of which can feed a different substance — such as metal, plastic, rubber, or glass — to deposit that material 60 times faster and 300 percent more accurately. Look at the two-minute video to see what I mean."

"Regarding supply-chain management in our company, supply was trying to catch up with runaway demand (presenter uses a gesture of going around and around) and never did quite make it."

Feeling and intensity

These gestures can be captivating when a speaker uses his entire body to help describe, amplify, and focus on an intended, meaningful emotion — enthusiasm, rejection, openness, or frustration — connected to a key point being made. Here are two examples:

"We have got to fight (presenter waves a clenched fist) these suffocating regulations that are destroying our businesses and jobs!"

"Our department must aggressively cut and clash (presenter uses a abrupt chopping motion) this out-of-control waste that's robbing us of profits!"

Making a grand gesture

Make grand gestures by extending your arms far from your body, which enlarges you as a presenter. Use these gestures in front of large audiences to increase your stage presence and charisma. If you want to add dynamics to your body language, expand your gestures outward and animate them as needed. Gestures that keep your arms close to your body are more appropriate for smaller groups where grand gestures would come across as too flamboyant and extravagant for the occasion.

Don't think that your arm and hand gestures have to be animated the whole time you're talking. You can, on occasion, use a specific gesture and hold it in place (*static*) for 3 to 15 seconds, which can be a very dramatic, sustained way of communicating a key point.

An organizational change consultant is making a presentation about his idea for a new vision for his client's corporation. He says, "The enticing vision we're discussing is right over the horizon." He raises his arm and points his finger in the direction he's looking toward (as if in the distance). While keeping his arm up, pointing toward the invisible vision, he continues, "Even though that vision is beyond our sight now, we will find it, travel toward it, and reach it. It's a vision that all of you said you would be excited by, and one that is worthy of your hard work. The vision is there (as he slightly pulls his arm back to thrust it forward in the pointed direction) for all of you to see very soon." Think of using static gestures that spotlight and reinforce your spoken words.

Avoid the following gestures, which send the wrong message:

- ✔ Keeping your hands in your pockets
- ✔ Holding your arms stiffly at your sides
- ✔ Pointing or wagging your finger at people
- ✔ Folding your arms across your chest
- ✔ Using the same gesture over and over
- ✔ Tightly clutching your notes or folding, rolling, or fiddling with them

To use gestures to your best advantage, do the following:

- ✔ **Plan** the important gestures you will use.
- ✔ **Practice** gestures to look natural and spontaneous.
- ✔ **Time** your gestures to coincide with a major point.
- ✔ **Reinforce** your messages with appropriate gestures.
- ✔ **Apply** a rich variety of gestures to your talk.
- ✔ **Use** your entire body, not just your arms and hands, to fully gesture.

Eliminating distracting gestures

Even seasoned speaking professionals often have a bit of stage fright or anxiety, especially when giving a new presentation or speech. In new or nerve-wracking circumstances, some mannerisms you don't even know you have come out of hiding. That's why videotaping yourself can be a real (surprising or perhaps shocking) revelation.

Don't let nervous mannerisms hurt your professional image and affect your presentation results. Watch your videotaped presentation and see if you do the following, then work on being conscious of them in your future presentations:

- ✔ Fidgeting with something in your hands — a marker, rubber band, paper clip, laser pointer, or your slide remote control.
- ✔ Frequently adjusting your tie or jacket or smoothing a part of your clothing or rubbing your clothing as if getting rid of a piece of lint.

✔ Taking your glasses on and off or putting a pen in and out of your mouth.

✔ Drumming your fingers on the lectern or playing with your microphone or its cord.

✔ Tugging at your ear, scratching the side of your face, smoothing your hair, twisting your mustache, or pulling on your beard.

✔ Playing with a necklace or other piece of jewelry. Men often tug at cufflinks.

Like it or not, chances are you use unconscious gestures even in everyday conversations; if you become more aware of them during daily activities and curb them, you'll be less likely to use them during your presentation. Years ago before laser pointers, we would often see people with retractable pointers continuously extending them and collapsing them without the slightest idea they were doing it. Or some people using a flipchart or whiteboard would hold a big marker in one hand and repeatedly snap the cap on and off.

Don't despair, you can work on one skill at a time to perfect it, then move onto the next one. The best tool to evaluate and shape your progress is to either audio record or videotape your actual presentations or rehearsals to spot what you do. While looking at your video, pay attention to your volume, rate, and pauses. Check to see what your body — facial expressions, gestures, posture, and body movement — is really saying. Most importantly, analyze how you're relating to your audience, especially with eye contact.

Chapter 8

Choosing Resources and Rehearsing Your Presentation

In This Chapter

▶ Finding great resources

▶ Improving your performance

Communication that positively impacts people translates into the language of leadership. When you discover how to not just use, but leverage, the powerful five secrets of presentation success to help reimagine, reinvent, and remake your presentations, you see new vistas opening up and a world of opportunities coming your way. By applying these secrets, your ideas sparkle, your audience welcomes your recommendations, and your presentations rise to new levels.

In this chapter, we explain the fifth secret of presentation success: presentation resources and rehearsing. First, we talk about the different types of presentation resources you need and relay a story about what happens when you don't take the time to consider the resources you must have for your presentation. We then discuss the one indispensable resource — you, the presenter — and give you pointers for rehearsing your way to presentation success.

We show you how to use the secrets for presentations, but don't stop there! — You can apply these secrets to your daily communications. Well-known business icon Lee Iacocca said, "You can have brilliant ideas, but if you can't get them across, your ideas won't get you anywhere."

Considering the (Re)source

Resources are important components of both creating and delivering a stellar performance. Ray lives close to a pavilion that seats several thousand people. The venue features many top-name rock, country, and contemporary singers, bands, and musicians. Ray watches a dozen 18-wheeler trucks pull up and unload huge amounts of equipment for just one show. These events are major productions that involve hundreds of pieces of complex equipment such as amplifiers, speakers, mixer boards, stage rigging, complicated lighting systems, fog machines, instruments, costumes, and special effects devices. Some touring bands and singers have from 50 to 100 people behind the scenes to support them. Aside from the *roadies* — guys who set everything up in record time — you find the *techies* who operate complex digital gear used to create a spectacular sound and light show.

Like live entertainment performances, presentations and speeches also need varying resources for success. Simple business presentations may require just a laptop (or iPad or other tablet), cables, remote control, accessories, LCD projector, and a projection screen or large television, and maybe a flip-chart or writing board. After you become a presentation rock star doing innovative presentations, major seminars, or motivational speeches in front of large audiences, you may need even more complex additional resources such as sound reinforcement systems, props, video recording equipment, lighting, elevated and decorated staging, and multiple-screen displays.

Resources can be physical, such as your laptop and a microphone, or part of the presentation content, such as anecdotes or data. Based upon the size of your audience and your presentation goals, determine all the resources you need to both develop and deliver your presentation. In developing it, consider where you can get the ideal, most compelling information such as true stories, shocking statistics, fascinating facts, memorable metaphors, and powerful examples. Keep these three types of resources in mind while developing your presentation:

- ✔ **People:** Find subject matter experts, graphic or multimedia designers, videographers, or technical professionals to assist you in putting together your talk.
- ✔ **Media:** Identify the apps and resources you need for your slides and visuals, such as custom or stock photos, animations, illustrations, diagrams, graphics, video, audio, and virtual and augmented reality.
- ✔ **Hardware:** For your delivery, consider resources including a laptop, iPad, or tablet; stands; projectors and screens; Apple TV, Internet, or phone connectivity; PA (public address) systems; tables and chairs; cables and connectors; props; flipcharts, storyboards, or writing boards; and handouts.

ving:

t to bring a small item like a RF (radio frequency) remote
op and slides. Consider using a checklist like the ones in
nsure you take everything you need.

dsomely to bring your own equipment to ensure your
othly. How many times have you experienced delays
neone else's projector because you don't have a sup-
w to operate it or sync it to your laptop? Even the
xtension cord can create delays.

l fully test all your equipment before your presen-
re your laptop or tablet works with the projector
levices. If you're using a PA system, check out
e adequate volume and coverage without feed-
t people available to help in case of technical

s and have contingency plans and extra time
if your pitch involves closing a huge deal for
on the projector burns out, or you suddenly
e's a freak problem with your laptop or
ntation on it? For critical presentations, you
dy, in place, connected, and adjusted for
ou need to switch.

ing it twice

few resources, but for major produc-
onventions, and workshops, you need
dio, and visual resources to support
nners generally use comprehensive
ofessional speakers, people who
as meeting facilitators will find
ale events.

es, headsets; note
dynamic or con-

me great ideas on things to
e, you may not have thought of
may add meaningful value to

back)

Laptop and tablet equipment and accessories

If your presentation relies on a laptop, make sure you have the follo

- Laptop computer(s) and power cords
- Accessory to hold tablet with one hand while presenting
- Apple TV
- Apps needed for presentation
- Cables and adapters for laptop and tablet
- Computer monitors
- Credit card reader
- External hard drives
- Laptop or tablet stand(s)
- Mouse or trackpad
- Remote control for computer
- Stylus pen
- Tablet(s) and power cord(s)
- Wi-fi router

Sound equipment

To make yourself heard, check that you have

- Speakers (passive or powered)
- 8-, 12- or 16-channel mixer (for powered speakers)
- Amplifier (for passive speakers)
- Corded or wireless microphones (handhelds, lavalier whether you need omnidirectional or unidirectional denser type)
- Extension cords
- Graphic equalizer (to adjust sound and reduce fee
- Headphone(s)
- iPod to play music or other audio files
- Microphone cables
- Microphone stands and booms
- Monitor speakers (for stage)
- Plastic cable ties (to secure wires)
- Power strips with multiple outlets

- ✔ Speaker cables

- ✔ Speaker stands

- ✔ Various audio cables, adapters, and connectors

Projection and display equipment

Projection equipment must-haves include the following:

- ✔ LCD or DLP projector. Choose resolution of XGA, WXGA, SXGA, or UXGA and brightness (in ANSI lumen output typically between 3000–6000+) and size/weight (pico, pocket, portable to large room size); format: wide-screen or standard; keystone correction

- ✔ Extension cords and multiple-outlet power strips

- ✔ External powered speakers (optional powered subwoofer) for projector or television screens and connecting cables

- ✔ Flat screen television (HD or UltraHD); specify size and connectivity to Internet

- ✔ Green laser pointer (much brighter than red)

- ✔ Projection screen (choose matte white, glass-beaded, or other); typically screens are 60-x-60 or 70-x-70 inches, or 8-x-8 feet and larger

- ✔ Stands for televisions

- ✔ Table to hold projector

- ✔ Wireless keyboards and remotes for television

- ✔ Zoom/wide angle lens for projector

Photo, video, and audio recording and playback equipment

You may want to record your presentation or use recorded pieces as part of your presentation. The checklist of things to bring follows:

- ✔ Audio mixer (to connect extra microphones to camera)

- ✔ Camera batteries and charger

- ✔ Camera remote controls

- ✔ Compact flash (CF) and secure digital (SD) cards

- ✔ Digital still camera (whether DSLR or compact camera) and extra lenses

- ✔ Equipment case(s) and cart(s)

- ✔ External microphone and cable for video camera

- ✔ Headphone(s)

- ✔ High definition video camera

- ✔ High-quality audio recorder

- Lights, stands, dimmers
- Monitor, stand, and cable for video camera
- Photo printer
- Tripod with fluid head (for smooth pans and tilts), tripod spreader for cameras
- Video camera with wide angle and zoom lens adapters

Flipcharts, writing or storyboards, easels

Possibly your largest presentation tool is a flipchart, writing board, or custom-made storyboards. Your checklist for them includes the following:

- Blank (or grid) writing pads
- Corkboard (with pushpins)
- Custom-made storyboards
- Easels to hold storyboards or signs
- Erasers and cleaning liquid for dry-erase board
- Felt-tip writing pens (in several colors and sizes; specify erasable or permanent ink)
- Flipchart stand (single or double-size)
- Magnetic dry-erase board
- Masking tape
- Multi-function reversible board
- Multi-touch interactive white board (optional: integrated printer)
- Sticky notes (in various sizes and colors)
- Writing boards (porcelain or chalkboard surfaces) and stands

Miscellaneous equipment and materials

Especially if you're making a large-scale presentation, you may have to consider the items in the following list:

- Banner stands
- Bulletin board
- Director chairs (cool-looking to use on stage if interviewing people)
- Display kiosks
- Elevated stage and steps
- Floodlights and stands, special-effects filters
- Floor displays (typically used in trade shows)
- Floor posts (to form lines)

- Fog machine
- Glass display cases
- Large-scale props
- Literature racks/dispensers
- Miscellaneous drop boxes (to collect business cards, evaluation sheets)
- Partitions and backdrops
- Pop-up displays
- Portable PA system, bullhorn
- Portable stage
- Ramps, risers, and platforms
- Spotlights and stands
- Stage sets and decorations
- Tables for exhibits
- Teleprompter
- Trade show truss systems for your exhibits

Handouts and giveaways

Dispensing materials with your name or message helps your audience remember you. If you have handouts, use this checklist:

- Activity and entertainment itineraries
- Attendee list
- Award certificates and frames or holders
- Biographies of speaker(s)
- Brochures from the resort or conference center
- Business cards
- Business proposals
- Copies of the executive summary of the presentation
- Digital copies of select slides (for each attendee) used in your presentation
- Diplomas and certificates
- Illustrations, drawings, and/or renderings
- Invoices
- Letters of intent or contracts
- Manuals or instruction booklets

- Meal menus (for conference attendees)
- Meeting/presentation agenda and objectives
- Motivational pins
- Order forms
- Plaques, trophies, and awards
- Presentation evaluation sheets
- Product/service technical booklets or brochures
- Purchasing quotations/estimates
- Questionnaires
- Scaled models
- Training materials

Meeting aids

Even a simple presentation at a meeting requires some equipment:

- Badges or name tags and lanyards or other holders for them
- Director chairs
- Flags
- Lectern with light
- Literature and brochure stands
- Name tents
- Pads, pens, pencils
- Registration table
- Sidewalk messenger
- Sign-in sheets
- Signs (in front of entry or in the room)
- Snacks, candy, fruit
- Table displays for your products or exhibits
- Table skirts and tablecloths
- Table tents (giving table numbers, if arranged seating)
- Table toys, stress balls
- Water for speaker and attendees/other beverages

Office equipment and supplies

With any presentation you need some mundane office supplies including the following:

- 3-hole punch
- 3-x-5-inch cards
- Blank writing pads
- Calculator
- Erasers
- File folders
- Flashlight
- Hot glue gun and glue sticks
- Label maker
- Laminator and supplies
- Lamps
- Multipurpose scanner, fax, printer
- Paper clips
- Paper glue
- Paper shredder
- Pens and pencils
- Presentation folders
- Rubber bands
- Rubber cement
- Scissors
- Stapler, staples, and remover
- Sticky notes
- Swiss army knife
- Tables and chairs
- Tape (duct, masking, strapping)
- X-ACTO knife

In Chapter 13, we have another valuable checklist relating to preparing and designing your presentation.

How resource mistakes blew an important event

About a year ago, Ray was invited to a big product unveiling and motivational event that more than a thousand people paid money to attend and were eager to see. The presence of the charismatic company founder added celebrity and built excitement for the enthusiastic group, eager to hear him and the other speakers. Unfortunately, presentation problems marred the occasion. The speakers provided for the PA system were inadequate and positioned in such a way that, when turned up to high volume, they produced howling, squealing feedback that only irritated and distracted attendees from what the presenters (including the company's founder) were saying. (For proper audio and to minimize feedback, a graphic equalizer and at least two other speaker cabinets should have been positioned a short distance from the wall and stage and closer to and tilted down toward the audience so the sound would not go back into the microphone and create feedback loops.)

The wireless lavaliere microphones were attached too low on the presenters' bodies (which contributed to sound problems). When speakers moved their heads to the side away from the microphone, the sound volume decreased. When they looked down at their notes, their mouth got closer to the lavaliere mic and suddenly the volume jumped, accompanied by feedback. And when they gestured, their clothing moved and rubbed against the microphone, producing annoying muffled sounds.

Professional speakers know that with lavaliere microphones, you have to position them high up on your body, keep your head in a fixed position relative to the microphone at times and know what type of fabrics to wear and how to fully gesture without causing sound distortions. Many presenters choose an inconspicuous microphone headset to avoid these types of potential problems.

More than ten times the main speaker interrupted her presentation to alert the audience that she would physically move to certain safe spots on the stage to reduce the audio feedback. But, in standing in most of those places she blocked part of the view of the projection screen (which should have been raised so the lower part was positioned over her head) that displayed important photos critical in selling the products to the audience. On top of that, the other event's speakers, who invited several people from the audience on the stage to give live testimonials, did not have separate hand-held wireless microphones to use. Instead, the speakers asked the guests to lean over very close to them to talk into the small lavaliere mics clipped to their clothing! Not only were the invitees' voices not clear, but it was extremely awkward and uncomfortable from a visual standpoint.

The meeting planners (who were probably just people from the organization, but not professionals) should have had the right audio equipment set up properly. The credibility of the people running this much-anticipated event was tarnished and their goals were compromised.

This is not an isolated example. We have seen too many off-site business meetings where poor selection and use of various resources negatively impacted the event. Even though presenters are not expected to be well-versed in the selection and use of various audio equipment (other than microphones), it is a decided plus when they are at least familiar with basic operation. Professional speakers, who earn from $5,000 to over $15,000 per talk, bring their own wireless microphones, laptops or iPads, and other transportable equipment to ensure those critical resources work exactly as expected.

Making room for improvement

The room where you give your presentation is a resource too. When you have the option of moving tables, chairs, and other items around, make sure you set up the room for best visibility to your screen and for best interaction with your audience. Plan to arrive about an hour before an off-site presentation and enter the meeting room to arrange furniture and supplies in a way that creates an ideal climate for your presentation. Simply straightening up a room and making it look neater can help.

We know one terrific corporate trainer who did something he didn't realize would help him close his biggest contract ever with a Fortune 50 company. The potential client escorted the presenter to one of the company's small meeting rooms where he would present to four people involved in making the buying decision in an hour. The presenter asked if he could rearrange the room and promised to put the room back in its original configuration afterward. He moved a lot of extra chairs and clutter out of the way and arranged two tables in a V-shaped configuration so audience members could better see the projection screen and flipcharts. He made ample room for his attractively and creatively arranged sample training materials, which he used as references and handouts. He'd printed name tents with the attendees' names in gold-colored ink and personalized the handouts with each person's name printed on a set. He personalized — without going overboard.

When the four people entered the room, they were surprised, and apparently impressed, with the way he set everything up. Although his small company was competing with some of the top national training firms for the huge contract, the main decision maker later told him that there were several key reasons they picked his company: One reason was that his simple act of rearranging the room in such an attractive and unique way symbolically communicated that he and his company would go way out of their way to customize, personalize, and perfect the training program for the client. He was quite surprised since that was his normal way of dealing with presentation rooms. The other bidders just presented in the crowded, cluttered room and made no extra effort to turn the room into a place more conducive for their presentation.

William N., an ex-Army officer, is an accomplished trainer and presenter, who, when he sets up a room, calls it his table *gig line*. In the military, you better make sure your dress appearance is perfect: A gig line refers to the vertical alignment of belt buckle, shirt edge, and trouser fly. When William sets up a room with handouts, writing tablets, pens, name tents, and anything else, he creates perfect uniformity and alignment, so if you were to look at the end of several tables, you would see a perfectly uniform line of handouts with everything in a perfectly straight line. Most people, when they walk into a room like that, are duly impressed.

Practicing Makes Perfect

Highly accomplished actors and entertainers train for years to perfect their craft. They practice saying different lines while expressing different emotions and experiment with subtle body language variations in the quest to come across as real and genuine to their audiences. Those in film and especially live theatre go through rigorous rehearsals to ensure that they're ready to give flawless performances.

Practicing is different than *rehearsing*. You practice to become better at a skill — playing an instrument, singing, performing a sport, or doing any activity that requires developing a particular talent or ability. Rehearsing is going over a specific presentation to become articulate with the information and smooth use of your visuals. You want to get your timing, transitions, and delivery to be as perfect as possible.

Developing any worthwhile skill should begin with instruction from a highly competent teacher or coach. So, if you want to elevate yourself to masterful status as a business presenter or professional speaker, get formal presentation and speech training and be ready for lots of practice.

Taking every opportunity to practice

If you are keen to become a poised, polished, and powerful speaker, give as many talks as you can in front of audiences in organizations, chambers of commerce, and other associations. Practicing speaking helps you practice and fine-tune your tone and body language as well as develop compelling content.

Consider joining a local chapter of Toastmasters International (www.toast masters.org), the non-profit organization that teaches public speaking, to sharpen your techniques while building confidence in front of an audience. Toastmasters has locations all over the world.

If you aspire to be a professional, highly paid speaker, consider becoming an active member of National Speakers Association (www.nsaspeaker.org), which has 36 chapters throughout the United States. Don't neglect to become competent in smoothly using your laptop or tablet and its features, accessories, and, of course, your presentation apps.

Practice does not in itself make perfect. Practice makes permanent. If you practice something incorrectly over and over, it becomes hard to fix and do right later on. But if you regularly practice something correctly, then the correct way sticks with you.

Repetition actually builds hard-wired neural networks in your brain that create a permanent skill. Famous football coach Vince Lombardi said something profound that we're sure you've heard but is worth repeating, "Practice does not make perfect. Only perfect practice makes perfect." That's why it's so important to get accurate, honest feedback from competent speakers, professional presentation coaches, and others who will help you hone your skills to a fine edge.

Recording yourself

Video helps you become a skilled presenter. It's like watching your golf swing — seeing everything you do right . . . and do wrong. We know what you're thinking: "I HATE seeing myself on video." Well, we can tell you that we never had a person in our presentation training or coaching sessions who looked at themselves on video and said, "Wow. I was absolutely phenomenal!" Seeing and hearing yourself can be a humbling experience as well as somewhat painful because you tend to be overly and unjustifiably critical of yourself. Many years ago Barbara attended an in-house speaker training session, and videos were taken to provide feedback. She discovered that she rocked the whole time, shifting her weight from one foot to the other. Painful to watch, yes, but so helpful to improving her stage presence.

Audiences are nowhere near as judgmental and harsh regarding your presentation as you are yourself. Eddie Redmayne, an English actor, singer, and model said, "Most actors hate watching their own films because all you see are the glaring mistakes — your own tricks and ticks." Accomplished actors including Dame Judi Dench, Denzel Washington, Johnny Depp, and Robert DeNiro have said they don't watch their movies. Even Meryl Streep, considered one of the best actors of all time, is a member of that group!

We all tend to see the minor, insignificant mistakes we make and blow them out of proportion. Keep in mind that your audience is not sitting down with an evaluation sheet and rating you on the tiniest performance slip ups!

When you look at your video afterwards — as difficult as it may be — try to be easy on yourself and be objective. Look for things that you can improve immediately and things that you know you'll have to work on over time. Judging yourself harshly is counterproductive and definitely not warranted. Use the video as a vital feedback tool. Professional speakers try to video themselves every couple of months to make sure they don't fall back into bad habits.

The more you practice your speaking skills in front of audiences, the more you relax and reduce any stage fright you may have. That results in a more confident and self-assured demeanor. Do many different types of speeches and presentations to experiment with your style. Try new content, humor, and creative ways to use your visuals, props, equipment, and accessories. The road to phenomenal presentations is through the tunnel of practice — perfect practice.

Rehearsing is not practicing

Rehearsing differs from practicing, which is improving your general speaking techniques through a simple form of repetitive behavior with the goal of becoming articulate and polished with a custom-designed presentation or speech, especially one that you give for the first time. Rehearsing is standing up, using your presentation visuals, and delivering your material word-for-word out loud — without missing any detail — as if you were doing it for real. Even though actors, theater performers, and entertainers of all kinds are seasoned, successful professionals, they still have to thoroughly rehearse a new movie scene, play, or musical show so that it looks effortless and natural when they do it for real.

Regardless of the venue, numerous rehearsals ensure that a performance is silky smooth, credible, and of utmost professional quality. When you can communicate your information and key messages fluidly and effortlessly, you can then better engage your audience because you're relaxed, sincere, and conversational. Knowing your material cold enables you to be at ease and enjoy speaking in front of people.

Ray worked with two senior partners from an international Big Four accounting firm who were given just 30 minutes by a client to discuss their proposal for one of the biggest deals in their expatriate tax division's history, ultimately worth over $100 million. Ray rehearsed the partners for three straight days to perfection. The partners said the rehearsals clearly contributed toward their winning the deal, especially in view of the surprising fact that their accounting firm was initially considered to be the least favored of three competing firms to clinch the huge deal. Apple's Steve Jobs often rehearsed intermittently for weeks to make sure his new-product presentations were absolutely amazing. Unlike others who rationalize that they don't have the time or the need to rehearse or wait till the very end to hastily rush through one or two rehearsals, Jobs knew otherwise, and it always showed and shined. With important team presentations, team members must rehearse handoffs, transitions, answering questions, and flawless use of laptops, tablets, equipment, and presentation visuals (see Chapter 23 for more information on team rehearsals).

Even though everyone has her own method for rehearsing, the following sections offer some tips to further help you make them as successful as possible.

Knowing your lines

There's something about speaking out loud that helps you retain and communicate your content effectively. Depending upon your knowledge and comfort with the topic, we recommend you have anywhere from at least five to as many as ten out-loud rehearsals using your laptop and prepared slides. Move and gesture as you would in the real situation. Gauge your success by having the last two try-outs being the best you can do.

Rehearse digestible sections at a time. It can seem overwhelming when first doing entire rehearsals from beginning to end. Consider working on five-minute sections at a time, then link them together to rehearse the entire piece.

Acing your introduction and conclusion

Always rehearse the opening of your presentation more than any other part. You want to start off in a smooth, self-assured, and polished way. Doing so helps you make a great impression, sets a positive tone for the rest of your talk, and reduces your speaking jitters. Consider having memory-jogging notes (not full sentences) in the event you need them; most presentation apps have a presenter's view feature in which you see the slide or visual and your notes but the audience only sees the visual. The same advice applies to giving a compelling summary and confident call to action at the end of your presentation.

Internalizing your message

You give the most impressive presentation when you have such a mastery of your topic that the content seems part of your DNA. With repeated rehearsals, you won't read from your slides but use visuals primarily to help your audience better understand the value and application of your information.

During your preparation and rehearsals, don't memorize your presentation as if reciting from a script — that's not only difficult, but also comes across as rigid and produces anxiety because if you lose your place or forget one line, you may stall the whole presentation. Aim to internalize and familiarize yourself with the stories, points, facts, and connecting messages that are most important for you to highlight and make sure you have the flow of your talk down pat. Know what comes on each following slide so that continuity is fluid as well. You want to be conversational and be able to randomly talk about any information in your presentation using different words to get you there.

However, we do recommend that you memorize select, priority facts, statistics, financial numbers, and anything else that shows your full command of your topic. That way you can effectively answer practically any question without referring to your notes or scrolling through your slides.

Timing is everything

Many presentation apps have a timer that gives you the individual time for each major part of your presentation as well as the total time — or you can time yourself with your smartphone. Remember, it almost always takes longer than you think. By timing each section, you can gauge how the total presentation time is divided and decide which parts you want to dedicate more time to and then make appropriate adjustments. And, we can't say this enough: If you are given an hour (60 minutes) to deliver your presentation, allocate at least 15 minutes (one quarter of the time) for questions, comments, and discussion time. Don't think because you have an hour, you need to talk for an hour. Most audiences expect to interact with you. If you find they only ask a couple of questions, and you end before your scheduled time, they will love it!

After becoming familiar with the material and working out the timing, videotape yourself and write down areas you need to work on in the next series of rehearsals. Tape your last rehearsal to see the difference you've made.

Getting feedback

Any presentation with a lot riding on it deserves to have a group you select to sit in on a rehearsal and give you constructive feedback and advice. Choose people who closely resemble your audience in terms of job positions, expertise levels, and needs as they will give more useful comments. You may also consider hiring a seasoned professional presentation trainer or coach to help fine-tune your content, visuals, and speaking skills.

Many large corporations offer in-house employee development courses on public speaking, meeting facilitation, and using presentation apps. Take advantage of these opportunities when they're offered.

Part III
Giving a Great Presentation

Innovate! ꟷNNOVATE! **INNOVATE!** Innovate! Innovate!

In this part . . .

- ✔ Follow the laws of communication impact.
- ✔ Create an effective introduction.
- ✔ Add intensity to your message.
- ✔ Get the audience involved and interested in what you have to say.
- ✔ Learn how to close your presentation to get the response you want.
- ✔ Use repetition to emphasize your message.
- ✔ Learn to deal with difficult questions and hecklers.

Chapter 9

Captivating Your Audience

. . . .

. . . .

*G*ame-changing presentations embody the Five Big Cs:

✔ Clear

✔ Concise

✔ Compelling

✔ Captivating

✔ Convincing

Inspiration, motivation, and, perhaps, entertainment take your communications to new heights and success levels. You can imbed those characteristics, not only in group presentations, but in everyday conversations and discussions.

Starting in this chapter, we explain the *Laws of Communication Impact,* which provide the tools to craft stimulating, intellectually persuasive, and emotionally driven communication. We offer specifics on how to influence and affect how people think, feel, and even act. When you follow these laws, people eagerly listen to you, better understand what you're saying, and are persuaded to follow your recommendations or requests, adopt your proposed solutions, or buy your products and services.

Touching on the Laws of Communication Impact

The *Laws of Communication Impact* help you engage, fascinate, and intrigue people — even hardcore, buttoned-down business types who may otherwise be inclined to yawn, suffer restless leg syndrome, or work their smartphones during the typical presentation.

This is the first of several chapters that provide specific guidelines to boost your creativity and professionalism as you communicate. Use them and see for yourself the amazing results you get.

The words *information* and *communication* are often used interchangeably. However, they signify quite different things with different results. Of course, you need to provide people with good, solid, useful information. Information is *giving out.* Communication, though, is *getting through,* which should always be your goal.

Innovative presentations create an impact with the audience. Champion presenters creatively use information (including various forms of media) along with their energetic, passionate, and polished delivery style.

If you want to change something in your organization or sell something, you have to get through to people in a potent way to change how they think, feel, and act. In today's frenetic, stressful business world where many are overworked to the point of distraction — a ferret on double espresso has a longer attention span — getting people to give their full, undivided attention and listen to what you're presenting and then agree and act upon your ideas, plans, or proposed solutions is a tall order. The information and examples we present about the five *Laws of Communication Impact* give you the ammunition to fight inattention, apathy, and decision-making procrastination.

The Laws of Communication Impact are:

1. **The Law of Primacy: the first thing people see, hear, touch, taste, or experience**

2. **The Law of Highlighting and Emphasis: the points, messages, information pieces, and visuals that are critical for your audience**

3. **The Law of Engagement: getting people to interact with you**

4. **The Law of Interest: communicating that you understand what's important to your audience**

5. **The Law of Recency: the last thing people see, hear, feel, or experience**

In this chapter, we explore the dynamics of the first law, the *Law of Primacy*. We cover the other laws in Chapters 10 and 11.

Whether you're presenting a business topic, giving a motivational speech, or hosting a training workshop, webinar, or virtual meeting, leveraging the Laws of Communication Impact helps you achieve results that far surpass your expectations.

Starting with the Law of Primacy

Think about your first romantic kiss, your first car, your first job, or the first time you achieved something you were so proud of. Now, think about a negative first occurrence, a painful or embarrassing memory. Positive or negative, you remember meaningful firsts of any kind quite vividly, often for a lifetime. Here, we show you how to leverage the Law of Primacy — of firsts — in an advantageous way: Start your presentation with a B-A-N-G! to wake people up and perk them up.

The *Law of Primacy*, first conceived by Frank Hansen around 1925, was initially and primarily focused on advertising. This law states that information or impressions first in sequence have a greater impact on people than anything that occurs later on. Whether it is advertising or a sermon, this psychological principle says that people are impacted emotionally, intellectually, and behaviorally more by the very first things they see, hear, smell, touch, taste or otherwise experience than things they encounter later on. Imagine seeing a good friend for the first time in a decade, and the very first thing she says to you with a big, welcoming smile is, "You look terrific . . . WOW!" That statement warms your heart and sets the stage and tone for your reunion.

The nature of the *Law of Primacy* means that you get one chance only to make a first impression. If a speaker delivers a captivating, riveting, and attention-grabbing introduction, it has more influence than anything he says later in his talk — with the exception of a stirring conclusion which involves the *Law of Recency,* which we address in Chapter 11. People typically remember the middle part of a presentation the least. A presenter must work harder to maintain, or recapture, a group's naturally fluctuating attention and interest after a strong presentation beginning.

The old adage rings true: You don't get a second chance to make a good first impression.

First impressions — in appearance or behavior — create a strong, often unshakeable opinion of someone. Even before you begin your presentation, you send signals: Your clothes and grooming, your gait, the manner in which you interact with team members or people in the audience, and your overall bearing and body language contribute to the impression others have of you.

You make your first impression before you even step up to the mic. That's why skilled presenters spend a disproportionate amount of time crafting a structured introduction that's interesting, stimulating, and appealing to the audience. The great movie mogul Samuel Goldwyn said that a great movie "starts out with an earthquake and works its way up to a climax." That's great advice for a presentation, too! A strong introduction does several vital things: sets the tone, mood, quality, purpose, intent, and oftentimes the urgency of your presentation. It encourages people to pay serious note to the rest of your talk.

If you can find a way to evoke the audience's curiosity, add suspense or intrigue, ignite their imaginations, add a depth of anticipation — maybe even tantalize them — you will have them firmly in the palm of your hand, with their eyes fixed on you, sitting up straight, and ears perked to eagerly hear what comes next. But, if you have a slow or lackluster beginning that comes across as lifeless, rambling, or anxious, the audience will tune out in a heartbeat. Although you can overcome a negative first impression, it takes a great deal of effort to recapture the interest of your audience.

The first two minutes of your presentation or speech say so much about your credibility, image, speaking style, personality, and your topic. Done well, the introduction conveys that you are prepared, enthusiastic, poised, confident, and a consummate professional with competent leadership abilities. Spending extra time preparing, rehearsing, and fine-tuning your introduction pays great dividends. Consider memorizing the first two sentences of your beginning and then continue smoothly in a natural, conversational way.

How you start determines how you finish!

Laws of Learning

The Laws of Communication Impact are based upon prior research and models called the *Laws of Learning,* a set of rules that affect the extent to which a person absorbs information, remembers it, acts upon it, or is otherwise mentally, emotionally, or psychologically affected by it. Edward L. Thorndike postulated several *Laws of Learning* in the early 1900s.

Based upon fundamental psychology and the brain's processing of information, these laws were almost universally applicable to the learning process, regardless of age or background of people. Over the years, the laws have been enhanced and modified by others. In this chapter, we adapt and apply those general learning laws to the communication process for presenters and speakers of all kinds.

Starting Off on the Right Foot

Your introduction should be suited to the audience and the situation. Developing and delivering a well-prepared, attention-grabbing introduction has many psychological advantages to it. Whether you decide to use a straightforward, conservative beginning or a creative kick in the audience's pants depends upon your comfort level and the goal for your talk.

Making a dynamic first impression

Regardless of whether you choose a mild or slightly wild start, your introduction should highlight your credibility, professionalism, and expertise and get your group's ears, eyes, and minds focused on your topic. First impressions can be fragile and that's why getting it right from the get-go is critical. Saint Jérôme put it in colorful perspective, "Early impressions are hard to eradicate from the mind. When once wool has been dyed purple, who can restore it to its previous whiteness?"

In Ray's advanced presentation training workshops, he asks participants to share metaphors that describe a really effective introduction from a unique perspective. Read a few of the responses he has gotten:

> "It's like the first bite into delicious food from a great restaurant, whether it's an appetizer or entree. Wow . . . your taste buds explode with pleasure and expectation of more — what yet is to come."

> "Experiencing a great speaker from the start is like the takeoff of a plane. Your adrenaline kicks in even if you are sitting down!"

> "I have a powerful Ducati motorcycle. When you twist the throttle to accelerate, it's amazing how incredibly smooth, yet thrilling, the "launch" is. Presentation introductions should be like that."

Use these guidelines to develop your own dynamic and effective introductions:

- **Make it dynamic.** Nothing is worse for a group than to hear a presentation start off in a dry, boring fashion such that they feel they have to put up with 30 or 45 minutes of dreadfully droning pain. So ask yourself:

  - How can I immediately grab the attention and interest of my group?

  - What methods can I use to ignite their intellectual and emotional response right from the start?

✔ **Keep it concise.** A lumbering, long-winded introduction of your topic is a recipe for failure. As a general rule, limit your introduction to between one and three minutes before going into your topic. Some experts recommend a flexible, approximate five-percent rule, which says that in an hour-long presentation, your introduction should be about three to four minutes — or about five percent of the alloted time.

✔ **Be confident and cordial.** Audiences really enjoy a speaker who is relaxed, comfortable, and confident from the very beginning. Even if you are somewhat nervous, you can fake it by starting off with a strong voice volume, a slower speech rate, a smile, and good direct eye contact with your audience — look at someone who's smiling or friendly to boost your courage. People respect a speaker who comes across as confidently in charge without being domineering, authoritative, or smug.

✔ **Avoid credibility and image killers.** We're sure that you've seen business presenters or public speakers say things like, "I'm not really an expert in this area. I was chosen to fill in for (name) who could not make it. So I will try to get through this presentation using his slides that I'm not totally familar with." Or, "I am feeling very nervous right now, so please bear with me because I had to quickly put together this presentation and there may be some minor errors in the slides."

Never start off with an apology, an admission of being inadequate, unworthy, or unqualified (in any way). Don't alert the group, who may otherwise not notice what you perceive as being nervous or unprepared.

✔ **Connect with your audience.** Accomplished presenters strive to get their audiences to like, respect, and trust them right away. It may sound like a monumental task to accomplish all three in the first few minutes in front of a group that's never seen you before, but using a friendly speaking style, demonstrating your good intentions, and giving a natural and sincere opening puts the group at ease while arousing their interest at the same time.

Using mild-to-wild creativity

Nothing says boring like a predictable, conventional (a nice way of saying slow and dull) introduction to a presentation or speech. Ramping it up just a couple of notches with *ah!*some creativity can make all the difference. And, in some cases, going from mild to wild with your imagination fires up your audience.

Imaginative, unexpected approaches to starting a presentation are eagerly welcomed by an audience weary of typical talks. The audience appreciates an entertaining, yet professional and relevant, presentation that sets you far apart and above the crowd. Famous comedian and late-night television host Johnny Carson profoundly said, "People will pay more to be entertained than educated." We say, "Do both!"

You may be a bit hesitant to attempt something different and untried because you risk the audience not accepting it. The fact is — and we repeat it again — groups love interesting, enjoyable presentations that display meaningful creativity, which captivate and rivet their attention. So, what are you waiting for? When it comes to being creative in your presentations, and particularly the introductions, your comfort level limits you far more than your imagination. The more you experiment in small ways, the more you feel confident and assured in your ability to successfully apply your imagination. Professional creativity that is neither silly nor lessens your credibility grabs the audience's attention when you begin your talk.

Start out with milder forms of clever ideas, test them out, and then escalate up the creativity ladder as you become more confident and comfortable with your blossoming communication imagination.

The following sections recount scenarios that ascend the scale from mild to wild. As you read, think about what tactics you could use in your presentations.

Scenario one: Opening with a video

An account manager along with his chemical engineer from a specialty chemical company gives a talk to a group of manufacturing managers from an international company. They begin by just introducing themselves and immediately start showing a 30 second video of several different manufacturing operations (that have successfully used their products) with these numbers superimposed over the running video: "Proven Averages: 30 Percent Savings . . . 25 Percent Productivity Increase . . . 50 Percent Return on Investment . . . 4 Month Payback." When the video finishes, the account manager warmly smiles and says, "Those are real numbers that report the benefits that over 70 of our customers have experienced to date. Now we will discuss how your company can and will achieve some remarkable returns from using three of our breakthrough coatings in your manufacturing operations."

This atypical introduction immediately begins with something of obvious value to a potential customer, without a long-winded buildup, transition, or wasted time. These two presenters raised eyebrows right away and snatched their group's attention from a 30-second, bottom-line oriented video.

Scenario two: Going dramatic

The CEO of a small, innovative software company is one of the key speakers at a business conference. The person who just verbally introduced him walks to the extreme side of the stage where the speaker has been standing unseen by the audience. He walks the speaker by his arm very slowly and carefully toward the lectern and the audience sees that the speaker is blindfolded. The speaker gropes awkwardly for the location of the microphone to adjust it toward him and the audience wonders what might happen. He begins, "A tsunami of data covers the world, doubling every 18 months. We are drowning in data, but dying of thirst for information that will help run our businesses more effectively. Unknowingly, we wear blindfolds, just like me, that prevent us from seeing the rich sea of information deep within the waves of data flooding our businesses. I'm going to show you how to remove the blindfolds you don't even know you're wearing, giving you the vision to see and use the invaluable, rich information that will make your organizations more productive, more efficient, more innovative — and more successful." As he takes off the blinfold, he smiles and puts up his first slide of a person successfully reading an eye chart for 20/20 vision.

Scenario three: Starting with a story

The Director of Innovation for one highly effective government agency (yes, it is possible!) was asked to give a presentation to another large, bureaurcatic agency that struggles with inefficiences and waste, which prevent it from meeting aggressive goals set by the administration. After being introduced, she starts in a most unique and unexpected fashion by saying, "Let me tell you a story." She recounts the compelling, captivating tale of three organizations that struggled with essentially the same types of problems that burden this agency. Like a mini-epic, the five-minute story mixes facts and statistics with the personal struggles and emotional highs and lows of the managers who ultimately overcame the obstacles and changed the operations and culture of their organizations.

The presenter tells a story each person in the audience relates to and understands. She mesmerizes the group, but stops short of telling how the story ends to build anticipation and curiosity.

In those five brief minutes, she makes a connection with the audience, conveys her understanding of their situation, and instills hope and optimism for a solution. The story gives a valuable, teasing glimpse into how to fix their set of problems. For the next 40 minutes, she describes the plan, process, and solution she advocates. (She does tell them how the story ends — at the end of her presentation.)

Scenario four: Overcoming obstacles

The regional sales vice president (VP) for a leading customer relationship management (CRM) application company puts on a public seminar in a hotel and invites sales executives and sales managers from dozens of small to large companies. As attendees walk into the meeting room they find not the expected rows of chairs and projection screen but an obstacle course laid out on the floor, as shown in Figure 9-1. Yellow duct tape defines the course interupted by paper building blocks, signs, plastic figurines, model buildings, and a metal bridge. A large remote-controlled (RC) car waits at the start of the obstacle course. Needless to say, this unexpected display intrigues the attendees.

Photograph courtesy of Ray Anthony

Figure 9-1:
An unexpected and entertaining demonstration grabs the audience's interest.

When everyone gathers in the room, the vice president says, "Welcome to our seminar! As sales professionals, you know how difficult it can be to navigate the accounts with whom you want to do lots of business. You meet gatekeepers, people change jobs, competitors want to gain an edge over you. Right?" People nod their heads in agreement. He continues, "This morning, we're going to show you how to drive past your competitors, maneuver around all kinds of obstacles, get into that account, and make a difference — quickly. My assistant here will show you how to *really* drive that business."

The VP introduces a young man holding the remote control, and then shouts, "Go!" With that, the fellow drives the RC car and knocks down the paper blocks that form temporary barriers on the road, navigates over the bridge, steers around the plastic figures of people representing gatekeepers, and passes the finish line in such a quick, masterful way that those in the audience are awe-struck with his expert driving. They've never seen anything like it. (The clever VP went to a well-known hobby shop where competitive RC racers hang out, and he hired a champ for the demonstration to make it look absolutely easy.)

The group spontaneously erupts in applause and when the din dies down, the VP says, "Our CRM software offers seven specific solutions that will drive your sales organization revenue growth. I'll show you how you can see increases from 15 percent to well over 45 percent within two years. Our median increase for more than 400 customers in this geographic is about 26 percent. Let's start with the first innovative application for you which is. . . ."

Building Your Introduction

A stirring, get 'em excited introduction relies on building-block components in various combinations. Knowing how to develop a structured introduction radically changes your presentations with the potential for over-the-top results.

Depending upon your purpose and goals of your introduction, think through how to best construct the building blocks. This list shows the components we recommend, numbered not because they are to be completed in that order but to indicate which ones we used to build the introductions in the examples that follow.

1. **Greeting**
2. **Theme**
3. **Introduction(s)**
4. **Housekeeping (goals, agenda, timing, process, handouts)**
5. **Confirm findings**
6. **Executive summary**
7. **Quotation**
8. **Media reference (publication, website, or broadcast media)**
9. **Remarkable or startling facts or statistics**
10. **Questions**
11. **Prop(s)**
12. **Demonstration**
13. **Humor**
14. **Story/anecdote**
15. **Transition**

Connect the blocks in various combinations to create an introduction with purpose (to position your presentation), style, and a tone designed to get your audience to intently listen while establishing your credibility and professionalism.

Sticking with tradition

This straightforward, low-key (but professional) scripted introduction combines components 1, 3, and 4 to build the intro:

1. **(Greeting):** "Good morning. For those of you who don't know me, my name is Jennifer M. and I'm the lead cryogenics engineer on this wonderful project. We certainly appreciate the opportunity to be here today to

tell you about our new breakthrough in superconductor technology. And we thank audience members Bill Y. and Yolanda H. for their help in supporting our development of this presentation for you."

3. **(Introductions):** "My engineering and science team are here to assist me in the four major topics that we'll cover. On my left is Jonathan B. who holds a Ph.D. in electrical engineering and has been on our team for the last three years. He'll jump into opportunities around our breakthroughs. Next to him is . . .."

4. **(Housekeeping):** "Our goal today is to give you a condensed, but important overview of our new superconductor innovation that translates into exciting new energy-related products and services for our customers. Looking at your agenda, you can see that we'll focus on four primary areas, with each of my team spending about ten minutes on the topics of . . . . Feel free to ask questions at any time during the presentation or after. Since this is a simplified overview, we have a 25-page handout for those hearty souls who want to dig into the technical details of this key innovation. We'll spend about an hour going through our information using a combination of slides and animations. We also have some interesting videos taken in our laboratory that will give you an overall understanding of our discovery. Jonathan will now get into. . . .."

Spicing it up

These are elements to give credibility and punch to your topic and can be used in any combination within your introduction. Assume the presenter has gone through the cordial greeting and other introductory remarks and now transitions into these components of the introduction.

8. **(Media reference):** "In its April issue, *Innovative Aircraft Weekly,* the industry's leading publication for small aircraft, highlighted the potential for dramatically escalating sales. In their article, *The Jetsons Are Almost Here,* it says, 'We are literally just a few years away from making flying as easy as driving a car, as affordable as owning one, and as safe, practical, and financially feasible as well.'"

7. **(Quotation):** "The well-known Professor of Aeronautical Engineering, Q.J. Razzintop, stated, 'The company that achieves major improvement in avionics, composite aircraft design, simplicity of flight, and low cost of operations will own an industry that explodes exponentially in growth — at least 25 percent per year or more.'"

9. **(Remarkable facts or statistics):** "While our company is only five years old, we have discovered the golden formula for engineering a quantum leap in technology to create an aircraft that will be today's 'Jetsonmobile.' Our engineers found a brilliant way to reduce avionics costs by almost 90 percent and cut fuel consumption by an unimaginable 70 percent with our radically efficient, ultra-reliable, low-cost engine. It normally takes a year to get a flying certification. It would take less than a week with our

plane! Last year about 2,500 small aircraft were sold. Our conservative estimates for our plane's sales exceed 1,000 the first year and 5,000 the second, and the trend curve looks like a vertical takeoff. We have over 156 patents pending that would give us a rare, and exclusive, competition-free field lead for at least five years or more.

"Our management team is the best in the industry, our factory is ready, our employees are all experienced, highly-trained experts, and our entire operations and marketing infrastructure is primed for takeoff. The skies are incredibly bright. And so could be your investment in our company. As potential investors, you will learn — in the next 60 minutes — about our superb small aircraft and our company's plans to grow and prosper so you can prosper with us. But most importantly, you will be convinced, I'm sure, that an investment in us will be one of the finest you will ever make. I'm turning the next part over to Denise R., our senior design engineer who has over 30 broad and deep years of experience designing some of the most advanced planes in the world. She will cover our radically bold and supremely tested engineering and designs. Denise . . . ."

Engaging the audience with questions

In this example (of part of an introduction), you pose questions to get a response and ask *rhetorical questions,* those for which you don't expect or want a reply, to stimulate thought or consideration. Since we're big fans of using startling facts or statistics to grab people's interest, we use that component again in this example. Notice the choice of targeted words used to appeal to the emotional, not just logical, sides of the audience.

10. **(Questions):** "How many of you have made investments in stock, bonds, or other financial instruments within the last five years or so? Please raise your hands. Now, how many of you are satisfied with the returns you got on those investments? I see that only two of you raised your hands, so . . . about 95 percent of you are not happy. Please raise your hand again if you think it's difficult for most of us to survive and maintain a good quality of life in this uncertain and downward economic climate? Okay, now I see everyone's hand up."

9. **(Remarkable or startling facts or statistics):** "Let me tell you about a 'super survivor.' It's called a tardigrade (presenter shows a photo of one). Not too pretty, is it? It's an eight-legged creature that's about as big as a speck of dust. They can resist temperatures just above the lowest temperature possible, absolute zero, which is about minus 460 degrees Fahrenheit, to way over the boiling point of water. They can withstand pressures in the deepest part of the ocean that are about 6,000 times that of atmospheric pressure. They can live after being bombarded with radiation hundreds of times greater than what would kill a person or animal. Tardigrades can live in the searing heat, frigid cold, and the total

vacuum of space for weeks, even months at a time. And some have been known to live without food or water for over 50 years! They are the ultimate survivors and seem like the stuff of science fiction, but are real and some may even exist in the soil in your backyard.

"I tell you about this fascinating creature because a vast majority of economic and financial experts predict that the world economy is entering the most dangerous economic climate experienced since Adam Smith became known as the Father of Modern Economics in the 18th century. Unfortunately, we will feel the enormous financial heat, pressure, and likely an empty vacuum in our lives."

10. **(Rhetorical questions):** "So I ask . . . is it possible to be a survivor in this economy? Is there a way for us to transform our portfolios into a financial tardigrade who can weather the extremes of higher taxes, increasing inflation and prices, and debilitating healthcare costs, among other financial downfalls? Are there any genuinely safe, proven ways to get back on a financial track to not only survive, but actually thrive? The answer is a resounding YES . . . Absolutely!

"This evening, I will share with you four specific financial strategies combined with our exceptional portfolio of promising and diverse investments that will give you more than hope — they will give you back the optimism and quality of life you so need and deserve. So, let's think like a tardigrade, that little critter who survives and lives through anything! Let's get right into our extensively tested strategies and then the impressive portfolio components . . . ."

Adding a little humor

Decades ago, public speaking couses advised, "Open with a joke." Unfortunately, well-meaning speakers were generally disappointed with the outcomes when they tried it. Unless you're a professional funny person with tested and proven jokes, starting out risking how people might respond can hurt your credibility and tank your ego if the joke falls flat. That's why even giants in the comedy industry test out new jokes in comedy clubs before going onto bigger, high-paying venues. They don't want to bomb either.

Nonetheless, including a somewhat humorous comment, insight, or anecdote that makes people smile while highlighting or reinforcing a point can be useful and can be an entertaining and enjoyable surprise to the audience. Humor, as part of an overall introduction, can add a bit of snap, crackle, and pop to your presentation.

13. **(Humor):** At a conference a presenter, speaking about Grabbing Opportunities, shows a cartoon illustration in his introduction — one he'd tested dozens of times before with excellent results. It shows two cute-looking dinosaurs sitting on a mountaintop surrounded by water. They look at Noah's ark sailing away with the animals gazing over the sides of

the ship. One dinosaur dejectedly says to the other, "Oh, crap! Was that TODAY?" Some in the audience laughed out loud, some chuckled lightly, but most smiled as the speaker said, "Now there's an example of a major opportunity missed. See . . . when was the last time you saw a live dinosaur?" as a few in the audience laughed again. The mild humor (not a joke) both amused and made a memorable point.

Use toned-down, and safer, aspects to amuse as opposed to telling jokes, which many in the audience may have heard before, and which may be met with stark silence and blank looks instead of the intended belly laugh. Always make sure any humor attempts tie into your topic to get people to think about and appreciate your information and messages that follow.

Setting the stage

If you propose a plan, a change of some kind, or are attempting to sell something, try combining these two components in your introduction. In just about any presentation, we advise giving an executive summary up front to preview the highlights, benefits, and key messages of your presentation so the audience knows what to expect.

5. **(Confirm findings):** "As consultants, you asked us to help develop a change management plan for your organization. You told us that you: 1. need to have a more streamlined workflow; 2. want to improve employee productivity; 3. need employees who respond faster to customer inquiries and requests; 4. have to reduce transaction error rates; and 5. need an improved system for all your employees to better communicate with each other in a more responsive fashion. Have we accurately and fully summarized your needs as described to us?"

6. **(Executive summary):** "Based upon those needs, our presentation today will highlight our proposed solution, which involves:

   • Improving your overall employee productivity by 35 to 40 percent

   • Speeding up response to your customers by over 60 percent

   • Reducing transaction error rate by an impressive 80 percent or more

   • Creating a seven-step process to ensure significantly improved employee communication

During our presentation, we will also highlight how our proposed changes will minimize disruptions to your operations, communicate to your employees the benefits of these changes, and specify the various payback and returns on investment you can expect within the next six months. Now that I've given you an overview, let's get into specifics starting with . . ."

Starting out bold and interesting

Don't hesitate to get creative, even in boardroom presentations. In this example, the vice president of research and development (R&D) wants to get approval from the board of directors for more funding to commercialize a significant breakthrough in materials development. In his introduction, he uses a metaphorical theme, a demonstration, and a prop to get his presentation off to a compelling start.

2. **(Theme):** As the vice president (VP) begins, "Today's presentation is really about 'Thunder' — you either create it or someone steals it from you." With that, he presses his remote control to bring up a video of thunder and lightning accompanied by several deep thunder claps of audio sound echoing around the room. "We have a unique opportunity to create a thunderous new product that could boost our gross revenues by an estimated 30 to 45 percent in the next two years and carve out a huge new market for a radical product we commercialize. With your approval for funding, we can beat our competitors to the market before they steal our thunder."

   He then briefly highlights the latest information about their new materials invention that combines nanotechnology and ceramics to produce a lubricant and coating unlike anything on the market. It reduces friction in moving parts by an amazing 95 percent and, as a coating, strengthens metal parts to resist wear in engines and equipment.

11. **(Props):** The VP holds up a two-foot long chain of molecules created with a 3-D printer to represent a blown-up model of the lubricant and coating and says, "This is a model of what our amazing discovery looks like. There is no other molecular structure like it in existence. It's part carbon as you can see by the red atoms and part ceramic as you can see by the blue atoms. I'm going to pass it around for you to look at more closely."

12. **(Demonstration):** The VP of R&D moves to the side of the room where a table and eight-foot long wooden board is set up like a table top. He holds up a hockey puck and says, "This is an ordinary hockey puck with no lubricant on it. Can I get a board member to come up and just push this with a light force on the wooden table?" A woman comes forward and pushes it with moderate force and it travels about two feet. He hands her another puck and says, "This one has our best lubricant and coating on it. Try this one." She does and it goes about four feet. "Now our new 'miracle' product is on this hockey puck. Push it gently." She does and it flies right off the end of the table! You see the stunned and amazed looks on the board members' faces.

   The presenter purposely pauses for about eight seconds, looks around the room and says, "Now I am going to discuss what it will take to get this to market quickly, what our expected financial returns look like, and the support and resources for which we need your approval. In the next 30 minutes, I will cover the details you need to make an informed decision to make some thunder and lightning happen." With that he brings up a four-second video with more lightning accompanied by an audio of room-shaking thunder.

Phrasing transitions

It's often a good idea to use a transition (also called a *segue*) statement as the final part of your introduction to alert your audience that you finished your initial opening and will begin the main body of your presentation with your detailed substance. Here are examples of number 16:

- ✔ "I hope your curiosity is sparked with the introduction of our new product line benefits. Let's get into the specifics of how these exceptional products will transform your operations. . . ."

- ✔ "You're probably anxious to find out more about the seven ways our proposal can achieve the impressive returns on investment that we teased you with a minute ago. Now you will see as I begin to discuss number one with you . . ."

- ✔ "So how will your company actually get those savings and revenue increases in process improvements, which you just glimpsed? Now it's time to move on to the mainline of our presentation starting with . . ."

Chapter 10

Keeping Your Audience on the Edge of Their Seats

You've heard the idiom perhaps hundreds of times before, but do you know what it means to "keep the audience on the edge of their seats?" In movie, theater, or sports parlance it means that people intently follow the action and excitement of a performance, sometimes in a mesmerized way. If it's a story being told or shown (as in a video), it means riveting the audience's attention so that they absolutely must find out what happens next. Entertainment professionals such as producers, actors, comedians, and magicians use suspense, curiosity, surprise, empathy, paradox, humor, and realism to keep people engaged. In innovative presentations when the audience sits on the edges of their seats, you own the room and have the audience's attention and interest locked in tight.

An audience on the edge of their seats focuses on what you say, do, and show. They have laser-like focus on you. They ask many questions to find out more about your topic. Their heads nod in agreement when you cover your key points, and many come up to you after your presentation to talk with you more. You own that group. If you see people glancing around, fidgeting, looking at their phones, conversing with their neighbors, or sitting back with the glazed look of boredom, you've lost possession of the group.

In this chapter, we cover four Laws of Communication Impact including the *Law of Emphasis and Intensity*, the *Law of Engagement*, the *Law of Interest*, and the *Law of Effect*. These laws serve to rev up any audience's attention span and interest. Apply them and you elevate the effectiveness of your presentations to a new level. For each law, we describe innovative presentations that focus on galvanizing and stirring people to committed action, which means getting the results you want.

These laws can be used in any type of oral or written communication, not just formal business presentations.

Standing and Shouting Out: The Law of Emphasis and Intensity

Suppose you're driving at night, and from far away you see the high-intensity lights of a police car. The brilliantly vivid, flashing, colored lights immediately capture your sight, even with all the traffic around you. They stand out! If you attend a symphony performance and in the middle of the *adagio* — the slow, soft passage of the musical piece — two cymbals clash, that instantaneously adds musical thunder to the ensemble and gives you an auditory jolt. It shouts out! Or you attend a conference in Las Vegas in an air-conditioned casino and then step outside in the July summer to suddenly experience an oven-blast temperature of 118 degrees Fahrenheit that seems to singe your skin. Immediately, you feel the sensation, the overpowering difference — that, again, stands out! Each of these audio, visual, or physical sensations exemplify the *Law of Emphasis and Intensity* in action. The sudden and strong change you experience with sight, sound, touch, taste, and other sensation affects you in an intense way.

If you want a key statistic, vital fact, or point to vividly stick out in your presentation, use the Law of Emphasis and Intensity. During your presentation, the audience watches and listens to you, so you can appeal to either, or both, their visual and auditory senses. Physical sensations are a bit harder to conjure during a presentation.

For example, say you fill the page on a flip chart with about 100 round dots using a black felt tip marker then in the middle of those dots, draw one much larger red dot or a big black square. Would eyes be drawn to the red dot or large square immediately among all the other dots? Of course. The non-conforming shape stands out from the uniform crowd of dots. The different color, size, and shape distinguishes it among the dots and emphasizes it.

The other part of the Law of Emphasis and Intensity involves intensity, be it mental, physical, or emotional. It can be an intense sight, sound, smell, touch, or emotional impact. Think back on something you saw, heard, felt, or experienced that surprised, shocked, intrigued, or otherwise got your instantaneous and undivided attention. Intense pleasure or pain, joy or sadness, overwhelming pride or shame — these all share some eruptive feeling, which at times brings a clear, intellectual insight or creates a simple, positive stranglehold on your emotional state.

The more intense the feeling — positive or negative — the more likely you are to remember it. Any sharply vivid or forceful experience causes you to dwell or ruminate upon it long afterwards. The intense feeling you get from a rousing standing ovation is unforgettable and drowns you in a sea of churning emotions. The Law of Emphasis and Intensity creates and sustains that sensation.

In any type of presentation, you convey your key points and also disseminate other needed, but less relevant details to explain, describe, or expand upon those points or link the key points together. During your presentation, you want to draw attention to certain aspects and make sure your audience immediately digests and remembers those aspects more than other supporting pieces of information. You need to use imaginative ways to separate necessary, yet supporting, information from your most critical message, main point, or key data.

To apply the Law of Emphasis and Intensity to the key points of your presentation, you have to, in some way, highlight and give special importance and prominence to the point apart and above everything else. As you develop your presentation and identify those key points, think about imaginative ways you can define, stress, and separate the critical points and messages from subordinate information. The next sections give you some ideas to churn your creative juices.

Comparing and contrasting

Despite echoing Composition 101, comparing and contrasting remains an excellent tool to show big differences and highlight and emphasize specific information. When Apple started shipping their radically redesigned and engineered small cylindrical Mac Pro computer server in December 2013, its diminutive size and raw computing power not only broke major new ground in technology advancements, but its small footprint shocked people who saw it for the first time. But when photos emerged of the tiny, elegantly designed cylinder computer next to the former huge rectangular box of the previous Mac Pro, the comparative difference stunned and awed audiences — it looked like a lizard next to a dinosaur.

Make a list of adjectives that describe your product, service, or idea in terms of size, color, quantity, speed, age, time, and other aspects, and then make a similar list for your competition or the existing way of doing something. Use comparison and contrast to emphasize the point you want your audience to absorb, remember, and consider when you reach the call to action part of your presentation.

Consider adding an element of controversy, curiosity, intrigue, or purposeful exaggeration to evoke an intense reaction from your audience.

Changing your voice

Your voice is a powerful and persuasive tool. Try repeating the same sentence but place emphasis on a different word (indicated with **boldface**) each time. For example:

- ✔ **Our** multi-slice tomographic radiation device can treat up to 15 patients an hour.

- ✔ Our **multi-slice tomographic radiation device** can treat up to 15 patients an hour.

- ✔ Our multi-slice tomographic radiation device can treat up to **15 patients an hour.**

Your voice guides the audience to the points you want to emphasize. Change your vocal inflection as you mention your key message, facts, or statistics. Raising your voice, like a cymbal clash that interrupts an adagio, jolts the audience to attention.

However, after several minutes of a rousing, fevered monologue, a measured statement spoken in a soft tone can have an enormous impact. The key to the Law of Emphasis and Intensity is differentiation. To further separate the ordinary from the important, use a brief, two-to-three second isolating pause both before and immediately after highlighting your significant piece of information.

In addition to inflection and volume, consider repeating that main point for emphasis. Repetition holds the audience's attention on the important point you want to stand out.

Adding pizzazz

Striking, unique, or provocative visuals, photos, and illustrations drive your message home to your audience members. A humorous photo often highlights your point best.

The director of innovation for an international farm, forestry, and construction machinery company gives a presentation to new engineer and technical hires about her company's culture of change and how it has always been ready and willing to embrace new things. She says that ideas — whether incremental or monumental — are the foundation of change and progress, but that it's necessary to unclog the mind of old ways of thinking and doing things that have led to past successes but no longer work in today's environment. With a wry smile, she projects the photo shown in Figure 10-1.

Figure 10-1:
Humorous images, when appropriate, reinforce your point.

Photograph courtesy of Ray Anthony

She leaves time for the group to laugh and then follows up with the interesting photo shown in Figure 10-2 that emphasizes her point of keeping an open mind to new opportunities.

Figure 10-2:
Use surprising images to stress your point.

Photograph courtesy of Ray Anthony

From a physical standpoint, when a person laughs, especially a hearty guffaw, the facial and abdominal muscles relax and blood and oxygen circulation increase, which lead to better attention.

Highlighting specific aspects

A powerful way to draw attention to an intended part of your text, illustrations, diagrams, photos, or videos is to use other visual attention-getters to precisely emphasize and contrast what you wish. Your imaginative ideas can create almost unlimited ways to do that. Here are just a few examples:

✔ With text, use a different color, font, size, bold, heavy underline, or italic to make it stand out. Also, consider putting a rectangular box filled in with color around the text. Without overdoing it, have your graphic designer manipulate your text to make it shout. Animating text is a sure-fire way to make it pop — not to mention a low-cost way to add visual interest to your presentation.

✔ Blur out the areas you want to de-emphasize so the part that stays in focus gets the attention — what photographers call a *wide depth of field*.

✔ Use a build or dissolve function in your slide show or video to reveal and selectively disclose parts of your visual to construct it sections at a time.

✔ If you have a pie chart or bar chart, make the key sector or bar a bright color, while keeping the rest of the illustration black and white.

✔ Spotlight a certain part of a diagram, illustration, or anything else by enlarging that part over the entire graphic as if a magnifying glass focused on it. Or lower the opacity of your graphic to 25 percent, while keeping the opacity at 100 percent for the part you want to stand out.

✔ Use shapes, colors, and geometric elements to draw the audience's eyes to where you want their concentration. For example, in a process flow chart that displays each step of the process in a box or other geometric shape, change the shape color as you talk about each step in the process. Use color arrows to dissolve onto the visual to point where you want. Consider using color circles, squares, and ellipses to overlay the parts of the visual you want to emphasize.

By using contrasting shapes or colors and showing single parts of the whole image at a time, you guide the viewers' eyes to precisely where you want them to be.

Using special effects

If you're using a presentation software app that lets you overlay (or composite) a QuickTime or other video format file on your slides, consider using stock animations typically called *revealers, motion elements,* or *blinkers.* These animated elements, such as a blinking arrow, lights that go back and forth, animated circles, or other visual effects immediately bring a viewer's attention to specific text or parts of a photo, diagram, illustration, or chart in a video or static slide. Digital Juice (www.digitaljuice.com) sells many of these.

You can customize powerful ways to direct a viewer's attention to specific pieces of information on your slide or video by using the custom effects of *Adobe After Effects* or Apple's *Motion* software. Selectively add audio to one of these animated effects for further emphasis.

Don't overdo these creative ways of drawing a viewer's eye to specific parts of your visuals. Special effects should support what you're saying, not replace or overwhelm your message.

Telling a story

People are more likely to remember a story than a list of facts or figures. A short and compelling story brings life to your presentation and can illuminate the critical point(s) you want to showcase. The moral of a well-crafted, captivating tale should convey the message or information you want your audience to remember.

Humor is a captivating way to stress something. An amusing cartoon or illustration with a simple but profound message often turns out to be a sudden sharp insight for your audience. If you tell an amusing anecdote, use the type of humor that makes people smile, chuckle, or laugh, but that also makes them ponder the underlying substance of your key point long after the laughs fade.

Demonstrating your point

Remember show-and-tell day in kindergarten? If you do, you began preparing for demonstrations then. Nothing proves your point as powerfully as showing what you discuss. Years ago when Kevlar bullet-proof vests were coming on the scene, some company owners actually took live-fire shots from a powerful pistol to demonstrate the real protective power of their vests. The manufacturer of a commercial-grade cordless drill pitted its product against a competitor's, connecting each drill to a winch to pull a 4,000 pound tractor. The competitor's drill pulled the tractor about half the distance and stopped as it began to smoke, while the featured product easily pulled the heavy vehicle the whole distance with no damage and a remaining battery charge, obviously highlighting its power, durability, and performance.

Effective demonstrations not only prove the claims you make, but stress the main points you want the audience to know and produce the greatest psychological impact.

Propping up

Physical props support and reinforce both your spoken word and visuals. For example, a sales trainer gives a presentation about how to deal with high-strung, overly-sensitive prospects. She takes a large inflated balloon, puts it directly over her head and compares it to a potential customer's highly inflated, but delicate, ego. She says if you blatantly disagree with such a person during your sales conversation, her ego will be damaged (as she sticks a pin in the balloon), and you will lose a sale. The abrupt burst with the loud POP! gets people's attention, and long after the training ends, they vividly remember that each time they face a sensitive prospect.

In addition to props, consider using relevant theatrical techniques such as skits, acting, focused lighting, music, and the aforementioned special effects (see "Using special effects" earlier) to add novelty, drama, curiosity, or entertainment around your most important concept.

In addition to props, determine what types of interesting handouts can further showcase what you want. The more concise, creative, and attractive your handouts, gifts, or giveaways, the more likely people are to read or view the main points you want them to absorb and remember.

Tech-ing out

If you lend a tablet to each attendee, you can communicate directly with each person from your computer or tablet. (We guide you through the technical side of doing this in Chapter 18.) Tell the audience that you're sending something important for them to see for themselves. While you're alerting them, transmit what you want to emphasize, and then discuss it.

If you have a small group of three to six people, you can use a theatrical technique by blanking out your projector or monitor and telling the group you want to show them something close up. You then put the highlighted information or visual on your large tablet screen, move close to each person and show it from about two to three feet away. This transition from screen to large tablet, combined with your movement and close physical proximity to each person, adds intensity to your information and your relationship to the audience.

Use your stylus and tablet to circle, underline, or put an exclamation point next to what you want to highlight. You can draw something around it or next to it and otherwise think of ways to isolate something on your visual to pull the audience's attention to it. Also consider using your presentation app's laser pointer function on your tablet to highlight key points. (See Chapter 17 for information about specific presentation apps.)

Involving Your Audience: The Law of Exercise and Engagement

As it applies to learning, the *Law of Exercise and Engagement* states that people who are engaged and active are more interested in continuing an activity, learn more from it, and are otherwise impacted to a greater degree than those who aren't emotionally involved. For our purposes, we interpret the law to mean that you should have people participate in your presentation.

A presentation, like a conversation, has at least two people — one who speaks and one who listens. However, both situations need balance. If two people have a conversation and one person dominates it, talking solely about her interests without regard for the other person who passively (supposedly) listens, the listener probably isn't interested in what the talker has to say, especially after an extended period tolerating a long-winded monologue. But, if the non-stop talker asks the listener a question, makes eye contact, and smiles, the (polite) listener becomes more involved in the discussion. You want to elicit the same reaction from your audience. By showing interest in reciprocally listening, your one-sided monologue becomes a meaningful, active dialogue.

Speaking about topics that don't interest or aren't pertinent to your audience's needs is a waste of time for everyone. See Chapter 4 to discover how to analyze your audience during the presentation planning stage.

Involving the audience

An engaged speaker creates an attentive and interested audience. Studies show that people mimic what they see and hear. It's a form of social reciprocity. So, when you show interest in your audience, they in turn show interest in you.

Great speakers use lots of eye contact to connect with their audiences. They encourage questions and comments and ask thought-provoking rhetorical questions. When the room setup permits, move into and among the audience instead of isolating yourself at the front.

Presenters who share stories, examples, quotations, and other specifically tailored content (that addresses the groups needs and wants) capture the audience's attention. (See the earlier section, "Telling a story.") And speakers who call on people in the room to interact with them as much as possible — "Hey, Grace, what are your thoughts on that?" — create a dialogue that makes people feel more attended to as a result.

Some speakers and presenters mingle with individuals before, during, and after their talk. If they know some of the people in the group, they use personal anecdotes about them or use friendly humor relating to them. Frequently seeking out a group's opinions, reactions, and ideas helps you turn an otherwise passive audience into an active — and interactive — one and significantly increases the chances of your presentation breeding success.

Encouraging interaction

The exercise part of the Law of Engagement and Exercise, while similar to engagement, indicates a high level of direct involvement. Trainers use learning exercises, case studies, role playing, and questioning to get people to use the information they have acquired in real-world simulation in the classroom — to just do it. When coauthor Ray Anthony sold computers for an international company, he would ask potential buyers to bring their real accounting data with them to a demonstration of his company's minicomputers (at the time, actually sophisticated accounting machines the size of a big desk). With a prospect sitting down beside him, Ray would lead the person through the process of inputting the data to do accounts payable, accounts receivable, and general ledger postings. The potential customer would then use the keyboard to type in the data and see for herself just how fast, accurate, easy, and beneficial it would be for her accounting operation. It was not Ray telling or doing it, but the person following the Law of Exercise.

The exercise part of this law combines sight, touch, and even sound (in this case the computer's printer gave an impressively quick printout) to present a real situation that convinces the audience of the point you make. By employing these types of product demonstrations using the Law of Exercise and Engagement, prospects became buying customers.

It's becoming more common, especially in large groups, to use a tablet or iPad to enable those in the audience to express their opinions, ideas, or questions. In large events, for example, hundreds of people in the audience can tweet comments for you to display on the big screen for all to see in real time.

Whether you're a fan or not, social media taps into a desire to share and encourages people to express thoughts and feelings toward an interesting or concerning topic. For many people, liking, commenting, or sharing have become second nature. You can take advantage of the social mentality in your presentation. You can respond as you wish to the comments people are making for as long as it's productive or entertaining.

Today's interactive technology allows you to create virtual situations where the audience inputs data or manipulates information or images, along with you, to reach the conclusions you want. Augmented reality apps show the viewer the solutions to the problem or situation at hand. (See Chapter 19 for information about augmented reality.)

By providing tablets or laptops that have a presentation or collaboration app pre-loaded (or inviting your attendees to download the app to their own devices before beginning your presentation), your traditional talking-head presentation becomes one involving the *Law of Exercise*. Attendees actively participate and can see for themselves the outcomes you pose and forecast as well as comments and ideas from others in the group. Search for "collaboration" in the App Store and you discover literally hundreds of apps designed to facilitate interactive brainstorming. Check out BaiBoard (www.baiboard.com), a free Mac and iOS app (and a forthcoming Android version) that lets small workgroups collaborate on a shared whiteboard and PDF document annotation, and iBrainstorm (www.ibrainstormapp.com), a multi-device collaboration tool that's also free.

We predict that in the near future, most meetings and presentations will effectively take advantage of the Law of Engagement and Exercise where involvement is much more two-sided (involving a back-and-forth between audience and presenter) as opposed to presenter-directed, sequentially ordered talks.

Hitting Their Hot Buttons: The Law of Interest

Why do people intently listen to or watch something with rapt attention or enthusiastically engage in an activity? Obviously because they want to. They're interested and enjoy doing it. Simple as that.

When people lose interest, they lose attention, concentration, and focus and become bored or distracted. They start thinking of something else or vaguely daydream. At meetings, training workshops, presentations, and speeches, you see people whip out their smartphones or tablets and start to review their e-mails, send text messages, surf the Web, or just work on something else. Although some people try to be discreet, many engage in these activities with total disregard for how you may feel. What was once considered quite rude before the popular advent and use of addictive digital devices is now accepted as commonplace behavior in many organizational cultures. However, research studies prove that a great majority of those multi-taskers who rationalize and justify their selective attention really cannot listen and do something else with equal effectiveness.

If you're giving a presentation and attendees become mentally and emotionally detached, they can miss vital information that affects their decision making and possible desire to commit to what you are asking them to do, such as approve, support, buy, or endorse. They may misinterpret something because of attention gaps in their listening. So, it's important that you strive to keep the interest level high for the person(s) listening or watching.

When it comes to capitalizing upon the Law of Interest, use techniques from the Law of Exercise and Engagement we discuss in the previous section. Use these extra tips to capture and hold the interest of as many in a smaller group or even larger audience as possible:

- Do an effective audience analysis to determine the general makeup of the group so that you can personalize and tailor your talk to give them exactly what they need and want. Focus on the priorities your audience wants addressed.

- Throughout your presentation, tell your audience how they will directly (personally or professionally or both) benefit from your talk. For example, say "I'm going to show each of you four things that promise to make your job easier, faster, and better. These will reduce your stress, hassles, and tedious workloads."

- Have as compelling and captivating a presentation introduction as you can. Set the bar high for what follows.

- Get creative. If appropriate, use fun (but always professional) activities such as information guessing games, interactive exercises to get feedback, ideas, and recommendations based upon your presentation. At well-planned segues in your presentation, consider sending useful bits of topic-related trivia, photos, or illustrations from your tablet or laptop to their devices.

- Ramp up your speech delivery technique. Show energy, enthusiasm, and dynamism to make it easier and more interesting to listen.

- As much as you can, use stories to communicate fascinating and riveting facts, statistics, testimonials, research results, or analogies that apply to, are meaningful for, or engrossing to your audience. Give vivid examples that entertain, amuse, or emotionally affect people.

- Use rhetorical, thought-provoking questions at specific junctures in your talk to reignite declining interest. Ask "Why should you be interested in knowing this?" or "What effect would it have if you began using this new process tomorrow — what three surprising differences would you discover right away?"

- In a smaller group, use the teacher's trick and call on a specific person (who seems to be inattentive or fixated on her device) to ask a relevant question or get feedback. Be subtle. By casually and randomly going around the room to stimulate discussion, you involve those who may have lost interest and will likely rejuvenate their flagging attention. Bear in mind that a distracted person may re-engage or may feel embarrassed or guilty for not contributing to the group discussion.

Sometimes people drift off because they don't understand what you're saying, so with a small group you can ask, "Does my point make sense to you?"

Facing the Consequences: The Law of Effect

Use the *Law of Effect* to activate or change people's behavior. Politicians, sales and marketing professionals, and others who strive to influence and persuade people to act in certain ways use this law. Edward Thorndike, the American psychologist known for his work on animal behavior and learning, developed this law. Based upon a stimulus-response reaction, the *Law of Effect* essentially states that responses that produce an enjoyable or satisfying effect in a particular situation become more likely to occur again in that situation, and responses that produce uneasiness, discomfort, or some other negative effect are less likely to occur again in that type of situation. Common sense, right? If you give an innovative presentation and your audience obviously got a lot out of it, then they will be more eager to attend and participate in your future presentations.

You can say that the Law of Effect relates to carrot-on-a-stick rewards and punishments. For example, if a person regularly gets speeding tickets while driving too fast, at some point, after spending lots of time in driving school and court appearances or paying fines and lawyer fees, she's likely to slow down because of the unpleasant and undesirable consequences.

Competent skills trainers, motivational speakers, personal trainers, and business coaches use the Law of Effect to help people learn, develop new skills, build confidence, and be inspired to excel. When it comes to giving a presentation or speech, evoke the Law of Effect in the following ways:

✔ From your laptop or tablet, show brief, compelling testimonials or success stories about how your products, services, programs, or innovations generate positive consequences for the users. Likewise, subtly communicate the negative consequences for people who don't take advantage of your recommendations. Before-and-after examples often persuade people to act.

✔ If you recommend change of some kind, focus on the (greater) probable positive gain versus the (lesser) possible risk, problems, or inconvenience associated with the proposed change.

✔ Compliment and praise people in your audience when they provide constructive comments about your presentation points. This way of psychologically rewarding people's supportive comments encourages more of those in the audience to speak up in ways that approve of and endorse your information.

People are fearful of taking unnecessary risks. Be very mindful about how you communicate things that may indirectly or subtly invoke fear, anxiety, concern, remorse, or guilt — unless your strategy is designed to solicit negative feelings to further your goals.

Chapter 11

Ending on a High Note

*T*oday's action movies start like a lit fuse in sticks of dynamite — a sizzling spark heading toward a shock wave with a scene that immediately envelopes you in the unfolding drama, suspense, or action. Many movies have the raw visual firepower and adrenalin-building punch to ignite our attention and transfix us. But . . . the ending of a great movie matters most in creating an explosive experience that impacts us emotionally and psychologically. Everything in a good plot builds up to the ending, the close, the climax — and releases it.

If you attend a live performance by a terrific singer or band, you notice that they start off with a lively, heart-pumping, foot-thumping number — their introduction. However, they bring down the house by saving their very best, most dynamic song for last — their conclusion — to leave the audience on a high emotional plain. Singers want their fans to cherish their act long afterwards so they sing a blockbuster as their closing song, and some save that blockbuster for the encore, making it the last of the last.

This chapter takes inspiration from movies and concerts to explain how to create and deliver a compelling and rousing conclusion to your presentation or speech.

Concluding Effectively: The Law of Recency

The closing effect — the *Law of Recency* — is the fifth of the Laws of Communication Impact, and carries more weight for your message than the primacy (beginning) effect, because the last thing a person sees, hears, tastes, touches, feels, or experiences is actually the first thing they remember.

The acronym LIFO, used by computer scientists, stands for Last In, First Out and applies to list processing and data structures. You can use it to remember how to structure your presentations.

Think about it: You had a great dinner, but you still want that delicious dessert — that last, lingering wonderful taste before you leave the restaurant. Or, you're saying goodbye to a potential client, who firmly shakes your hand, gives you a warm, ear-to-ear smile and says, "This was a terrific meeting. I see us working with your company!" These endings send you out on a high note, long felt and well remembered, don't they? Or, in a converse situation, your boss looks at you sternly and in a cold, steely voice simply says, "Okay," as he walks away after you explained something. That last message also digs in and sticks with you, unfortunately.

For your talk to be a success, you must use the *Law of Recency* to construct a strong conclusion, which has the following features:

✔ Encapsulates and brings everything together in a simple, concise, and memorable manner

✔ Highlights your most important points and messages in a convincing and compelling way

✔ Leaves a group on a high note and motivates them to act upon your recommendation, plan, solution, or idea (the call to action)

✔ Cements your rapport and credibility with the audience

✔ When necessary, inoculates your group against any subsequent discussions or presentations, such as competitive sales presentations, designed to counter what you advocate

Avoid the flapping swan conclusion

Too many presenters let their conclusion trail or suddenly and abruptly die off with weak, disjointed, or indecisive ramblings as if they had not prepared any well-thought-out final remarks. This is what we call the Flapping Swan: A speaker comes to the end of his talk and raises both arms to the side about shoulder height and lets them quickly fall to his hips while saying something like, "Okay...that's it, I guess. Ah... any questions?" or "That's about all I ... sort of have to say ... uhm ... thanks." Ending this way is definitely neither dynamic nor smooth and certainly not memorable (at least in a positive way).

Impacting Your Audience Right to the End

Your conclusion can be soft-spoken or electric, depending on both your personality and your audience, but every type of conclusion should follow the guidelines in the next sections to be effective.

Conclude, don't include

If you forgot minor, unimportant pieces of information, don't add them to your conclusion as afterthoughts. A conclusion wraps up and tightly summarizes what you said and is not a forum for new information. What's more, if you forget something important and discuss it during your conclusion, your may jeopardize your credibility and leave the audience wondering, "If it was that much of a priority, how could he not have focused on it during the presentation?"

Signal that the end is near

Audiences snap to when they hear the magical words that tell them it's the beginning of the end. When a presenter says something like, "I'm going to wrap up now with my summary and final thoughts," listeners perk up with renewed attention, which you can take advantage of. Use transition statements such as:

- ✔ "I'll conclude with the profound quotation of the eminent business giant Catherine Wittner who said . . . "

- ✔ "The main points I want to leave you with before I end, are . . . "

- ✔ "As I finish up, I want to leave you with a stunning four-minute video that perfectly encapsulates and dramatically amplifies the dire importance of my message to you today . . . "

- ✔ "I end today with three recommendations, which are . . . "

End it already

Your conclusion should be direct and concise, yet smooth, not choppy. After you alert your group that you're heading down the homestretch of your talk, conclude with brevity and panache. Some presenters frustrate audiences by giving the impression things are wrapping up and then continue talking with no sign of ending soon. Some people do this multiple times to the great dismay of the audience.

Be neither meek nor weak

Finish in a confident, strong, and self-assured manner that conveys positivity and optimism. Never apologize or appear submissive as in the following:

- ✔ "I am so sorry it took this long and that we didn't have enough handouts for all of you, but . . . "
- ✔ "I'm embarrassed I forget to prepare details about . . . "
- ✔ "This is a new presentation for me, and also I'm not an experienced speaker . . . "
- ✔ "Thank you for your patience during my talk."

Instead, offer a solution, such as, "If you didn't receive the handouts, please write your e-mail on the list on the table by the exit and I'll send them to you this evening." Or "It was a delight to speak with you today about my new responsibilities."

Leave with a strong message

In certain types of presentations or speeches, a thought-provoking, memorable finale embodies the epitome of the Law of Recency — like the last lyrics of a song or the final words of a play. Consider the following examples of punchy closing statements:

- ✔ "Our company's debt is a disaster teetering on a precipice. We still have time to avoid economic catastrophe, but only if we act right now. Right Now!"
- ✔ "Innovation in your corporation is absolutely critical as never before. Apply it, accelerate it, and benefit from it in ways you've never imagined before!"
- ✔ "There are three things to remember about great leadership: Take care of your people . . . take care of your people . . . take care of your people. And they will take care of you and your company!"

Giving a Tactical Conclusion

Innovative presentations demand powerful, unique, unpredictable, and thoroughly imaginative conclusions. A genial capstone separates you from the crowd of other presenters. In the next sections we provide examples of superb conclusions to spur your creativity and turn a Flapping Swan (see the nearby sidebar) into a Soaring Eagle.

Repeating a theme (with a twist)

In Chapter 9, which covers the Law of Primacy and explains how to compose a good introduction, one of the examples describes how the CEO of an innovative software company begins his presentation at a business conference by being led blindfolded to the lectern. The theme of his key message drove home the point that extracting useful information from the continuous mega-explosion of data around us is difficult because we can't distinguish between useful and useless — it's as if we're blindfolded.

In his conclusion, the CEO concisely and compellingly summarizes his key points and then says to the group of about 200 people, "Now I've got a couple of surprises for you today. Reach under your chair and open the plastic bag." The audience finds a black blindfold with the four main points the CEO emphasized in his summary printed on one side of the cloth.

"Now, I have a couple of more surprises," in which he teases the group. "I'm going to ask you to put on your new blindfold. I have six assistants around the room, who will throw soft foam rubber balls to you while blindfolded. Those who catch them will get prizes. Ready . . .throw the balls!" he yells out. No one caught one, even by accident. "Take off your blindfolds. Not one of you out of about 200 here today caught one." He said. "Not surprising, is it? I hope you enjoyed this fun exercise that reinforces my point about being blindfolded. I still have one more surprise for you, though. Ready? Everyone gets prizes. As you walk outside, pick up a free stylus pen you can use with your smartphone or tablet, a 25 percent discount coupon for our information-gathering software, and a $10 gift card. It was great being with all of you today!" He ended with power and passion. The CEO got a standing ovation and probably lots of business from his talk.

Leaving them smiling

A senior account manager gives an innovative sales presentation using video, animation, and a live demonstration about his company's latest computer-activated plasma- and laser-cutting tools for steel plate to a defense contractor who builds naval combat ships. His crisp summary highlights the extra speed, reliability, and precision of his company's heavy-steel cutting machines that results in reduced waste, increased productivity and quality, and the ability to better meet stringent deadlines and budgets — critical components of getting renewed contracts in the defense industry. Following his summary, he points to a man sitting on the side and says, "I introduced Travis H. in the beginning. While he was quiet throughout my talk, I'd like to bring him up now."

The well-dressed, professional-looking man in his 40s pushes an open cart with a small tablecloth over it, obviously hiding something underneath. Travis opens with, "This is the end of our structured presentation. We hope you understand the excellent information about using our latest equipment to give you the benefits Sam mentioned. Since we have 15 minutes left, we would like to give you a dessert while we briefly chat with you. Don't worry, we'll still finish ahead of schedule." With that, he uncovers the cart and reveals a large cake under a glass cover, which he also removes. "Quality inspection is critical in your industry. Can I get someone up here to do a quality check on this cake?" he asks, as some people laugh while others are curious as to what's going on.

A smiling engineering vice president (VP) steps up, looks it over as Travis queries, "Is that cake marked or otherwise defective in any way? Does it look like a tasty, normal cake that our account manager baked just for all of you?" More laughs and smiles from the group as the "inspector" says, "Yeah . . .looks okay to me." "Now, check the cart out," Travis requests and continues, "It's a regular cart, with just a flat top holding the cake and nothing under it right?" The VP affirms it.

Travis takes the small tablecloth, covers the front of the cake and shouts the name of the account manager's company while lifting the cloth straight up to the amazement of everyone. Not only is the cake now bigger with a different color and decoration, but it has 18 perfectly equal slices in it, exactly the number for each person in the group! The account manager steps forward as jaws are still hanging down and says, "I told you we offer precision! We'll work the same magic for your company — growth and perfect cuts." To those who asked, he explained that Travis was really a highly skilled magician hired to entertain the group. Needless to say, his innovative presentation was a cakewalk that had a tasty win to it.

Offering impressive incentives

The construction industry is among the most highly competitive of all industries with those who submit the lowest valid bid winning the deal a huge percentage of the time. Lori V., a senior project manager, as shown in Figure 11-1, works for a successful, respected construction firm that made the short list for building an upscale lakeside community of expensive residences, offices, four-star restaurants, and retail stores. She and her team compete against two other firms to win the prized project. Her strategy is simple: prove they are the absolute best firm to bring the project in on-time, on-target, and on-budget with some important extras. She and her team plan a superb presentation that conveys the expertise, professionalism, teamwork, and valuable creativity their firm brings to the project.

Figure 11-1:
Lori's presentation makes use of creative, professional-looking displays and handouts.

Photograph courtesy of Ray Anthony

The presentation is extraordinary and spellbinding, both different and significantly better than any of the other construction firms. Their bid, however, is the highest, although not by an unreasonable margin. Lori has a strategy for that as well. Like any great presenter, she summarizes the highlights and superior benefits of her proposal that include:

- Her firm's record of successful projects completed
- Their strong financial health and growth trend
- Their industry-winning quality awards and safety records
- The impressive qualifications of their firm's leaders and personnel

For her imaginative finale, her presentation team gives each of the five meeting attendees — the decision makers — a special set of handouts, as shown in Figure 11-2. Each includes a model dump truck with a unique binder inside, which you can see in Figures 11-3. Lori then uses a standard sales tactic called the trial close, "Based upon your questions, comments, and body language, I get the impression you would like to seriously consider us for this large, beautiful project. Have I sensed that accurately?" She sees several smiles and slight head nods, but knows someone will mention their higher price, which two people do. So she counters, "Let's see if we can fix that."

She continues, "You'll find two important items in that cool-looking Plexiglas cover handout: a compelling, detailed summary of all aspects that we will excel in for your lakeside development. Secondly, on page 14 you'll find a pleasant surprise! In our previous discussions, you mentioned that you like the idea of further developing the lakefront with numerous amenities and recreations. But you said doing that was in the budget for Phase 2 about three years from now.

Well, page 14 details the designs we came up with based upon your ideas to do just that." Lori holds up a real-looking bill and says, "My firm is offering you an attractive incentive — a free bonus — of $1 million dollars out of our pockets to further enhance the lakefront and offset part of our higher fee!" She instructs her team to give each of the potential clients the realistic one million dollar bill. That spectacular presentation with her unexpected, over-the-top finale clinches the deal.

Figure 11-2:
The model truck contains a binder summarizing her presentation.

Photograph courtesy of Ray Anthony

Figure 11-3:
The binder is more than just a folder and paper.

Photograph courtesy of Ray Anthony

Although many presentation coaches warn against communicating important incentives at the end of a presentation, Lori's risk-taking pays off, and her team's innovative presentation captivates the audience, giving the eleventh-hour unveiling a stronger psychological buying effect with positive results.

Engineering Your Conclusion with Building Blocks

Putting together a well-structured and well-delivered ending amplifies and confirms the excellence of your entire presentation. You can construct a memorable, impressive, send-them-forth-marching conclusion by connecting building block components in various combinations, just like those we suggest for building introductions, as covered in Chapter 9.

Together, your creative introductions and conclusions are critical in developing and delivering the ultimate innovative presentation. Use the building blocks we suggest, but don't stop there. Use your imagination to come up with something new, unique, maybe even bold and daring. Your conclusion — the last thing they heard — is the first thing they'll remember.

Depending on your presentation's purpose and goals, select and combine these building blocks into an effective conclusion that matches your compelling introduction. Start building your conclusion with these components and then add anything that your imagination cooks up:

1. Theme

2. Quotation

3. Challenge

4. Executive summary

5. Humor

6. News reference (publication, website, or broadcast media)

7. Remarkable or startling facts or statistics

8. Thought-provoking questions

9. Multimedia (video, audio, photo, illustration, animation)

10. Story/anecdote

11. Call to action

In the next sections, we give you several examples of how to connect these building blocks in various combinations to construct a conclusion that adds to the overall excellence of your presentation and elicits the results you want.

Ending with motivation and inspiration

This scenario includes building blocks to pump people up about a challenging situation. A management consultant specializing in innovation and change gives a presentation to managers and professionals on how to best navigate and deal with a big change initiative in their organization. The presenter finishes his summary and now wants to leave the audience with a sense of control, power, and optimism. He uses two quotations and leverages a metaphor as part of his stirring conclusion, combining three building blocks in this scripted example:

> **1. (Theme):** "Throughout this project and this presentation, we highlight our theme of victory. It is not contrived or artificial, but a genuine rallying cry to turn this company around 180 degrees — to steer that ship hard to starboard, so we can not only save jobs and security here, but give each of our careers an opportunity to grow and prosper in the most effective ways."

> **2. (Quotation):** "Attitude, optimism, and a drive to win — in spite of the odds and obstacles facing us — are everything when confronted with a tough challenge, as we have here. Muhammad Ali told one opponent, 'If you even dream of beating me, you'd better wake up and apologize.' We need that kind of confidence and bravado to keep us going when the going seems stopped. We must have an unbeatable attitude and drive to succeed and win!"

> **3. (Challenge):** "This fine company's CEO and board of directors have committed abundant resources and continuous support to help you turn our ship around and head full speed toward destinations that are full of promise, opportunity, and prosperity for all of us. My challenge to each of you is to look forward to the voyage. Though there will be some choppy and rough seas ahead, hold the helm steady and sure and don't let up or give up for one moment. I challenge you to show your best and be your best during this transformational voyage in which we are setting sail."

> **2. (Quotation):** "Many of you who have been here for a decade or more have told me that you're worried. That's understandable. Sometimes a situation, though, is at its best when it is shaken and stirred. I will leave you with what I think is a truly profound thought that should sustain us. Anne Morrow Lindbergh, the wife of famed aviator Charles Lindbergh, was herself an aviator and author and one who experienced numerous difficulties and tragedy in her life. She waxed philosophic as she noted, 'Only in growth, reform, and change, paradoxically enough, is true security to be found.' Let's keep that always in mind!"

Advocating a new strategic approach and direction

Organizations must constantly adapt to meet new trends, discoveries, threats, and to take advantage of emerging opportunities. The scenario here is about a vice president of a large research and development (R&D) group in a Fortune 100 company. He gave an hour-long presentation to a group of over 100 division presidents and senior executives from worldwide locations. He followed the guideline of keeping his summary points between three and five, but decided to give adequate detail in the summary to meet his goals of convincing the executives to endorse his new, visionary plan. Here are the building blocks the VP used in his conclusion:

> Transition statement: "Now it's time for me to wrap up my presentation and summarize."

> **4. (Executive Summary):** "Unprecedented, groundbreaking innovations in material science are happening at breakneck speeds and the trends, implications, and consequences will significantly affect our company. I want to leave you with three defining points:

> 1. **Expect radical change.** Nanotechnology, microceramics, and exotic multi-material alloys will dramatically change what we build, process, and use in chemistry, engineering, energy, medicine, travel, environment, space exploration, and literally, every single industry. It will impact the most minute aspects of life and business as we know it.

> 2. **We are positioned for success in that change.** Our company is in an enviable position to leverage the 234 patents we have developed in the last two years to not only take advantage of this change and to master it, but to lead that change, while both creating and riding the tidal wave for many years to come.

> 3. **We are ready to capitalize on enormous opportunities.** The bold plan that my team created and that I discussed today is meticulously researched, developed, and analyzed in ways to minimize risk, maximize gain, and have an extraordinarily high probability of reaching the estimated goals of revenue increase of $65 to $75 billion over five years, annual returns on investment of between 25 to 30 percent, and impressive industry market share gains of at least 8 percentage points.

> For those extremely critical three points, our company is perfectly positioned to be the leader in a monumental way in a monumentally important industry."

6. (News Reference): "Coincidentally, in this month's issue of *Advanced Materials Engineering Journal,* in an article titled, 'The Coming Revolution of Exotic Ceramics, Polymers, and Nanotubes,' 20 prestigious university research center directors in America, Europe, and Asia cited how expanded investments in research in precisely the areas in which we have been successfully creating breakthroughs will create sustained massive returns and exploding exponential growth in new, evolving markets."

7. (Remarkable or Startling Facts or Statistics): "During my presentation, I gave you many eye-opening financial figures and statistics to prove and justify what I will ask of this group in a moment. But I saved this rather shocking projection for last: The International Association of Materials Scientists has conservatively projected the worldwide market for commercializing the quantum-leap material innovations we and others are working on to be over $7 trillion in U.S. dollars by 2030. That's trillion, not billion, which is an amazing ten percent of the world's estimated gross domestic product! That financial value would be larger than the combined worldwide industries of aerospace, computers, electronics, energy, automotive, communications, and construction. The scope of this opportunity is almost unimaginable!"

11. (Call to Action): "Because each of you here today is a leader in one of our international business divisions in your country or geographic area, I'm asking you for two important things: One: To strongly support the commercialization of our advanced exotic materials innovations. By support, I specifically mean to convey what we are doing with your new product designers, your operations managers, and your sales and marketing professionals. Another way to support these plans is to start thinking of specific budgets for new products based on our patents. Two: I ask you to take about 15 minutes and fill out a questionnaire. Your answers will be included in my upcoming presentation to our board of directors."

2. (Quotation with Ending statement): "I want to thank you for your previous support and dedication, and for your insights on how our company can dominate this new business space. We look forward to your ongoing support, which is so vital to us. It was journalist and author George Will who said, 'The future has a way of arriving unannounced.' Not if we can help it. We intend to loudly trumpet our entry in science and business history!"

Giving the audience a happy ending

Conrad J., president of a national animal rescue organization, gives a fundraising presentation. His gripping talk shows heart-wrenching photos and disturbing stories of neglected and abused dogs, cats, and other animals. The stories, as expected, melt the hearts of potential donors. The president of the rescue organization wants to end in a special way that shows appreciation for the donors, gives hope and happy endings to many of these wonderful creatures, and leaves his audience ready to donate again. He briefly summarizes his key points and communicates his specific request for making a commitment to generous donations (his call to action) with the following conclusion building blocks:

10. (Story/anecdote) with music: Conrad tells stories about the animals, but saves the best one for last. Here is a condensed version of that emotional, heart-tugging tale. Conrad's team selects a moving piece of music to play softly in the background as a subliminal complement to the following anecdote: "Remember the sad story and photos of Pookie, the beautiful Golden Labrador that was literally a day away from death's door? Well, a wonderful family of five from The Woodlands, Texas, adopted him for their nine-year old son, Danny. You see, Danny is autistic. He has numerous communication problems, which limit his social interactions with other children. He demonstrates no interest in playing or showing enjoyment, regardless of the activity.

His heartbroken parents tried everything with no success until . . . they brought Pookie home from one of our shelters. Sweet Pookie bonded immediately with Danny. It was love at first lick for Danny, too. Pookie is now Danny's most beloved friend, and they do everything together — they're inseparable. Here's a photo of Danny with Pookie (who embraces Danny as he sleeps). This child, once trapped inside himself, is now free as never before! He talks fluently and takes the initiative for social interactions. He laughs, he hugs, he even tells jokes — all because of Pookie. All because you cared to save this beautiful soul of a dog, who saved the life of Danny. This is a genuine miracle that no medicine, no doctor nor treatment could fix. With your continued donations, we are aggressively expanding this program and many others to bring two-legged and four-legged hearts together!"

Luckily there were boxes of tissues on the tables, because there wasn't a dry eye in the hotel ballroom.

9. (Multimedia): "I can't express enough gratitude for the incredible support you have given and will continue to give to these needy or suffering animals who so deserve a good, healthy, happy, fulfilled life because they give us so much unconditional love, caring, and joy. I know it was uncomfortable and painful seeing the pictures and hearing the stories about Pookie (the dog), Samantha (the cat), Trumble (the horse), and Shadow (the dog). But because of your kindness, I will end showing the photos and short videos of the incredible transformation that results from our caring, our loving, and bringing them back to health. These pictures and 30-second videos are the proof and the thanks they give to you." With that, Conrad concludes with a fast-paced, dynamic 3-minute multimedia show with 30 photos and 4 videos showing the happy, well-nourished, playful animals running, jumping, and delighting in their renewed vigor and life. This time, the background music is lively and joyful, ending with a close-up photo of Pookie — along with a big, enthusiastic bark from him with the words below, "Thanks to you!"

For this type of happy ending finale, no words alone could have expressed the wonderful work that the rescue shelter provides for these beloved creatures as well as the heartwarming visuals and music does.

Offering an informational conclusion

Many business, technical, or scientific presentations are designed to simply provide information about something. It may be a product or service, a new process, a management technique, a scientific discovery, or anything that the audience may benefit from knowing about. In this example, a consultant gives an extended two-hour presentation to a group of doctors and other medical personnel on new software applications and diagnostic tools to better deal with radical changes in healthcare processes and laws at a medical conference workshop. This ending of this presentation consists of a crisp, concise summary, several thought-provoking questions, a bit of humor, and a different type of call to action. Notice how the presenter uses repetition to emphasize key points right to the finish line.

> **4. (Executive summary):** "Over the last two hours, we discussed four software applications for your computers, tablets, and smartphones. Keep in mind these four important points:
>
> - One: These applications will make your practice more efficient and profitable.
>
> - Two: We've had the finest firms rigorously test and exhaustively check and certify these apps as error free! (This veiled reference to the problems with the Affordable Care Act website got some laughs.)
>
> - Three: Transitioning to these new processes and procedures is much easier and quicker than previous applications — on average of about 65 percent quicker.
>
> - Four: These apps are designed to boost the productivity, effectiveness, and quality of all your administrative processing operations, but most importantly, they will give you great peace of mind by better dealing with the myriad of challenging and otherwise frustrating healthcare changes now and in the future."
>
> **5. (Humor):** Leaving people with brief humor that makes a definite point can be a nice addition to a conclusion. Here the consultant uses an amusing concise story to set the stage for the next building block of thought-provoking questions. "Oftentimes it pays to get a quick and sure head start on a situation — like this one — that could spiral out of control if you wait too long. It's quite like the story of the patient who told his doctor that he was thinking of getting a vasectomy. The conscientious physician asked, 'That's a big decision. Have you discussed it with your wife and children?' The patient shot back with a straight face, 'Absolutely! We took a vote and they're in favor 16 to 2.'"

8. (Thought-provoking questions): These set the stage for the call to action as a result of providing the comprehensive information during the two hours. "So to get that quick start, you may now be asking yourselves these questions:

- What are the next steps to take to begin implementation?

- How will I know the app is running successfully?

- What's the ideal way to train myself and personnel without disrupting our patients and practice?

- Where do I go to get immediate help in the future?"

11. (Call to action): Instead of asking the group for something in an information-giving presentation, you leave them with some thoughts on how best to use that information in their work or personal lives as this example shows: "The very next step to take is to pick up a package that consists of several brochures, a typical implementation plan, and a set of instructions and resources to truly make implementation of your apps easy. The packets are on tables on your way out. You will definitely know if your implementation of these apps is successful simply by using them and seeing the results. It's that simple! As far as training, we have a proven plan for that in the handouts along with links to our extensive online courses, where each session lasts only 15 minutes. For help 24 hours a day, we have answers to typical questions on our website, in addition to a live online chat capability with one of our specialists. If you need further assistance, we have the unthinkable: a real live person you can contact via phone or Skype. So, please capitalize upon these great resources to get started. I'm also available after the presentation to answer any questions you have right now. I'll be here as long as there are people who want to talk with me."

2. (Quotation): "As all of you well know, these major healthcare changes can be perplexing, upsetting, and time consuming. As Albert Einstein noted though, 'In the middle of difficulty lies opportunity.' That's exactly what these software apps are — opportunity. Take full advantage of them. I enjoyed being with you over these two hours, and I wish you great success in using these powerful applications to ensure your practice runs smoothly, efficiently, and profitably!"

Chapter 12

Reminding Your Audience of Your Message

*H*ow do people learn and remember? How can they be influenced and persuaded? The answer to both questions is through effective repetition. Whether learning how to play an instrument or trying to make sure that people fully understand and appreciate your main presentation point, repetition is critical.

Dale Carnegie's oft-mentioned rule of public speaking: "Tell them what you are going to tell them; tell them; tell them what you've told them" holds true for presentations. What you hear repeatedly, you eventually believe those in the influence and persuasion (and self-help) business tell us. Sales professionals discover on day one to repeat the benefits of their products or services. A carefully planned and smartly executed repetition strategy increases the effectiveness of your message. However, presenters who use this, the *Law of Repetition,* should also be aware of its pitfalls: overuse and misuse.

In this brief chapter, we explain the Law of Repetition and give examples of how sales and advertising experts use it and how you can, too.

Driving Your Message Home

Advertisers use the Law of Repetition all the time, in print, broadcast, and on the Internet. Television infomercials or those pitching on the shopping channels have mastered repeating key messages and the advantages of their products and services. They use a proven, highly successful formula that includes smooth, and often subtle, repetition of enticing buying messages sometimes dozens of times during their compelling sales pitch. They follow the advice of Napoleon Hill, personal success guru and author of the famous book, *Think and Grow Rich:*

> *Any idea, plan, or purpose may be placed in the mind through repetition of thought.*

Listen to the wide variety of numerous testimonials from satisfied users of a product or service in infomercials, for example. They say the same things but in different ways to drive thoughts about buying deeply into the minds of viewers. Each variation of a genuine testimonial amplifies its persuasive effect. (Chapter 20 gives more insights into the persuasive formula that makes infomercials a booming mega-billion dollar business.)

Finding repetitive balance

Moderate repetition becomes persuasive repetition when you build the main message over time. Using the Law of Repetition during the length of a presentation or speech creates a greater familiarity with the message and leads to gradual, yet firm, agreement as the intensity of repetition gradually builds. Too much repetition in a short time span can defeat the purpose of gradual acceptance by creating a stronger aversion to the idea, plan, or proposal you recommend. In general, carefully space repeated messages at equal or similar intervals throughout your presentation to achieve acceptance by the audience.

There is no firm guideline on what is the right amount of repetition. It varies with your audience, the goals you're trying to achieve, and the complexity of information you're delivering. Use your judgment and experience accordingly.

Advertising uses the Law of Repetition in television commercials, which reinforce efforts in other outlets such as print, websites, or social media. Repetition serves two advertising purposes:

- **Branding:** Commercials remind people of company and product names. *Branding,* or name recognition, means when people see a product or service, they know it and because it feels familiar, they're more likely to buy it or recommend it, even it they haven't used it.

- **Differentiation:** Advertising demonstrates and tries to convince people of the superior merits of the product compared to any competitor's product.

With the right amount, timing, and placement of content repetition in your presentation, people will realize the favorable implications and cogency of your persuasive arguments. Overdo it and tedium sets in, resulting in a negative reaction such as annoyance or, worse yet, a contrarian attitude of resistance toward your message, which defeats the purpose!

Consider this (fictional) 15-second commercial about a laundry detergent. In this example, the advertiser repeats the name of the product a dozen times within that limited time period:

> **Commentator:** Sudsy D cleans clothes like new because Sudsy D has patented SupaStuff that rips out dirt and grime. Martha uses Sudsy D on her 15 kids' clothes that have days-old spaghetti sauce, ink spots, and chocolate syrup on them.

> **Martha:** Sudsy D is the only detergent I use. Sudsy D works. Who can live without Sudsy D? I can't imagine life without Sudsy D. I strongly recommend Sudsy D. Before using Sudsy D, people thought my family had perpetual food fights!

> **Commentator:** Buy Sudsy D and live a clean life for a change . . . Sudsy D, the ultimate dirt terminator. Sudsy D.

Advertisers use the term *wearout* when referring to the negative result of over-repeated exposures to a commercial. Research studies show attention, awareness, and recall initially increase and then level off with moderate repetition but ultimately decline with overexposure to the repeated message. This wearout phenomenon happens when people no longer focus on a message and it loses its effectiveness as people either tune out or selective forgetting sets in.

Using verbatim repetition

Purposely — and purposefully — using the same phrase or term numerous times throughout your talk emphasizes your point.

In political, social, or other types of speeches designed to arouse, provoke, or galvanize an audience, repetition of key emotionally charged phrases can be deeply effective. Speech coaches cite Martin Luther King, Jr.'s "I have a dream" speech as the quintessential example evocative repetition. However, repetition of this nature works only because of the established emotional nature of an issue. Such techniques in general business, sales, or marketing have the opposite effect — turning off people — if not approached ever so carefully.

U.S. President Ronald Reagan gave a speech where he advocated a certain defined position. His persuasive strategy was to tell the viewing audience the hard evidence supporting his point. He stated the evidence, paused, then said, "Facts are stubborn things," paused again, and stated his next key fact or statistic, following each with "facts are stubborn things." Combined with President Reagan's great delivery, the repetition of "facts are stubborn things" stuck in people's minds because it was a perfectly timed, captivating, and convincing technique used for emphasis in his argument.

When using a theme in your presentation, repeating it several times at just the right times to stress your message is a good tactic. For example, a chief financial officer (CFO) proposes a major capital investment for her firm at an executive presentation. Her briefing involves four important aspects of justifying the costly investment in building a new advanced research and development facility that would enable the development of radically innovative products. After covering the details and attractive aspects of each financial criteria related to the decision to move ahead, she pauses, raises her voice and says "Excellent ROI Squared" a term she coined (and defined to the group) meaning "Excellent Return on Invested Innovation." She finds the balance to slam the point home without going overboard or entering the wearout zone.

A specialty financial firm looks to entice wealthy personal investors to buy into the a small island development called Crabb Cay in the Bahamas. The main presenter develops a creative strategy and theme around location that focuses on the attractiveness of this island for investment purposes. In her introduction, she says to potential investors, "Ladies and gentleman, you have, of course, heard the number one rule in real estate, 'Location, location, location.' Well, that mantra applies to Crabb Cay as you will firmly see throughout our presentation. And you'll appreciate how those three aspects of the location of this beautiful, untouched island, when magnificently developed, will lend itself to an investment that will give you a superb return for many years to come. Let's get into the first aspect of location — its internal and surrounding unmatched beauty includes stunning crystal clear waters." After fully describing this aspect of the island, the presenter pauses and says with increased voice volume and energy, "Beautiful location!" as she also puts up a slide with just that word *location* on it.

She then talks about the proximity of the island to other developed islands a short boat ride away and discusses the dining and entertainment amenities, water sports, and conveniences on large, nearby islands. Again, she pauses and vocally emphasizes "Conveniences location!" along with a slide of the word on it. As she continues, she discusses the geographical location of the tropical paradise island as a relatively short flight from major populated cities. As she finishes this part, she repeats "Getaway location" with the word slide shown.

She repeats the word "location" in about ten-minute intervals, so it's not overdone. The slide with the single word nicely reinforces the vocal repetition. As she concludes the presentation with a strong, compelling summary of the details and benefits of investing in the development of Crabb Cay, she says, "Your investment is guaranteed because of three most important aspects of location, location, location!" The verbatim repetition creates a persuasive effect.

Creating 360 degrees of repetition

Don't confuse using exact-wording repetition for emphasis, as in the examples in the preceding section, with saying the same thing over and over, which can be bothersome or even insulting to listeners. Instead, develop the valuable technique of repeating your main point with different words and from several perspectives: we call it *360 degrees of repetition*. You say the same thing, but with variations — just like successful infomercials do. Subtlety can be as important as the intensity and frequency of your message.

Finding more than one way to make the same vital point repeatedly effectively accomplishes your objectives of branding, name recognition, and message recognition. Attendees at your presentation respond more positively to the same argument stated several interesting and impacting ways rather than hearing the same message over and over.

Sheila G., a VP of operations, wants her company's executive staff to approve her new "Smart Strategies to Reduce Waste" program. She repeats articulate variations of her message throughout her 30-minute presentation:

- ✔ We need to cut waste right away. It is bleeding our profitability.

- ✔ Cutting waste is vital to our being more competitive and staying that way.

- ✔ We must minimize waste if we are to free up funds for our other important opportunities.

- ✔ Why tolerate this level of waste when the Smart Strategies program will slash it?

Notice how she uses repetition masterfully in different statements, but all focus on making her point about the critical necessity of dealing with waste that she identified in her company. Sheila takes a creative step in applying the Law of Repetition by using her laptop. On three of her twelve slides, she superimposed a *text crawler* — a message that flows across the bottom of the slides (like you see on the major news networks) — designed by a professional using a video editing program. The text crawler repeated her key points with other consistent, supportive messages such as "W.A.S.T.E.: **We Are S**quandering **T**he **E**fficiency of our operations!" She knew that the audience would be reading the moving text as she spoke, but was willing to cede some of the attention away from her during each of the eight-second scrolling — and somewhat subliminal — messages.

Think of imaginative ways you can use the spoken word along with text, images, illustrations, audio, or video from your laptop or tablet to repeat and reinforce your key points, messages, or overriding theme. By varying the phrases you use, you can still hammer home your message using repetition. And, besides voicing it, you can repeat and reinforce key points by using photos, video, visuals, props, handouts, and anything else that stresses, high-lights, showcases, or emphasizes the one or two things that are critical for you to meet your presentation objectives.

An architectural firm wants to close a deal to build a 15-story, multi-purpose building that includes office space, retail stores, and upscale restaurants. Their value proposition in their presentation focuses on what they call "Green Beauty." It involves communicating their strength in sustainability and superior energy efficiency through advanced technology and building materials (green) along with ultra unique architectural designs (beauty).

Rather than repeat their thematic value proposition in words, which they do in their introduction and conclusion, they decide to get creative with animation. At strategically timed points in their presentation, when they want to empha-size their strength in combining breathtaking, elegant (interior and exterior) design with impressive energy-saving engineering, they emphasize that part of their presentation with an animation that starts with a slide showing their value proposition "Green Beauty" in simple black text where, seconds later the word "Green" morphs into an exquisite green floral design and the word "Beauty" transforms itself into a stunning rendering of the proposed building. In addition, they cleverly include vital summary information (that dissolves) in that section of the presentation on the lower part of the visual after the animation concludes. The architectural team repeats the animation four times (each with new summary information) over a period of an hour. The Law of Repetition — applied using a captivating visual — proves to be an integral part of the presentation's winning strategy.

American motivational author Robert Collier noted, "Constant repetition carries conviction." That it does, indeed. Use it just right in your presentations, and the Law of Repetition will serve you mighty well.

Chapter 13

Dealing with Questions, Resistance, and Audience Hostility

*H*ow often have you seen a press conference or public announcement with a head of state or CEO of a major corporation facing a mob of aggressive reporters ready to pounce on him with tough questions? It's difficult enough to give a planned presentation or speech, but answering difficult questions takes more than intestinal fortitude and confidence. You need skill and a cool head. The unpredictability of the ubiquitous Q & A (question and answer) session may make you anxious or make you fear losing control or otherwise damaging your fine presentation.

Most audiences, however, ask mild, inquiring yet nonthreatening, questions. Boardroom presentations tend to generate a lot of questions during the presentation rather than afterwards. Nonetheless, questions are an integral part of any presentation, and you need to devote adequate time and effort to do well in this area. Anticipating, carefully preparing for, and masterfully answering questions is just as — and sometimes even more — important than planning and delivering your core presentation.

The mark of a true professional presenter is not just in how you give a structured presentation, but how you deal with all sorts of challenging questions, concerns, and points of contention from your audience. Master the techniques and tips in this chapter and you will be head and shoulders above other presenters.

In this chapter, we explain the critical points of effectively answering questions, dealing with difficult people, and handling likely objections. We discuss strategies and techniques to help you eliminate the frazzled nerves that might prompt an inappropriate response. Mastering these aspects of your talk will give you a decided edge over other presenters who don't prepare for them — often to their dismay.

Taking Advantage of Questions

Being an interactive presenter who eagerly encourages questions and engages an audience is a decided plus. Dealing with audience concerns by adjusting your presentation on the fly boosts your credibility and professional image.

The questions you're asked give you important clues about your audience. Take advantage of audience questions to reinforce all your key points and priority information from your talk.

It takes refined communication skill and oftentimes a bit of psychology to become good at answering questions off the cuff. Although you may have prepared for anticipated questions, you're likely to face a situation that requires you to present in an impromptu or extemporaneous way. A proven process can help you handle audience comments, queries, and feedback. Your answers are really mini-presentations in themselves and should have a goal, a strategy, and an organized flow of good information.

Handling the occasional tough — even provocative or hostile — question with grace and aplomb is a great chance to strut your stuff. A calm, confident, and composed demeanor in the face of a challenging question makes a mighty big impression with your audience.

Fortunately, you seldom face the verbal firing squad of character-building questions, objections, or other forms of resistance to your ideas, plans, or recommendations. Nevertheless, answering questions and objections effectively — accurately, thoroughly, and competently — and handling trouble-causing members of an audience with poise and grace strengthens your credibility, professionalism, and leadership image while improving the chances of reaching your presentation goals.

Planning, preparing, and rehearsing

Before your presentation, nothing helps more than preparing to answer any and all types of questions. Forewarned is forearmed. When you carefully think through what people might ask, not only will you be able to better answer questions, but you'll do so with a sense of relaxed and self-assured confidence. Here's how to get set for any eventuality:

✔ Develop as complete a list of questions, objections, or other forms of negative feedback or demands as you and your presentation group can think of.

✔ Identify all the facts, statistics, models, diagrams, and other information that someone might challenge or strongly disagree with. Then craft several versions of answers from different perspectives.

✔ Be a strategist. When encountering awkward or difficult questions from your group, think in terms of the best way to handle it, involving communication skills, persuasive arguments, and psychological factors. Consider which style is best to address a particular question in certain situations — for example, do you want your answer to be direct or subtle, soft or hard, stoic or passionate.

✔ Plan for the worst. Think about how to handle a hostile person who seems to want to sabotage your presentation and intimidate you, perhaps with an unexpected, emotionally charged outburst.

One of the best ways to diffuse a hostile manner is to remain calm and answer the question or objection — not the emotion. Regardless of what your audience asks, says, or does, keep your cool and don't get flustered or defensive.

✔ Spend adequate time rehearsing your answers to ensure clear, concise, and convincing responses. Videotape yourself, and if possible, get feedback from those whose opinion you respect.

Getting the ball rolling

Traditionally, the time for questions comes at the end of a presentation. However, with small groups or in informal settings, you should encourage questions throughout your presentation to make sure you're responding to the audience's needs — unless answering questions during your presentation really interferes with your flow or goals.

As you know, most people are reluctant to ask that first question at the official Q & A session at the end of your presentation. So, prime the pump in two ways. First, instead of asking, "Does anyone have any questions?" say something like, "Who has the first question for me?" Secondly, open up comments by saying, "With this topic, many people often ask me . . ." Then answer the question yourself and say, "What else are you interested in knowing?" If you don't get an immediate question, wait a few moments rather than thinking no one is interested and prematurely shutting down the Q & A session.

In larger meetings, audience members may be reluctant to stand up and pose an inquiry. Hand out 3-x-5-inch index cards before you begin your presentation and ask the audience to write down their questions and send the cards forward at the end. If you're set up for interaction with tablets, laptops, or smartphones, audience members can submit questions electronically. Even without a formal smart device set up, you can ask the audience to tweet their queries, which you can show on the screen during your presentation or during the question period (as long as your projection system is connected to the Internet).

Taking it step by step

After you carefully think through the types of questions you may get and the approach you want to take for each, memorize the process laid out in the next sections to answer questions you get during or after your presentation.

Step one: Propose rules

At some point during your presentation introduction, tell the audience how you prefer to handle their questions. With small groups, tell them you encourage their questions and feedback during the presentation, but that you also allocated time afterwards to answer extra questions. With larger audiences at conferences, association meetings, political events, or keynote speeches, tell people that they can shoot you questions during the formal Q & A session at the end of the presentation. If you're giving a speech and someone introduces you, remind that person to mention that you will answer questions at the end of your talk. Point out the microphones questioners should use and, if appropriate, where to direct questions through smartphones and other electronic devices. Always let people know how much time is allotted for the Q & A and stick to that time table. Finally, let your audience know if you'll be available afterwards to take on questions that require more comprehensive answers.

Step two: Listen

Relax and listen carefully and completely to each question. Too many presenters jump in, not realizing that a person may have two or more back-to-back questions and pauses briefly between them.

Make direct eye contact with the questioner and maintain a relaxed, open body position — don't cross your arms. Smile, if appropriate, or at least strive to guard against a facial expression showing angst, concern, annoyance, or any other negative reaction. Wait until the questioner finishes and pause for just a second or two before answering. Even if you can respond in a lightning quick way, don't rush to comment.

Step three: Analyze and understand

People generally ask questions for these reasons:

- They simply want extra information.
- They want clarification or confirmation of what they believe you said.
- They crave attention and want to make a positive impression by asking what they think are thought-provoking and unique questions. We call this *station identification*.
- They want to put you on the defensive by asking a loaded question.
- They have a hidden agenda they're hoping to present.

First ask yourself if the question is a positive one asked by someone interested in knowing more — for example a buying signal — a neutral one to better understand your point, or a negative one masked as a question, but used as a hostile tactic. Listen carefully to determine what you think the intent of the question is. Listening to the tone doesn't necessarily give you the intent.

Next, make sure you understand what the questioner is really asking. Often a person asks tangent questions around what he really wants to know. There are two techniques to get to that understanding — confirming and clarifying, which we explain in the next two sections — that not only makes your reply more accurate, but elevates your image as an effective communicator.

Step four: Confirm

In order to confirm your perception based on a quick analysis, you need to confirm, or verify, what the questioner wants to know. For example, someone may ask if your company has a certain number of employees and locations and also ask about clients who have benefitted from working with your firm. After answering those specific questions, you might ask a paraphrased question like, "Are you ultimately asking if our project teams can handle your large and complex project?" If the inquiring audience member says, "yes," then address that issue directly. If he says, "no," ask what the real underlying issue is that he wants addressed.

Step five: Clarify

If you're not sure what a person is asking because the question is vague or somehow unclear, then use a clarifying question to remove any possible doubt, ambiguity, or confusion as to what information that person is seeking. Some clarifying questions you can ask to ensure that you truly understand what someone is getting at are

- "I'm not sure I understand. Can you be more specific?"
- "Can you give me some examples of what you are asking?"
- "Please clarify that for me."
- "Do you mean . . .?" or "Are you claiming . . .?"
- "Why do think that?"
- "Based upon your question, how did you reach that conclusion?"
- "So are you saying that . . .?"

Always repeat the question, even in small-group situations. Sometimes a questioner is so soft spoken that you barely hear them or those farther away may not have heard what was asked. So, it's a good idea to restate the question loudly so everyone can connect your answer to the question. Besides, doing so will ensure you understand it and, if needed, give you some extra time to think through your reply. If it's a simple question, repeat it verbatim, but if it's a multi-part question that may be a bit vague or complicated, try paraphrasing it in your words and ask the questioner if that's what he's asking. Feel free to paraphrase by saying something like, "I've been asked to comment on our position regarding strategic alliances with other technology companies."

Step six: Answer the question

When you reply to someone's question, you do a combination of describing, explaining, providing more details, and justifying. Your answers should always be as clear, concise, and convincing as possible. Remember, your answers are really structured mini-presentations that last perhaps from mere seconds to about two minutes. Therefore, your answer should include facts, statistics, examples, comparisons, contrasts, analogies or metaphors, and even anecdotes to give a narrative and prove and justify your response to that question.

Using enumeration in your answer gives it a strong sense of legitimacy and can be quite effective. Imagine that in a sales presentation one of the prospects in the group says, "I heard your product has been prematurely released into the market without adequate testing." The presenter replies enumerating facts, statistics, and a competitive comparison such as, "I heard that rumor too, and it's absolutely not true for three very important reasons: One: This product was exhaustively tested for more than four months with thousands of run times simulating ten years of use — and even product abuse — and passed. Two: These tests were conducted by the prestigious, objective, and unbiased Commercial Testing Laboratory and received the highest ratings they give out. Three: In more than 400 installations of our product in companies like yours, we are running a 99.2 percent reliability rate — higher than any competitive products. I have full documentation for your review if you'd like. So you see, our product has been tested and brought to market in a timely fashion."

When you answer a question, direct your answer and eye contact first to the questioner for several seconds and then look at the rest of your audience — you want to involve them in the answer as well. As you finish, briefly re-establish eye contact with the questioner, and if needed, check that you have answered his query by saying something like, "Does that explain why our technical group chose to . . .?" If the person has another question requiring a short response, go ahead and respond to it. But, sometimes people want to hog the floor by asking a series of back-to-back questions after the first one is finished. If that is happening, one way to tactfully redirect attention is to say, "I see a bunch of hands up right now, and I'd be happy to get back to you as soon as I give others an opportunity to ask their questions." And then circle back to that person later.

As part of being an innovative presenter, why limit your answers to word responses? Remember that answering questions gives you a chance to reinforce and further emphasize key facts, points, or themes. Some clever presenters who anticipate specific questions have slides or visuals they can immediately navigate to show interesting photos, illustrations, diagrams, 3-D animations, or video and audio that can better answer an audience member's question than even an articulate reply. Props and product prototypes can come in very handy. Think of how you might use these nonverbal resources to further support your key messages, while answering questions in a novel and riveting way.

Step seven: Check the acceptability of your answer

After you respond to someone's question, ask the person something like, "Does that answer your question?" Mix up your words each times so as not to sound like a parrot. Say things like, "Is there anything else you need to know?" and "Do you need further information?" and "Have I given you what you needed?" and "Is that the kind of information you were looking for?" When that person responds, "Yes," you have a bridge that allows you to go to the next person who wants your attention.

Be concise: When someone asks you a detailed question about a specific aspect, such as, "Does your product's goesinta run in a quadraplasmatic echobit with a bleep speed of at least 80 megachiccups?" often, all you need to say is "Yes" or "Yes, and faster." If the person wants more detail, he will ask. If your answer is no, find out why he asked about it, and then reply as you see fit. Interpret a request for detailed information as a sign of interest in your product or service.

It is always a good tactic to be as succinct as you can without being vague or having gaps in your reply. Being brief is immensely better than going off on a tangent or starting a monologue.

Responding when you don't know the answer

You created a list of all expected possible questions based upon your presentation. Still you're likely to get a legitimate question or two that you never considered and that leaves you wondering, "Where did that question come from — out of left field. How did I miss that one?" Unless you're psychic, you can't anticipate everything, and unless you're omniscient, you can't know everything, although some in your audience may think they do.

When you're asked a question you don't have an answer to, follow these guidelines:

✔ **Be confidently candid:** If you don't have an answer to a question, just admit it in a matter-of-fact way without feigning embarrassment, disappointment, or any other negative reaction however slight. With a steady, sure tone of voice, say, "I don't know" or "I'm not completely sure, so I'd rather get you the exact and accurate answer by (give date)." Then, in a very obvious way, write down the question and person's contact information (or select someone else to do it), research it, and follow up on time as promised. Be specific, if possible, "I will contact our head of engineering today, and if his schedule permits giving me an answer quickly, I will get back to you no later than tomorrow afternoon. Is that okay?"

✔ **Defer to the audience or an expert:** Depending upon your topic and audience, you can redirect the question to the group if you know someone in it is capable of delivering the answer, "I know there are likely some folks here who are experienced in this area. Any thoughts on answering that (question)?" Oftentimes, people are quite eager to be engaged to speak and show their knowledge.

We know of a masterful speaker who deflects questions with humor in a rather effective way without being flippant. If she gets speculative questions such as, "Where do you think that technology will be in ten years," she replies, "I wish I were the technology equivalent of the Oracle of Delphi to give you an accurate answer, but the fact is this technology is advancing so quickly and its development is so unpredictable, I might as well look into a crystal ball for an answer. However I'll give you my thoughts on where I believe this technology will likely go in the next three years at least . . ."

If a question is outside of your field of expertise or experience, you can ask if a team or audience member with relevant credentials can answer it. For example, if you're an engineer and someone asks a financial question, you can direct the question to someone you know is a finance or accounting person. You can say something like, "Tanisha, you're an MBA. Do you have any insights about the rough payback and return on investment estimates?" Or, "Are there any financial people in the audience who might want to guesstimate those approximate numbers?"

Another tactic to use selectively if someone comes up with a real surprise question is to say something like, "That's a rather interesting slant on it that I haven't thought of. Before I give you my thoughts on it, does anyone in the audience want to give us your opinions on it?" This will give you time to think of an answer — that you may not need if other people eagerly jump in to reply to the questioner.

Handling loaded or attack questions

Whether you call them hostile, inflammatory, or emotionally-charged questions, some of these are biased and designed to instigate trouble, discredit your points or recommendations, put you on the spot, make you defensive, or even attack your credibility and competence.

If a questioner's tone is challenging, taunting, or aggressive, for example, and you respond to it in a defensive, sarcastic, or emotional way — even if you feel such a response is justified and fair — you're the one who pays the cost with diminished credibility and professionalism. Taking the high ground by not taking the bait and handling the person and the question with composure and a dignified bearing lifts your image and status ever higher during that session. You'll be seen as, well, magnanimous.

Always expect the unexpected attack. Be ready and stay calm and cool.

Luckily, belligerent questions seldom happen, unless a controversial topic or unpopular position is being advocated. The following sections offer some very effective ways to handle these situations.

Working your style

Anytime you address a group, strive to develop rapport with your audience, treat all of them with respect, listen well to their comments, and avoid any hint of being self-righteous, arrogant, or closed-minded. When you strive to be reasonable and fair, you automatically reduce the chance, right upfront, of someone going on the attack.

Using humor to defuse the person

Humor can amusingly reveal the true intended nature of an unfair question and show that you are unafraid and confident enough to deal with it. With a smile, you can say something like, "That sounds like a trap to me. Surely, you're not trying to make me fall into it, are you (with a bigger smile)?" or "Jane, before I answer, I'm afraid we'll have to call in the bomb squad to defuse that loaded and explosive question (said with a big smile)." Stronger still is this example, "Wow. Sounds like that question should come with a fighting piranha, although it has enough bite to it by itself!"

Employing crowd psychology

If you think the hostile questioner is alone in his attempt to disrupt you, query the group with, "To better understand the potential impact of that question, let me ask the rest of the group, 'How many of you feel like that to that extent?'" If you get no one or just a few out of many people raising their hands, you can say, "I see that no one else (or a bare few out of a lot of people) is concerned about that or feels that way. So for the sake of all the others, I can't spend their time on it. However, I will be happy to discuss it with you afterwards and give you all the time you need. So, we have to move on right now."

What this tactic does is to leverage indirect peer pressure and confirm silent disapproval (or at least apathy) of that person's unsavory goal. Usually, that's enough to dissuade him from continuing, especially if a senior manager is present. If you find a surprising number of other people sharing that person's feeling, try rephrasing the question as we explain in the next section. The question may indicate others feel a negative attitude toward the topic of discussion, not toward you.

Rephrasing the question to neutral or even positive aspect

Say you're giving a sales presentation and one of the decision makers in the group prefers your competitor. He says, "I notice your company's net profits have grown by an average of only about eight percent over the last ten years, while your competitors have averaged twice that percentage. Your firm doesn't appear that successful, does it?"

So you respond, "You're right about the rate of profitability growth of our company. I'll be happy to answer that, but I think the most important aspect to consider when deciding on a company like ours — or others — is to really ask, 'Who can provide you with the products and services that will give you the absolute best returns on your investment over the short- and long-term,' rather than simply focusing on a firm's profitability by itself, perhaps out of context.

"You see, our CEO and board decided to forsake three years of partial profit growth, which averaged more than 20 percent per year prior to that, to put extra money into research and development so we could come out with new and improved products for customers like you. Actually, 40 percent of all our products over the last two years are new, and we innovated and improved 35 percent of our other offerings. That's why our profit margins have decreased; we invested potential profit to out innovate our competitors. So, let me summarize again the four reasons our proposal to you today is the best one among all the vendors you are talking to . . . ."

Handling a legitimate confrontational question

You may get an angry question directed at you, not to sabotage you or your presentation, but because the questioner is righteously indignant about some issue. For example, someone may surprise you at the beginning of your presentation and say, "Your group was responsible for integrating that new company we bought six months ago into our corporation. I see nothing but delays and a series of problems that are jeopardizing the effective integration of their people, plants, and culture into those of our company. How did your team mess this up so royally?"

If you suspect this is a justified comment, it's always better to bring it up yourself and answer if before someone else does (see the following section on objections). In this example, though, you were blindsided prematurely. So, the painful and rather humbling thing to do is admit fault and accountability and reply with a proposed fix such as, "You are absolutely right!" With that direct, immediate admission, you defuse a chunk of a questioner's explosive anger. You continue, "I certainly understand your frustration and that you have good reasons for your displeasure." With that, you show empathy and likely dissipate even more anger. "We dropped the ball. No doubt. Let me explain. We missed the targets you mentioned for these reasons: One: Several faulty assumptions made by our corporation and theirs. Two: Insufficient human resources to get the job done on time and target. We were overly optimistic with our plan. Three: While we were behind in our project milestones, we believed we could make up for it in the remaining four weeks." With that you explain the situation without giving an excuse.

Finally, you communicate your solution to the problem, "So how do we make it perfectly right . . . and right fast? Let me concisely explain our new eight-part plan that was carefully crafted to address the situation."

What to avoid when answering questions

We like to accentuate the positive and tell you what you should do, but there are some faulty — albeit common — ways that presenters answer questions that you should try your best to avoid:

- **Switcharoo:** Politicians are notorious for ignoring the true nature of someone's question and instead giving a predetermined answer that does not fit the question. Audiences see this as a devious trick unless an exceptionally adept and smooth transition is used to go from a real answer to an add-on response.

- **Mini-filibuster:** An unnecessarily lengthy response comes across as rambling and will frustrate your group. Keep your answer concise and tightly focused. An economy of words is best.

- **Defensive bluster:** Never let anyone knock you off balance and goad you into shooting back to someone who has sharply disagreed with you, put you on the spot, or even attacked your presentation points. A tit-for-tat aggressive or defensive reply will detract from your professionalism and poise. A calm, dignified, and composed reply will win you major points with your group.

- **Winging it or faking it:** The euphemism may be improvising, but, let's face it, winging it is for the birds! The worst thing you can do is to provide an answer that you either don't have the real information for or that you simply make up. If you get caught in that unfortunate case, you will be seen as disingenuous and perhaps unethical. When you say something without sufficient forethought, preparation, or adequate knowledge, it lacks accuracy and believability, and it gouges a big chip in the credibility you built so carefully up to that point in your presentation. Your entire presentation is put in serious jeopardy with one unconsidered answer.

(continued)

(continued)

✔ **Ending on a question:** You want to avoid the Flapping Swan conclusion in which, after answering the last question from an audience, you lift up your arms (like wings) and let them fall to your sides saying, "Ah. . . I guess that's it. Thanks." Instead, you need to conclude with a strong final thought to stick in the minds (and maybe hearts) of the group such as, "My speech today has been about not just being a leader, but an innovative one. The difference that a creative, vital skill set makes can be enormous. With more innovative leaders in your company, your revenues and profits will continuously grow as never before. You will have a competitive advantage and market share increase and an organization filled with excitement, promise, and challenge. Implement the proven techniques I gave you today to not just have an innovative company, but a company of innovators and innovative leaders. I wish all of you great success in the future!"

✔ **Spinning:** In today's world of influence and persuasion, the spin is (unfortunately) in. *Spinning* is the art of constructing a favorable answer out of an unfavorable situation. Some call that the right answer, even if it twists and bends the truth. However, audiences respect and trust a presenter who answers honestly, candidly, and forthrightly even at the expense of disapproval or criticism. More times than not, the real answers dramatically elevate the credibility and respect of the presenter. An honest presenter who shuns any hint of an underhanded manipulation of the truth or a slick answer actually has a greater chance of meeting his goals.

✔ **Praising the question:** Sometimes it's tempting to compliment an audience member with, "That's a great question!" or "I'm glad you asked that." However, if other people ask questions and you don't praise them, they may feel as if you did not especially value their questions. Also, if you praise everyone's inquiries, you come across as insincere or perhaps patronizing. If someone asks a tough, but sincere (not loaded or hostile) question, you might say, "Thanks for asking that question" which will show you are unfazed, have class, and are open and receptive to difficult, yet valid, inquiries. Obviously, don't thank someone who asks a hostile or loaded question.

Remember: A real answer trumps the right answer.

Dealing with Distractions, Problem People, and Resistance

It doesn't happen often in presentations, speeches, or training sessions, but when it does you want to have some tactics and techniques to deal with audience members who cause problems. Despite your feelings of annoyance and frustration, let your fine character and professional demeanor rule the day.

Luckily, you're likely to run into just a few annoying, frustrating, or aggressive people who test your patience to the max. When you do, keep in mind that, even with the most unreasonable, inconsiderate people taunting and goading you, your goal is not to get even with them, punish them, or show them who's in charge or who's the smartest. Your goal is to deal with them in such a calm, effective, and reasonable manner as to fully counter their intent and take the sting out of their behavior. Developing good rapport with your audience and getting them on your side when a heckler or disruptor erupts is invaluable.

Besides developing rapport, take an escalated approach to dealing with problem people. This method involves first using gentle, indirect, and mild tactics instead of starting with a sledgehammer. If a mild approach doesn't work, then continue to escalate into more direct and stronger approaches. If you immediately go on the attack, the audience is likely to be more sympathetic to that person, however strange and unfair that seems to you. Remember, you want to avoid embarrassing or belittling the person who is — unintentionally or otherwise — causing havoc to or disrupting your talk.

Never let the heckler see you become flustered or afraid.

The next sections offer examples of disruptive behaviors and proven ways to handle them.

Talking on the side

People holding conversations with the person(s) next to them and sometimes talking loud enough for you and others to hear are a distraction to everyone in the room. People making occasional comments may actually be talking about something you discussed. But if you see a specific person or group repeatedly talking, smiling, laughing, and basically not focusing on your presentation, you have to cut them short — and fairly quickly.

Some people simply are rude and inconsiderate, and unless a senior manager is there to mete out some discipline, your best efforts may not work as planned. But here are some escalating tactics to employ:

- ✔ Ask a question of the person to the left of the talkers, then ask another question to the person to their right. They will start to feel encircled with the audience focusing attention next to them.

- ✔ Stop talking for five to eight seconds, look at a group loudly joking with each other, and smile. The sudden silence will make their talking evident.

- ✔ If possible, walk around the room and stand near them while presenting. All eyes will be on you (and them and their behavior). Don't make an obvious dash to them, be subtle in approaching them.

- ✔ Engage one of the talkers to ask his opinion about a presentation point you just made.

- ✔ Call out one of the side-talker's name (let's say Keith) in the context of a relevant point you are making, "Keith J. was telling me that one of his clients . . ." Hearing his name will usually force him to listen to be prepared to comment.

✔ Highlight a critical point in your presentation by saying this with increased voice volume and a sense of urgency, "I'm coming to a very important part of the presentation that all of you should benefit from, and I need everyone's total attention on this because I want your ideas, reactions, and comments."

✔ Mention that you notice their continual talking, "Denise, it looks as if you and Darius are going over something I was discussing (or something recently said). I'm wondering if there is a question the both of you have or a comment you would like to contribute to our discussion?"

✔ Approach the talkers during the next break (if possible) and say something like, "I don't know what your extended conversations are about, but based upon the body language of people in the group, it is distracting others. I would appreciate if you would refrain from those side conversations or take them outside the conference room."

Deflating windbags

Windbags have an opinion about everything, and they think everyone wants to hear them endlessly pontificate. They want to hog the floor and interject their comments throughout your presentation. They don't care if others mind. They never heard of a sound bite — that ultra-concise way of using an economy of words to make a clear point quickly. Vaccinated with a phonograph needle, windbags need a quick yappendectomy.

As a presenter, you have to deal quickly and decisively with a potentially disruptive individual. Use these tips:

✔ Actively call on other people by name to ask their inputs and ideas.

✔ Ask the chatterbox how his comment (or question) ties into the topic you're presenting or the discussion taking place.

✔ After several interrupting comments, look at the person while pausing for three to four seconds and simply continue without responding to the comment. Ignoring the person with stone silence and moving along without a response may discourage more interruptions.

✔ Say something like, "Marsha, you've been doing all the hard work asking and contributing comments freely. I really want other audience members to give their fair share of contributions for a change and give you a break."

✔ If someone is going on and on about a trivial matter or their pet opinion, interrupt them and summarize, something like the following, "I hear what you're saying: Cost control is critical. I wish we had more time to discuss that, but with so much more to cover on the how-to's during this presentation, we have to move on."

Handling phones during presentations

The world has changed. Besides showing up late for meetings or presentations, many people put their phones on the table in front of them, read and send text messages, surf the Web, and check their Facebook page throughout your presentation.

Ray Anthony worked with a special, highly elite U. S. military group (he can't say which one). What surprised and pleased him enormously was that prior to entering the meeting room, everyone has to shut off his phone and place it in a box outside the room. Wouldn't that be nice in corporate environments? No such luck, so as presenters here are a few tips for you to consider:

✔ Set the ground rules for phones accompanied perhaps with a slide showing a phone happily going to sleep. Communicate other guidelines designed to show courtesy and respect for other audience members. Suggest that if someone is expecting a really important call, he put his phone on vibrate and take the call outside the room.

✔ Take out your own phone and put it on vibrate. Then ask everyone to take their phones out and do likewise. Wait for them to actually do it. In the event a phone rings, stop speaking. That signals that you have been rudely interrupted and will not continue until the distraction stops. Don't look at the person or call out his name. When the phone is turned off say, "Thank you" and continue.

✔ Do something creative or use humor, which is especially effective in large-scale presentations or speeches. One keynote speaker, when hearing a phone go off in her large audience, hyperlinks to a video in her slide deck to show a flashing light (like on police and emergency vehicles) accompanied by a loud wailing siren audio blast with the words, "PHONE DISRUPTION!" that lasts about four seconds. She then smiles, laughs, and says, "Sorry, that's my automatic phone detecting device. You don't want to hear that, so please make sure your phones are off. Thank you." Just once is often enough to encourage people to follow phone protocol. Another professional speaker says "Is that call for me?" with a smile and playful intent rather than openly embarrassing the person.

One presenter has an interesting activity she uses to have fun with the message about phones during meetings. She buys cheap, used cellphones. She tells her group, "I love phones, but sometimes they can just disrupt others at meetings. I need a volunteer — well, actually two people to come up here and help me." As people are walking up, she slips an old phone into a transparent plastic freezer bag and locks it in. She throws it on the floor and tells each of the two people to "do a flamenco on it" while she plays flamenco music. She says it's amazing how some people enjoy smashing the phone to pieces with their feet.

She then says with a huge smile, "Okay, these two phone terminators will get $10 each to dance on your phone if it goes off!" Many in the audience chuckle and laugh while getting the point. Still the occasional phone goes off, but not nearly as much as before she started using this clever tactic.

Staying in charge

Your audience looks to you to lead and control the situation and the attendees during your presentation. Sometimes people in your audience want a soapbox or bully pulpit to expound their opinions, theories, or feelings about something or to promote themselves or their agenda, much to the detriment of others in the group. Give these tenacious talkers just enough time to spout and when they pause for a breath, interrupt and say, "Thank you for your thoughts." Immediately shift your eye contact and body position away from them and engage other people.

Other times, people ask irrelevant questions or specifics regarding their project (when theirs isn't the only project in the room). We don't recommend dismissing their questions if you can answer them briefly, and then say, "I hope I gave you some quick insights on your specific project (program, activity, requirement), and I'd be happy to give you more time afterwards with a one-on-one discussion, if you need that" or "That's a topic I am not familiar with since it was not part of this presentation, but I can get you an answer on it if you want one."

If a questioner inaccurately paraphrases something you covered in your presentation, politely and diplomatically correct the person, even putting the onus on yourself (which the audience will clearly see as tact) such as, "Perhaps I miscommunicated that point. Let me be clear as to what I either said or intended to say."

Dealing with objections

An *objection* is a statement, request, comment, or question from someone in your audience that indicates some form and degree of resistance — ranging from mild to extreme — regarding an aspect of your presentation. Salespeople frequently deal with objections to buying their product or service. The old-time method salespeople were taught to use was to overcome objections by wearing down the potential buyer, using scripted answers and techniques to counter concerns or reluctance to buy.

However, with today's sophisticated consumers and corporate professionals, those telegraphed techniques are not only ineffective, but offensive to the audience's intelligence. People want sincere, genuine answers and acceptable solutions rather than canned replies. Here, we give you powerful guidelines on dealing with people who have a mix of intellectual, logical, and emotional resistance to any aspect of your presentation.

There are numerous reasons why a person in your audience would communicate resistance to your plan, program, solution, strategy or recommendation. Some typical reasons are

- **No perceived need:** They feel that what you are proposing isn't really necessary.

- **Fear of consequences:** They perceive risks, problems, setbacks, or other negative repercussions if they agree to go ahead with what you advocate.

- **Doubt the benefits you outlined:** People feel skeptical and cynical about your claims regarding the projected results, outcomes, and advantages.

- **No sense of urgency or motivation to act:** Some in your audience may think what you are saying is useful, but they believe there is no real need to implement it right away.

- **Misunderstandings or lack of knowledge:** If someone misinterprets what you said or doesn't have sufficient experience or knowledge about your topic, he may make a wrong assumption, and then object.

- **Preference or taste:** Someone may agree conceptually with your proposal, but prefer to have or do something differently. It may have to do with planning, design, operations, implementation, or leadership. He wants to change something. Try selling a blue Ferrari to someone who loves a red Ferrari.

- **Financial concerns:** Someone may balk at the perceived high price, unattractive return on investment, payback terms, or any other financial aspect relating to your proposal.

- **Emotional or ego issues:** Maybe a person has had a previous bad experience with your topic or may not like you or your company (or internal department, team, or boss), and has a visceral negative reaction to whatever you propose.

Handling reluctance to change or start something new

People automatically reject change of any type — it's a part of the human psyche. Something new or different, whether it's starting a novel training program, buying a product or service from a new vendor, restructuring an organization, purchasing a new company, or implementing a different strategy, policy, or procedure creates fear, anxiety, or some kind of mental or emotional discomfort.

People may sense the change would involve more work on their part (without a proportionately larger reward or payback), or jeopardize their job or their current position and power. Maybe they see risk or new obstacles resulting from a change to their satisfactory status quo. Unknowns and unpredictable possibilities (however unlikely) are scary.

On the other hand, if you propose a viable solution to rid people of pain and problems that have been vexing them for some time and that have a stinging negative effect upon their jobs and lives, there's an excellent chance that they will jump on your proposal. But if there is little or no perceived pain, problems, hassles, or annoyances in their business, then convincing them you have something better to improve their operations, satisfy their customers, or improve their financials may very well incur apathy, which is a form of resistance to your goals.

The more creative, bold, different, or daring your idea, plan, or proposed solution is, the more innovative your presentation must be to get it accepted.

Even though some objections can be very specific to some factors in your presentation, look at the following list of common, general excuses, objections, and put-downs and ask yourself how many seemingly endless times you've heard them at meetings or even spouted them yourself. We guarantee you'll smile while reading these, maybe even laugh. Think of how you can best answer each one as it relates to your presentation:

- It won't work.
- We tried that before (or we've never done that before).
- It's too radical a change.
- No one else has done it.
- We don't need it.
- Another company tried it before.
- We've done it this way for years.
- It isn't in the budget.
- It's against our policy.
- Our competitors aren't doing it.
- Let's not rock the boat.
- We're overstretched as it is.
- Our business is different.
- Let's think about it some more.
- We don't have enough time (people, resources, expertise).
- Three people said it was a bad idea.

✔ People around here don't want to change.

✔ Management won't go for it.

✔ The idea (concept, plan, proposal) is way too far out.

✔ Let me play devil's advocate.

✔ It's not our problem.

✔ The timing isn't right.

✔ I just don't like it.

✔ We can't take a chance.

✔ It's more trouble than it's worth.

Strategizing to overcome objections

There are essentially three fundamental strategies to effectively deal with objections:

✔ **Preventing:** Doing a meticulous audience analysis that identifies your audience's key needs, wants, concerns, risk tolerances, priorities, and preferences goes a long way toward meeting your goals with little or no resistance. If possible, ask some of the people who are attending what they and others would absolutely want to hear about your topic and what areas of potential contention might be brought up. You can then develop and focus your compelling content in such a way as to better convince people, who might otherwise have reservations. Delivering an excellent, innovative presentation will significantly reduce the chance of problems. Planning and preparation for resistance is vital to success.

✔ **Analyzing:** If you get an unexpected objection, your goal is to quickly and accurately identify and understand the underlying nature and cause of the resistance. Perhaps someone has had prior bad experiences with a program like yours. Find out why and to what extent someone hesitates or shuns your recommendations. Just because one person feels a certain way does not mean others do.

Just like hostile questions, find out if others are aligned with the person who objected. Suppose someone says, "Let's think about it some more." Your response might be, "In your opinion, what specifically needs to be thought about and why?" Or what if a person says, "It's not in the budget," then you can counter, "Are you saying that you feel that the program I described is very worthwhile and if a budget was available, you would endorse and support it?" If the person says "yes," you can logically say, "So why don't we at least try to get it funded if you feel that positive about it?" These comebacks can smoke out any insincere answers by qualifying the objection, which is part of analysis. Empathic listening and smart probing are key.

✔ **Convincing:** After you fully identify the real reasons behind the objection, you can answer in a sincere, realistic, and persuasive way to see if you can influence the person's thinking or feeling. What if a person hits you with, "We don't have enough time or resources to get it done" and you reply, "What if I showed you a draft plan and informal survey that says, in spite of the fact that people are overstretched, not only can we be creative with time and resource constraints, but about 72 percent of people polled are interested in this idea?" Imagine an audience member saying, "Your concept is too far out." You can come back with, "Sure this approach may initially seem far out. I understand. But what breakthrough or quantum leap isn't perceived that way at first? We have a real opportunity to slam-dunk an increase in our market share with a new product like this. Let me quickly give you six incredible examples of bold, daring, and even outrageous ideas in our industry that created a treasure chest of new fortunes for them over the last five years." Being not just profoundly creative, but logically compelling with your answers will melt away resistance.

Never call an objection an "objection." That gives it undue weight. Call it a question, an issue, an item, a point being raised.

Try one of the following tactics when dealing with objections:

✔ **Pre-answer:** If you strongly suspect that several people in your group disagree with a specific part of your presentation or will bring up a point of contention or concern, it's a good tactic to anticipate the problem by bringing it up yourself and answering it beforehand. From a psychological standpoint, it shows that you are not only aware of a potential feeling or concern but not in the least worried about it.

✔ **Use a metaphor:** Aristotle said that one of the signs of genius was the use of metaphors. You often hear people using (muscle-developing) steroids as an example of metaphors such as: "This machine is productivity on steroids." A software company advertising their presentation software, which focuses on visuals more than text says, "This will give the eyes of your audience something to scream about."

✔ **Provide proof:** A powerful way to counter an objection is to use various forms of proof, such as facts, statistics, video, demonstrations, examples, and anything else that provides concrete substance to back up your claims.

Part IV
Mixing Creativity and Technology

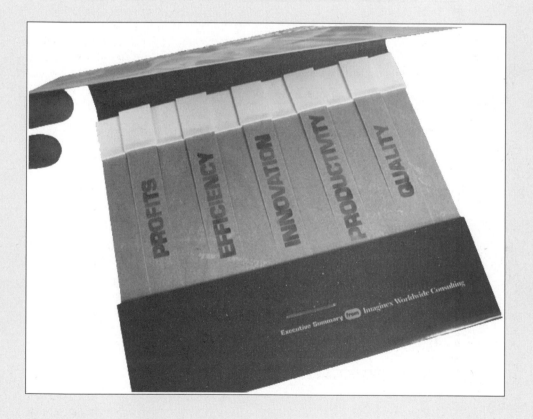

Check out www.dummies.com/extras/innovativepresentations for tips on adding video to your presentations.

In this part . . .

- ✔ Create captivating visuals.
- ✔ Incorporate color, text, and images to emphasize your points.
- ✔ Use boards and props to add three-dimensional interest.
- ✔ Make proposals and handouts that help the audience remember you.
- ✔ Understand the difference between linear and nonlinear presentations.
- ✔ Examine and choose the appropriate app for your presentation.
- ✔ Evaluate the situation to identify the correct hardware.
- ✔ Use laptops and tablets to control visuals and interact with the audience.
- ✔ Understand augmented reality and gesture apps.
- ✔ Conduct online meetings and webinars.

Chapter 14

Reinventing How You Create and Use Multimedia Visuals

*Y*ou probably don't drive the same car you did 25 years ago but your slides may look much the same as they did when PowerPoint was introduced in 1990. Much as you (and the auto industry) have learned about cleaner emissions, better fuel efficiency, and safety features such as airbags and hands-free radio, the presentation industry has studied how people learn in multimedia settings — and it's not from bulleted lists!

In this chapter, we re-educate you about making electronic visuals. The term *visuals* focuses on photos, video, animations, diagrams, illustrations, charts, and graphics much more than it does on ineffective text slides, although we use *slides* as well. For simplicity's sake, we use both PowerPoint and Keynote in our examples to show you that you can use apps you probably have. Keep in mind that you can apply these tactics to other slide/visual apps or create your slides in a page layout or photo manipulation app, save them as PDFs, and then use them in a different presentation app, like one of the ones we discuss in Chapter 17.

First, we give you an overview of the results from recent studies about how people learn, and then we give you concrete examples of how to turn that knowledge into effective slides.

Appealing to Your Audience's Sensory Perception

People learn through experience, and they experience through sensory perception. If you were to attend a guided honey tasting like those Barbara leads in her spare time, you would use all five of your senses: sight, sound, smell, taste, and touch. During a presentation, however, you communicate to your audience through sight — what the audience sees on your visuals — and sound — what you say.

Interestingly, this means your audience taps into both sides (right and left) of their brains, so if you can keep both hemispheres of the brain engaged in the same tasks, you're less likely to lose the attention of your audience. For example, rather than listen to you while reading e-mail or Twitter, the audience listens to you and looks at your visuals.

Another interesting thing about senses is how they link to emotions. When you tap into the audience's emotions, you've got them hooked. Think about the difference between seeing a confusing graph and seeing an evocative photo, stunning animation, or video. The image sticks with you, and when you think of that photo, you experience the original emotion it elicited and remember what was said or what happened when you saw it.

Conveying concept, solution, experience, and feeling

You may be asking yourself, "I sell widgets, how can I get an emotional response?" And we respond, "Let us count the ways:"

✔ Use your voice, gestures, and facial expressions to communicate what you want your audience to feel: enthusiasm, concern, satisfaction, or whatever. Studies about mirror neurons, although controversial on some points, do agree that when you see someone else's emotion, be it pain or joy, you empathize or experience it as if it were happening to you. When you're excited and energetic, it rubs off!

✔ Let your audience participate. When demonstrating a product to a group, ask someone from the audience to help you. Your audience will identify with the helper and laugh at or applaud her success.

✔ Show a short video of testimonials from customers similar to your audience who have had good results or solutions from your product or service.

✔ Tell an anecdote or metaphorical story analogous to your audience's situation. Personal stories that show you understand the pain or difficulty your audience has will strike a chord with them.

✔ Use a single, striking image that relates to your business or industry or use single words or phrases. Remember that what takes your breath away may not do the same for your audience.

✔ Use a consistent image, phrase, or color scheme and find ways to repeat it throughout your presentation. As something becomes familiar, people begin to identify with it and remember the emotion it brings.

You know an image or story works when you see the audience watching you, heads up, eyes alert, maybe even nodding in agreement. If you tell an amusing anecdote, laughter means you reached them. If, instead, your anecdote gives an example of a serious situation, an attentive audience will likely purse their lips and nod their heads in agreement with you.

Avoid slides that show a bulleted list. You can't expect your audience to be listening while they're reading, especially as they may be trying to copy down everything written on the slide. Your audience has enough distractions with their electronic devices, physical handouts, or a chatty neighbor, and then you go and put up a slide that's full of text to read? Don't do it!

Showing and telling

From the time of Homer — long before the printing press — stories have been used to communicate information. You may not have the oratory skills of Homer, but you can certainly learn to tell a story.

You probably began learning about telling oral stories at a young age in a natural way at kindergarten show-and-tell. You brought your favorite toy, the fossil you found at the beach, or maybe your great-aunt visiting from a foreign land, and told a story about how you found it or what's special about the object and why you like it. Remember the faces of the other children in the circle, listening and appreciating your story as if the object were their own (the mirror neurons at work); give your presentation with that same pure intensity and keep your audience in rapt awe.

You don't speak in bullet points, and you certainly don't dream in them, so why should you present that way? Not only does the audience remember a story better than a list of facts, you have an easier time remembering a presentation composed of stories than one composed of facts. That doesn't mean you don't talk about facts or concrete data points but that you communicate them in a narrative way while showing visuals that relate to them. Tell and show; show and tell.

Dr. John Medina, developmental molecular biologist and author of *Brain Rules,* (a great book to learn about how you learn) states that people learn in ten-minute chunks of time. For you, that means when you give a presentation, you must do something different at the 9-minute-58-second mark to re-engage your audience and snap their brains to attention. You can hand the presentation over to another speaker, show a video, open up a question-and-answer session, or start an activity.

Choosing Visuals Wisely

Taste is subjective, color trends change, and new production techniques can make a visual from five years ago seem old today. Using visuals to support your presentation increases audience retention six-fold: Research shows that three days after an oral presentation, the audience retains 10 percent of what you said, whereas after an oral and visual presentation, the audience remembers more than 60 percent of what they heard.

Your visuals must be appropriate to your presentation, so remember the following key qualities when choosing them:

- ✔ **Relevant:** It may seem obvious, but your images must relate to your presentation and provide insight to your message. That said, think about different ways to represent things. For example, if you want to reinforce the word *drive,* you can use a car image or a golf image.

- ✔ **Enhance:** The images you show should support your words. They should not distract, overpower, or replace them. Choose images that add value to what you say and help you make your point or convince the audience of your message.

- ✔ **Simple:** Don't confuse the audience; keep the data on each visual to a minimum.

- ✔ **Size matters:** Make sure your visuals can be seen from all the seats in the room.

There should be just one key point associated with each visual. For example, "Sales have been increasing at a steady rate and are predicted to continue their rise over the next three years."

Relating words and visual elements

When you begin developing your presentation, think about the main point you want to make and keep reworking it, asking yourself why or how, until it's solid. Change subjective adjectives into descriptive adjectives. For example, you have an appointment to present your services to a potential client and developing your main point may go something like this:

✔ We offer great travel services.

✔ We offer custom, full-service business travel arrangements.

✔ We take care of your company's business travelers from reservations and limousine pickup to meeting room and banquet arrangements. We do the price comparisons, so you don't have to. We track each traveler during the journey to pre-solve eventual problems and delays.

✔ We're your virtual, ever-present travel concierge.

Now you're talking. Come up with a visual of a familiar figure who takes care of everything, such as nanny Mary Poppins, maid Rosie from *The Jetsons,* valet Jeeves from stories by P. G. Wodehouse, or Jules Verne's traveling butler Passepartout (shown in Figure 14-1) to open your presentation.

Figure 14-1: Familiar images hit an immediate emotional chord with the audience.

PASSEPARTOUT

YOUR VIRTUAL TRAVEL COMPANION

Illustration courtesy of Ray Anthony and Barbara Boyd

After you develop your main point, begin building the supporting points and visuals that accompany them, going through the same honing exercise you did for the opening visual. Give your audience one piece of information at a time, repeating salient points and reinforcing them with related images to make them memorable.

Break your presentation into ten-minute chunks, and use your visuals to punctuate them. For example, use still images while you speak for ten minutes and then show a short video.

Building and directing the flow of information

As the presenter, you guide the audience through your presentation. You begin with a set of assumptions about what they know — gleaned from your audience analysis which we cover in Chapter 4 — and then move forward, essentially teaching them, giving them the information they need to move to the next step or idea.

Use your visuals to support the building blocks of your presentation. In old-style presentation slides, you would use bullet lists, and perhaps each point would shoot across the screen and come to a screeching halt one under the other as you introduce them, and you would read each bullet as it appeared. Yawn. In an innovative presentation, each idea (former bullet item) has its own visual or multiple points build a graphic. For example, for the fictitious travel service company, rather than show a bulleted list of services, your visual could be an open suitcase, and as you talk about each service, an animated icon (such as tickets and souvenirs) goes into the suitcase. The suitcase is closed and carried away by a traveller, thereby showing that the services are always with the traveller.

A single object can have similar impact, especially when the visual provides a metaphor, as in Figure 14-2, where the labyrinth represents a business problem. The presenter speaks about the difficulty of finding a solution when you can only see a part of the problem but how solutions become quickly visible when you see the overall situation.

Figure 14-2: Use visual metaphors to support your message.

Illustration courtesy of Ray Anthony and Barbara Boyd

At the present, companies of all kinds use infographics to communicate statistics, facts, research results, and processes. Study them to get fresh ideas for presenting your data or message.

Apps including Prezi (which we talk about in Chapter 17) use a new style of visuals, moving from point to point but then zooming out to show the entire image.

Highlighting and Emphasizing Points

Images, whether photos or illustrations, quickly emphasize the idea and emotion you want to convey. But taking a look at one of the historic presentations by Steve Jobs (late CEO of Apple) shows that printed (and projected) words can be just as inspiring and moving. As with images, you want to use words that directly express and support your message.

Using color

Sometimes two colors — one light, one dark — lend a stark importance to your data. This has become Apple's signature presentation style. It's up to you to decide if it fits with your presentation style, because there's nothing wrong with using color. In fact, studies of the psychology of color report that colors affect mood, and everyone from package designers to prison architects consider the correct color to use to garner the desired results.

Usually warm colors (reds, yellows, and oranges) are considered stimulating, creative colors, and cool colors (blues, greens, and purples) are thought to be calming and balancing. When designing your presentation palette, you can also adjust the hue, saturation, and brightness of the colors you choose.

To help you choose a palette of complementary colors, the Color Palette Generator at www.degraeve.com/color-palette generates a color palette based on a photo. Or visit www.colourlovers.com and https://kuler.adobe.com/explore/newest to view a wide range of color palette trends.

When scouring the web for the most recent research, as well as looking at presentations we like, we found some controversy about choosing a dark or light background color. Overall, our conclusions and recommendations are:

✔ **Dark room, dark background:** In a theater setting for a keynote speech or a professional conference, a dark background with contrasting light-colored text or bright images is easier on your audience's eyes. What's more, because your eyes are drawn to bright things, if you use a light background in a dark room, your audience's eyes will focus on — and be distracted by — the light screen and miss the dark images on it. Whereas with a dark screen, your audience's eyes look at and absorb the lighter words and images on the screen but then revert back to focus on you, even if you're dimly lit by the lectern light.

✔ **Light room, light background:** In a small, well-lit meeting room, a light background makes for a more conversational presentation, similar to using a whiteboard. High-quality LED projectors perfectly display color images on a white or light background.

You can find lots of inspiration by browsing the winners from design competitions; check out the AIGA (American Institute of Graphic Arts) website at `www.aiga.org/inspiration`.

Stylizing text

Like choosing a color palette, choosing a typeface can be an exciting, creative task or a daunting one. Typeface styles communicate the tone and intent of your company and presentation. Just by changing the typeface, the style of your presentation can go from juvenile to professional. Figure 14-3 shows how the same word conveys a different feeling just by changing the typeface.

Figure 14-3:
Fonts can be fun, professional, academic, or neutral.

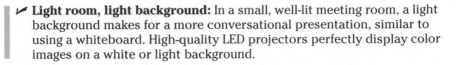

Illustration courtesy of Ray Anthony and Barbara Boyd

Sans serif fonts including Ariel, Helvetica, and Avenir are easy to read on a screen, big or small, because of their simple lines. However, for one or two words or a short phrase, we think serif fonts can work just as well as long as your display offers a high resolution (serif fonts are most readable at 1,000 dots per inch or higher). Experiment with different typefaces to see which one conveys your message best and looks clear on screen.

Serifs, those embellishments on the edges of letters in serif fonts, guide your eye from one letter to the next, which is why they're great for printed material (such as this book which uses the Times New Roman font). Your brain has to work a little harder to recognize groups of words in a sans serif font.

Your computer probably came with dozens of preloaded fonts and you can find hundreds more if you search the World Wide Web for "copyright free fonts for commercial use." Two sites you can try are `www.fontsquirrel.com`, which distributes free and fee-based fonts and has some neat tools for identifying and finding fonts, and `www.1001fonts.com`, which has a category named Free for Commercial Use.

Please read the terms and conditions for using any fonts that you download, especially if you plan to use them for commercial purposes.

Figure 14-4 provides an example of using the visual appeal of text to support your message.

Figure 14-4: Contrast is key to using text effectively.

Illustration courtesy of Ray Anthony and Barbara Boyd

If you work in a large corporation, you may be restricted to approved company fonts and presentation templates when giving presentations as a company representative.

Pointing and circling

One of the simplest ways of highlighting your idea is to point to it. When you speak to a large group and refer to a technical drawing, you can't avoid pointing to the part you're explaining, but you can choose how you point. You can approach the screen and point with your finger but probably only those in the front row will be able to decipher what you're indicating. One of the following is a better choice:

✔ **Laser pointer:** A hand held, pen-size object that shines a red dot where you point it when you press the button — just don't point it toward anyone's eyes.

✔ **In-app pointers:** Many, if not most, presentation apps come with a built-in laser pointer. If you're working with a computer, you use the mouse or trackpad to move a shining dot to the part you want to indicate. Better yet, if you're working with a touch screen, you put your finger on the part of the image you want to highlight and the shining red dot appears.

In addition to pointers, presentation apps have built-in highlighters and pens so you can write directly on your visual. See Chapter 17 to find out more about presentation apps for your computer and tablet.

Adding Variety and Interest

Don't limit your visuals to strong images and text; think about using other props, such as those we discuss in Chapter 15, and change up your presentation with video, animation, and guest speakers at ten-minute intervals.

Incorporating custom video

If you blanch at the thought of the cost and time involved in creating custom video, think again. With a smart device or handheld video camcorder combined with an easy-to-use video editing app, you can capture interesting testimonials or demonstrations, and then incorporate them with your slides and spoken message. Some presentation apps, such as 9Slides, let you capture video directly in the app from your iPad.

If your budget allows, you can also hire professionals — or talented amateurs — to shoot and edit video to include in your presentation.

Creating custom animations

The Royal Society for the encouragement of Arts, Manufactures and Commerce's RSA Animates (`www.thersa.org/events/rsaanimate`) uses compelling animation to explain facts and figures through animation. You see a hand draw the figures and numbers corresponding to the data the voiceover talks about. If you visit the RSA website, you can find out how to use their videos in your presentations, or you can create your own with an iPad app called VideoScribe (`www.sparkol.com/products/videoscribe`).

Another way to do ultra impressive animations is by using Adobe After Effects software. Find a talented expert on it and you can then show custom animated illustrations, bar and pie charts, technical diagrams, operation processes, and organizational charts in radical, stunning ways that make your information and messages POP!

Both Keynote and PowerPoint offer animation tools that bring your data and visuals to life. However, as with any media placed in your presentation, make sure it enhances your message, adds value, or better explains what you're saying — don't use tricks just to use them.

Using stock media

When you don't need specific, custom video, stock video or animation can provide the break your presentation needs. You can find a vast selection of royalty-free stock media — that means you pay for it once and can use it in various situations, worldwide, multiple times. As with stock photos, read the terms and conditions to make sure you don't infringe anyone's copyright.

A few sites that offer stock video, photos, animations, vector illustrations, music, or special effects with various price and usage structures are listed here, and you can find other providers by searching the web:

- www.istockphoto.com/video
- www.productiontrax.com
- www.motionelements.com
- www.stockfootageforfree.com

Just looking through them stirs your imagination. For example, iStock has a free, royalty-free video called Crazy Monkey that shows a monkey dressed in a blue button-down shirt and tie jumping from one filing cabinet to another. If you sell office organization supplies or services, this cute little guy could run in the background while you say something like, "Does this guy look like some of your coworkers?" and then go on to talk about your services.

Working with visuals

Refer to Chapter 7 for details about posture and gesture, but keep these tips in mind to emphasize visuals:

- Position yourself near the screen, but don't block it from your audience.

- Talk conversationally about the information on your slides. Practice makes perfect. Ideally, your visuals are enough to keep you on track, and you won't have to refer to notes. However, it's better to refer to written facts and figures than risk giving the wrong information.

- Communicate the main point you developed using the technique described in the section, "Relating words and visual elements." When creating your presentation, continually ask yourself, "Does this visual and point support my main message?" If not, leave it out.

- Black out the screen when you don't have or need an image to support your words. It's okay to have a blank screen now and then during the course of your presentation. The best way to do this is to create a black slide and insert it at the appropriate times during your talk.

Chapter 15

Using Presentation Board Systems, Flip Charts, and Props

In This Chapter

▶ Using presentation boards

▶ Posterizing your information

▶ Creating displays

▶ Handling props to add interest and meaning

▶ Winning ways with flip charts

*W*ith all the technology and special effects available, it's tempting to ignore the original visual showstoppers: presentation boards, props, and flip charts. Today's boards and charts are still superb tools for communicating concepts, strategies, solutions, and projects. You can use them as additional sources of visual information right alongside your stunning digital visuals.

An innovative presenter can win — hands down — any competitive situation using only well-designed presentation boards against an "average" presenter using a laptop or tablet; just like a great golfer will be victorious using a regular set of golf clubs against an average player using the best clubs available. It's about skill and mastery.

This chapter covers different types of presentation boards and gives you tips on using another staple of visual equipment — the venerable flip chart. In addition, we give examples of presentation props and displays that you can make or ones you can rent or purchase from companies who primarily cater to the trade show market.

Stepping Up to the Presentation Board

Aside from being effective visual tools, a key reason to consider using presentation boards alongside your tricked-out technology-based presentation is variety, change, and redirected attention. Think of your favorite food, one that you love. As tasty as it is, could you eat it three times a day for days or even weeks on end? As much as you love it, after a period of time, you'll want something different. Staring at a projection screen or large television — even if you have great visuals or videos — can be tiring after a while. Transitioning to another form of visuals breaks that visual routine and snaps and reinvigorates people's attention to something new.

Several years ago, a friend of ours attended a one-day training event along with about 2,500 other people. The famous speaker was (and still is) considered one of the most dynamic, popular motivational speakers in the world. Yet, our friend said that after about three hours, he really wanted to listen to someone else. He noticed people starting to become listless and restless. Sir Francis Galton, who wrote a paperback book in 1885 titled *The Measurement of Fidget,* observed that the more people slouched and leaned while listening to a speaker, the more bored and inattentive they were. While our friend was mightily taken with that speaking celebrity, like chomping down one's favorite dish for days on end, he craved a change. You could measure his fidget. This "master of the stage" talked for an entire day using few visuals or other attractions to enliven the experience for his audience. A great speaker, like a favorite food, can get tiring without some creative diversions.

In today's fast-paced world, we measure attention spans in minutes, not hours, and we often have to be ingenious about giving people variety to keep them interested and focused. This is where a presentation board (or several) can help. Say you're giving a relatively extensive business, sales, or technical presentation that lasts an hour or more. You're using your tablet or computer to project a great mix of compelling illustrations, photos, videos, and animations. Suddenly, the screen goes blank, you walk to the side of the room, pick up your easel holding the large presentation board (with the interesting graphics on it), and begin pointing to and talking about a specific captivating illustration of your new product. This simple change can make a difference with your audience.

Using presentation boards to your benefit

Why use a board when you can just project the same visuals on a screen or large television?

- ✔ Variety
- ✔ Change
- ✔ Focus

When you transition from the projector and physically pick up (if easily moved) the board or position it closer to a small group of people, you add variety to the pace, you change visuals, and you lead the group to shift and refocus their attention. The more you find ways to incorporate meaningful visual and physical body shifts, the better you can minimize fidgets and lulls in your presentation.

You don't want to get stuck in the technology-and-presentation-board rut either. Use this combination only when it makes sense to, and when you have a clear purpose in mind. Ask yourself, "What special visuals or select information can I put on a presentation board to help emphasize, highlight, clarify, or reinforce the ideas I show in my projected visuals and create needed transitions in my presentation?"

Reaching out to your audience

A presentation board enables you to position it and you nearer to your group. Your physical proximity helps you develop rapport with your audience and have more direct eye contact with individual people. It permits you to get up close to the group with your board and easily point out those things you want to stress.

Using attractive, professionally designed presentation boards helps differentiate you from other presenters who are less creative and flexible in their presentation style. With today's ability to print large, colorful, high-resolution images on large boards, these visuals are a worthwhile companion to digital presentations.

Using a clever, multi-part presentation board system where you put on and take off sections using Velcro-type or magnetic attachments, you can actually add a bit of theatrics (in addition to revealing information at the appropriate moment). Practice so that you can make the changes smoothly as you continue talking. We have seen groups be quite impressed with how competently presenters used these boards along with other digital visuals.

Combining a large board with projected visuals enables you to show the entire big-picture strategy, solution, plan, or engineering design on the board and use projected visuals to show details. You can then go back and forth between the details in the projected visuals and the overview on the board. This way, you keep the audience on track with a logical flow of information and points.

Sometimes companies develop attractive boards that stand on an easel in the corner of a room or are mounted on the walls of their meeting rooms. These function more as displays than as active tools, but they're effective in reinforcing the message the company wants to communicate.

Choosing the right board style

Presentation boards are best used with smaller groups of fewer than 25 people to ensure good visibility of the information. Figure 15-1 shows a simply designed, basic board with minimal information on it. When the presenter wants to repeat and reinforce certain points such as "Return On Investment," he transitions from his electronic presentation, which shows visuals about his product's benefits, and walks to the side of the room where the board is positioned close to the group, stressing that "no other competitive product can deliver such a high financial return," as he points to it. Or he can begin his presentation by using the board's four main points as his executive summary and be able to repeat his main messages on the board during his presentation.

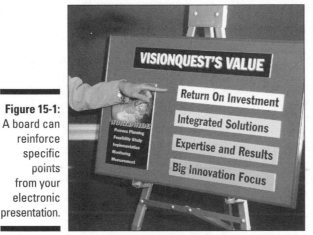

Figure 15-1:
A board can reinforce specific points from your electronic presentation.

Photograph courtesy of Ray Anthony

Tri-fold presentation boards

The presentation board shown in Figure 15-2 can contain a good many key ideas, and the three-panel design provides a flexible base to lay out information. These boards work in conjunction with an electronic presentation or as a standalone visual display.

With this type of board, you can choose to present this information in a random or organized way, depending on the needs of the group.

With groups of fewer than five people you can ask your audience to come nearer to the visual and then convey your information in a conversational style that encourages discussion.

Photograph courtesy of Ray Anthony

Figure 15-2:
A tri-fold board works as a flexible presentation tool.

Oversized boards

Most presentations benefit from being on a large board (5 feet wide, 3 feet high). Your text and images can be seen even from a distance, and details of complex figures are easier to understand.

Figure 15-3 shows an oversized board used to talk about the company's creative team, which comprises four executives. The foam-core graphics were glued onto the board's large black foam-core background, giving them a raised, three-dimensional effect. In addition the board is fitted with an attractive black metal frame (that also protects the edges when transporting).

Figure 15-3:
A larger board with oversized graphics and text works for an audience of 25 to 50 people.

Photograph courtesy of Ray Anthony

Storyboards

The storyboard system is borrowed from filmmaking. Each single visual represents a scene of the story. The storyboard system, shown in Figure 15-3, uses a background board consisting of a large ¼-inch piece of flat plastic framed with aluminum strips. The plastic background gives the board rigidity and durability and enables you to attach self-sticking black Velcro strips (that cannot be seen several feet away) in any configuration, creating a flexible, modular board where you can attach any number of visual panels as the presentation calls for. In addition, because of the strong, rigid plastic backing, you can add other novel functional and decorative items to your board. In Figure 15-4 vertical Velcro pieces spaced 12 inches apart hold the panels and a decorative, high-quality die-cast bulldozer rests on a metal platform (see Figure 15-5), adding extra visual appeal to a board a construction company might use.

Figure 15-4: Easily removable panels make a storyboard a powerful and flexible visual.

Photograph courtesy of Ray Anthony

Figure 15-5: Creative touches such as a model piece of equipment add interest to your board.

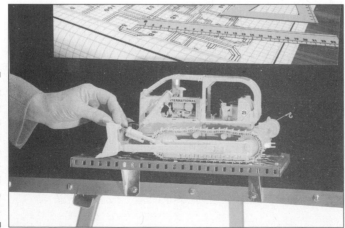

Photograph courtesy of Ray Anthony

By attaching visual panels of various sizes and shapes (as shown in Figure 15-6) at specific points in your presentation, you methodically feed your audience information only when you want to.

Figure 15-6: Add panels during your presentation to emphasize the points you want to make.

Photograph courtesy of Ray Anthony

Still another attraction is the ability to add objects (such as the large resin spark plug replica) to your board (see Figure 15-7) with a Velcro or magnetic backing system. By using the storyboard technique, your audience tends to pay more attention to you than they would while watching slide after slide after slide while you stand in one position. This activity of occasionally using your board in combination with your electronic visuals adds real animation and value to your talk.

Figure 15-7: Attaching objects to symbolize or reinforce your messages can add interest.

Photograph courtesy of Ray Anthony

Presenting at a Poster Session

Unless you're involved in medical, scientific, or other types of research, you probably haven't heard of poster sessions. Also called a *poster presentation,* a *poster session* is a systematic way to present research information at a professional or academic conference. Typically an area of an exhibition hall is dedicated for the poster session where researchers describe, explain, and justify their research using large, detailed posters. Conference attendees walk around, glance at posters, and socialize. The researchers stand by their posters to discuss their research with anyone interested in it.

A medical or scientific poster is essentially a journal article translated into graphic form by minimizing text sections, presenting key findings as bullet points, and including graphic elements to illustrate key research points.

Creating an effective poster can be challenging because you may have to squeeze results from a whole year's worth of research onto a 3-x-5-foot sheet of glossy photo paper printed from a wide-format printer. The poster has to succinctly and clearly convey what may be a complex and comprehensive topic.

The tricky part is determining what information is most meaningful and impactful. Depict too much and it may confuse or overwhelm the viewer; depict too little and people may not appreciate the research's value, urgency, and impact. Just like visuals in a business presentation!

Borrowing from poster people

You may be wondering why we mention poster sessions in a book about business presentations. We have a couple reasons: One, if your clients are in the scientific or medical profession, you may have to make a poster presentation at some point; and two, poster session tactics are valid for business presentations. Consider the following:

- **Everything on one visual:** A poster is usually a single PowerPoint slide or visual (from Adobe Photoshop or Illustrator) developed into a large-format paper visual that contains numerous key headings, text boxes, and graphic objects. The benefit is you don't have to sequence through slides or any other visuals. Everything of an important and relevant nature should be on that poster. Figure 15-8 shows a version of a smaller poster-type visual to use with one to four people as a presentation aid. As you can see the entire presentation is on one foam core poster, so the presenter can randomly talk and answer questions about any item on the visual.

The poster format forces you to think almost excruciatingly about what to put in; what to leave out; how much should be text; what should be illustrations, photos, diagrams, or charts, and much more. The goal is to say and show a lot using the fewest words and graphics. The same should apply to business presentations.

Figure 15-8:
Having one visual with the major parts of your presentation gives you flexibility.

Photograph courtesy of Ray Anthony

✔ **Order and flow:** A researcher at a poster session has scant minutes to cover results that have taken perhaps years to complete. He has to tell a story his listeners can quickly and easily follow. Laying out the string of information and key points in a logical order is critical. The same should apply to business presentations.

✔ **Getting it:** Too many visuals make a poster too busy, too disjointed, too indecipherable. Consummate designers create posters so that viewers can quickly comprehend what the research is about as they walk by. Great visuals are self-evident, self-explanatory, and speak for themselves. The same should apply to business presentations.

✔ **Focus and proof:** The key to crafting a good poster is to focus as precisely and sharply as possible on the central ideas you want to convey. The same should apply to business presentations.

Taking a cue from poster sessions, presenters who discuss projects, strategies, plans, processes, or technologies might want to create that big visual (for example 4-x-6 feet) that tells the whole story on it. With a large visual to accompany your electronic presentation, you can refer to it as long as your group can see it. In addition, you can use a miniature version of your large board to create a valuable laminated handout using the front and back for graphics along with detailed text for descriptions, explanations, and examples. Consider using a horizontal format to print your project summary on an 11-x-17-inch sheet of paper.

Considering Your Display Options

It's rare for a general business or technical presentation to need a background or display such as those you typically see at trade shows or larger promotional events. But, some speeches and presentations you give and videos you shoot lend themselves nicely to a smaller display or exhibit system. (Background displays are often used at TED talks. The stage is decorated to make it more attractive and interesting for the audience to look at rather than a bare stage with only a projection screen on it.) Smaller displays leading into a presentation hall reinforce your image, message, and product.

Using tabletop displays

You may want to consider bringing your own portable custom displays when giving presentations or speeches at conferences, large corporate events, conventions, association meetings, multilevel marketing sessions, or at larger training workshops. Displays with custom graphics can help you with your presentation objectives.

Professional speakers and authors often sell their books and other materials at the back or side of a presentation space and could advertise their goods with tabletop displays inside the room and eye-catching banner stands and pop-ups by the entry door or in the lobby of the hotel or organization where they're speaking.

Many of these displays are easy to pack in compact, transportable cases and can be set up in minutes. Several companies, such as Displays2Go (www. displays2go.com), offer a wide variety of traditional displays, signs, and banners, as well as tablet stands and presentation-related products. Three other leading trade show display companies you might want to visit for ideas for your larger presentations or training workshops and seminars are Nomadic Display (www.nomadicdisplay.com), Skyline (www.skyline.com), and Apple Rock (http://applerock.com).

Making attractive, active displays

Another category of displays to consider using for those speeches or presentations that warrant them are items that you can buy or build or hire someone else to build.

Figure 15-9 shows an example of a display that adds flavor to a presentation. You can place something like this near you or somewhere in the room. Or you can have it as an attractive sign at an entrance beckoning people into a meeting room.

Figure 15-9:
Creative signs and displays can set your presentation apart from others.

Photograph courtesy of Ray Anthony

When Stoddard Construction's (not their real name) business development professional gives a presentation, the presenter brings along this eye-catching sign to accompany her electronic presentation. The company constructed the display by gluing a laminated graphic to foam-core board. Notice she's wearing a prop construction helmet; both the sign and hardhat add spice to her presentation.

The construction company attached real aluminum strips around the edges and used real bolts drilled through the foam core to give the display a sturdy look and feel. Then they built a stand for the detailed model crane out of various metal pieces, including some from an Erector Set. They purchased the museum-quality die-cast model crane (shown in Figure 15-10) from TWH Collectibles (www.twhcollectibles.com). To reinforce their image as an innovative construction company, at a certain point in her presentation the presenter dons the light-bulb helmet as a prop. This product-related costuming goes over very well with even the most conservative customers.

Figure 15-10:
High-quality replicas of symbolic objects make for a stunning display.

Photograph courtesy of Ray Anthony

For presenters dealing with the construction, automotive, aerospace, or shipbuilding industries, attaching die-cast, wooden, or other models and objects to displays can help differentiate you and your presentation even in small but important ways. Check out companies like Fairfield Collectibles (www.fairfieldcollectibles.com) and Magellan Models (www.magellanmodels.com) to get ideas and purchase items.

Consider using your own image: Next to the entry of the room where he'll be giving a speech, a professional motivational speaker places a two-foot photo of himself that is cut out as an outline and attached to the back of the display with a thick backing to create a three-dimensional look. A real microphone is attached to this display. As people walk in to the room, this attractive sign helps build his credibility and professionalism. Or, consider creating an eye-catching *standee* — a self-standing display — of yourself or something relating to your presentation to promote or highlight your presentation. These custom-designed displays typically are made of thick cardboard and may include three-dimensional objects, devices, moving parts, and lights. These are useful at the entrance to your public seminar, conference, convention, or other (non-corporate business) presentation. For ideas, check out Shindigz (www.shindigz.com), Standees.com (www.standees.com), or Pixus Digital Printing (www.pixus.com).

To see really creative things that you can use and build into displays for automotive, truck, and motorcycle themes, check out Genuine Hotrod Hardware, Inc. at www.genuineHotrod.com.

Tinkering with quick, inexpensive displays

Throughout our book, we aim to give you ideas you can synthesize from various sources. Often you can borrow ideas from the most unlikely places. Who would think that you could make cool, funky-looking, inexpensive displays and operating props from Tinkertoy construction sets? Although we don't recommend these kitschy displays for business presentations, if you give training workshops, seminars, or speeches to small gatherings, you can do wonders with these small poles and connectors. You would be surprised at the tall, complex structures you can build for signs, activities, or games.

For example, Ray created the display (with iPad attached) in Figure 15-11 to sell his books and other products for his presentations at smaller local associations, chambers of commerce, and some company events. He had the sign on top printed, laminated, and mounted on a foam-core board that attached with Velcro to the round Tinkertoys. Parts are glued together using wood glue. However, it disassembles into three major sections for easy transport. The iPad hanging down plays a looped video (without sound) to attract the attention of potential buyers.

Figure 15-11:
A Tinkertoy display used to help promote and sell materials.

Photograph courtesy of Ray Anthony

Another example of a Tinkertoy display, shown in Figures 15-12 and 15-13, was built as part of a creative project to show how to make a display for less than $100. The signs attached with mounting hardware to the Tinkertoy structure were printed, laminated, mounted on foam-core boards, and cut to size and shape. The developers even constructed a small model train diorama (see Figure 15-13) on top using gravel, shrubs, and a track to give it a sense of realism.

Photograph courtesy of Ray Anthony

Figure 15-12:
Great displays often require more imagination than money.

Figure 15-13:
Creating scenes and attractive dioramas can give punch to your displays.

Photograph courtesy of Ray Anthony

The large, animated display in Figure 15-14 was made quickly, easily, and inexpensively for a workshop on business ethics. The structure has a hardwood cutout of a "greedy man" attached to the top with a hinge who swivels when hit by workshop participants using a Nerf gun dart (the trainer is holding one). When hit, the greedy man swings and activates an electrical contact, causing a bell to ring and a light on top (not shown, but later installed) to flash. Workshop attendees love to use the Nerf gun to score points as part of one of the session's fun activities.

Figure 15-14:
Large, fun, inexpensive display used as a game in a training session.

Photograph courtesy of Ray Anthony

Think about displays or props you can build using Erector Sets or Tinkertoys combined with metal pieces, foam-core signage, and other items that make interesting additions to your presentation.

Propping Up Your Audience's Interest

Cool props are a mainstay of the innovative presenter and professional speaker. The best business props — used selectively — reinforce your points and add an element of interest and novelty to your topic.

Props are ideal at large meetings, public seminars, training workshops, or sales conferences. Props make your talk more animated and entertaining. And they are terrific in your videos as well.

Make sure you use props that your audience can easily see and that add not only meaning but also a new perspective or dimension to your message.

You can choose static props that don't move or operate in any way or mechanical, electric, or electronic props, which, when they work as planned, are wildly impressive. Search the Internet for "Markus Fischer: A robot that flies like a bird" to see a breathtaking example of a presentation built around an incredible prop: a robot SmartBird that looks like a seagull and flies by flapping its wings.

Take a cue from improvisational comedians, actors, and imaginative speakers in turning ordinary, everyday items such as brooms, fruit, toilet paper, empty metal cans, tennis balls, whistles, hats, duct tape, balloons, a metronome, a wind-up alarm clock, thick telephone directory, or practically anything into a prop that adds special effects to your story. Even cordless electric tools, laser pointers, and battery-operated toys or devices can effectively slam your points home or reinforce a theme. Because of their informal nature, you wouldn't use these in a professional business presentation, but in a talk or speech designed to amuse, entertain, and motivate while still informing or educating your group the more creative you get, the better!

Aim to maintain a balance between the props and your message. Overusing props or using too many props may hurt the polished image and credibility you work so hard to establish.

Watching props in action

Ray's firm built the realistic-looking detonator prop shown in Figure 15-15 and bought some fake plastic sticks of dynamite as part of the illusion. In one of his training programs with larger audiences, when Ray talks about explosive ideas, he has his co-presenter Kathie push down on the prop's plunger (see Figure 15-16) as Ray uses his remote to activate a video of an explosion on the projection screen complete with a loud audio of the explosion. During his talk, Ray asks volunteers to come up and explode their own ideas as each uses the detonator prop accompanied by another explosion video and resounding audio.

Figure 15-15:
Look for ways a play on words can rein-force your message with your prop.

Photograph courtesy of Ray Anthony

Figure 15-16:
With a team presentation, props keep each member involved.

Photograph courtesy of Ray Anthony

This participation from the audience energizes people, and this activity gives variety to the presentation. Ray's other co-presenter Lance uses the prop shown in Figure 15-17, a sign and a fake hand grenade, to communicate another aspect of dangerous ideas that explode mediocrity.

Figure 15-17:
Keep the prop theme consistent throughout your presentation.

Photograph courtesy of Ray Anthony

Lori is a trainer who facilitates workshops on creative thinking. When she talks about the human brain, she uses a life-size model as shown in Figure 15-18 to discuss how people can channel both right and left sides of the brain to develop winning ideas. In a video she produced, she uses a close-up of the prop shown in Figure 15-18 combined with her trained acting skills to help unravel the mysteries of the brain.

Figure 15-18: Use props that give audiences extra insights.

Photograph courtesy of Ray Anthony

In her seminars about coaching for managers, on certain occasions during her session, Lori uses her megaphone (see Figure 15-19) and whistle to amusingly portray a sports coach. Finally, in another one of her videos, she uses a conductor's baton as shown in Figure 15-20 along with music and accompanying photos and videos to give tips on orchestrating performances of teams using the analogy of a maestro working with members of an orchestra to have them perform flawlessly together.

Figure 15-19: Working props can be powerful attention-getters.

Photograph courtesy of Ray Anthony

Figure 15-20: Consider using props as metaphors and theme-builders.

Photograph courtesy of Ray Anthony

Alfred is part of a construction company's presentation team that covers the specific pieces of the latest productivity and quality equipment used by his firm. As he discusses several pieces of the heavy equipment, he uses models as props like those shown in Figure 15-21 in addition to videos to make his piece more interesting. In Figure 15-22, Alfred is holding a prop made out of big Scrabble letters with strips of wood glued and screwed to the individual pieces to create one structure. These larger props can also be used as displays in the room where you're presenting. Check out `www.greatbigstuff.com` for Scrabble letters and other oversized props and objects to use in your presentations, training sessions, videos, and trade show events.

Figure 15-21: Use only relevant, professional props in your business presentations.

Photograph courtesy of Ray Anthony

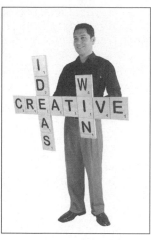

Figure 15-22:
Be creative
in building
and applying
oversized
props.

Photograph courtesy of Ray Anthony

Printing 3-D prototypes

Product designers, engineers, and manufacturers who give working presentations to discuss their designs for aerospace parts, automotive equipment, energy equipment parts, or consumer products such as tools, eyewear, housewares, electronics, or apparel can produce functional prototypes with a 3-D printer to communicate their concepts. Handling real prototypes or end-use products can be invaluable to people in the audience who have to make informed decisions and recommendations about them. With accurate, full-size or proportional-scale prototypes, people can see, feel, touch, wear, or use these items in ways that greatly help them give their input about improvements to initial designs or select those options worthy of further evaluation, testing, and use or purchase. For example, salespeople can give presentations about new designs for jewelry printed in 3-D so that these real items can be closely scrutinized and even worn to evaluate buying options.

Today's 3-D printers are actually not just used for conceptual prototypes, but are doing *additive manufacturing,* which is creating actual, useful components for various industries including aerospace, medical/dental, architectural, and automotive. Check out commercial-duty 3-D printers from companies including Stratasys (www.stratasys.com), 3DSystems (www.3dsystems.com), and Mcor Technologies (www.mcortechnologies.com). Many companies offer design and 3-D print services that start with using powerful apps like SolidWorks (www.solidworks.com).

These commercial 3-D printers use a wide variety of materials including more than a dozen different colors and types of thermoplastics, ceramics, carbon fiber, metals (including titanium), concrete, and other materials that can create complex, realistic, even functioning objects made of a combination of rigid, flexible, and transparent materials. For those vital presentations where showing the audience several variations of concept models, prototypes, or real parts are important, to help close a deal consider using the service bureaus that can provide printed examples or get approval to produce it from your audience. 3-D printing will become ever more important to innovative presenters as their already impressive capabilities continuously improve.

Flipping over Flip Charts

Another low-tech visual that still has a place in today's digital world is the flip chart. Flip charts continue to be excellent presentation media, if used effectively in groups of 25 people or fewer. A flip chart is simple, does not require electricity, and is reliable, low-cost, and easy to use. Like presentation boards used in addition to your electronic presentation, a flip chart adds welcome variety and spontaneity and can offer a bit of professional theatrics that nicely complement your other visuals.

One presenter, who focuses on performing in a subdued, showman style, often uses a flip chart in addition to projected visuals for sales presentations to smaller groups. Purposefully moving his focus between projected visuals and a flip chart, he breaks the potentially fading attention span of his prospects and reawakens it by having them wondering what he's going to write or show on the flip chart. He knows exactly when and how to use the flip chart to give his presentation a unique flavor and flair. He transitions from showing visuals to writing on the flip chart. He writes what he calls, "really important numbers" about financial returns on investment from his products on the flip chart, thereby focusing the audience's interest on those numbers.

 Many digital flip chart apps work on a computer or tablet. Alternatively, Quartet Kapture (www.quartetkapture.com) uses a special digital marker, Kapture self-stick easel pads, a USB receiver, and software to record and transmit every thing written or drawn on the pages to your laptop computer, saving the need to have someone transcribe all the flip-chart pages.

Another creative technique an account manger for a printing company employs that impresses her audiences is to use an illustration showing the major components of her company's 3-D printer. She prepares ahead of time by projecting that graphic onto a blank page of the flip chart and then carefully sketches the entire outline of it with a very light pencil that only she can see from up close on the page. During a key point in her sales pitch, she tells her group that she will quickly draw the key parts of the printer and explain how each one works to produce a product prototype in less than a minute. Using three different color markers, she quickly traces over the light pencil outline to create an almost perfectly drawn illustration — explaining each part of the illustration as she draws it. Not seeing the pencil lines guiding her, audiences are duly impressed with her ability using this clever approach. Even if they did see the light outline, the smooth and seamless way she draws and talks while still maintaining eye contact with the group is indeed captivating. This is what we mean by an example of a theatrical effect using a flip chart.

Customize the cover page of your flip chart with not only the prospect's company name and logo, but also the names of the key people attending the meeting. Something about seeing their name professionally printed on a flip chart pad (rather than written by a marker) seems to captivate people more than simply viewing their name on a screen from a visual.

Here are some helpful tips for making the most of your flip charts:

- ✔ Write only five to seven words per line using printed letters two or three inches high with your title line four inches high. Keep to a maximum of about six lines per page.

- ✔ Try to avoid using all capital letters, with the exception of titles or few words in very large print. A mix of upper- and lowercase letters is easier to read.

- ✔ Flip chart pads are sold in plain white or with thin grid lines on them. Grid lines make printing and aligning words and drawing straight lines and shapes easier.

- ✔ Use only the top two-thirds of a flip chart page. And either leave blank pages between to avoid bleed or see through or staple every two pages together to make turning them easier.

- ✔ Lightly write your text in pencil before using markers. This lets you make any adjustments with text spacing and diagrams you draw. Also consider writing notes on the page with light pencil to help you remember key points or numbers.

- ✔ Place your flip chart where it can be seen by every person in the group and, if necessary, arrange seats so that the person farthest from your chart can read the smallest lettering or figures.

- ✔ When you finish writing on the pad or finish showing something, flip to a new blank page to keep your audience focused on your presentation.

- ✔ To draw perfect circles on a page, use a large-diameter plastic bowl, lid, or a special flip-chart compass.

- ✔ Use dark-colored (black, blue, brown), wide, chisel-tip markers to print or draw in bold ways easily seen by everyone. Use red and green markers to highlight areas, give contrast (to distinguish types of information), and to add accent and variety to your text or drawings. Avoid using orange, pink, yellow, or light colors that are difficult to see.

- ✔ Write or draw on the pad, then turn around to face the audience and talk to them. Avoid talking to the flip chart with your back to the audience for extended periods of time.

Pre-printed flip charts

You can have a flip pad pre-printed in color by FlipCharts2Go at `http://flip charts2go.com`. Send them select visuals from a PowerPoint presentation or Word file via e-mail, and within days they will send you an impressively printed flip chart pad back.

Consider doing the following with pre-printed pads:

✔ Have blank lines next to the pre-printed words or numbers to interactively fill in extra information while you discuss it.

✔ Have diagrams, illustrations, graphics, or photos printed on those large pages. Using different color markers, write in explanations; draw circles, boxes, or underline to highlight information or emphasize parts as you go.

✔ Buy several books on simple origami projects. Practice and learn to quickly take a pre-printed page of an illustration off your flip chart pad and make an impressive object (building, vehicle, plane, tool, eagle) out of it that reinforces your presentation theme, key message, or objective.

Two excellent books about doing creative things with flip charts are *The Big Book of Flip Charts* by Robert William Lucas (McGraw-Hill) and *Flip Charts: How to Draw Them and How to Use Them* by Richard C. Brandt (Pfeiffer).

Chapter 16

Winning Proposals and Presentation Handouts

*"W*ow! That's impressive . . . let's do it!" Wouldn't you like to get that reaction from clients or decision makers in your organization who have experienced your stunning, unique proposal — one that includes compelling, superbly organized information and illustrations that creatively communicates an ideal solution to their needs or problem, packaged unlike anything they have seen before?

Whether you're initiating a new program or project or trying to close a business deal, many proposals have to be structured to tightly conform to very specific questions and requirements from a Request For Proposal (RFP), where the customer has already decided to buy but must select from whom. When you have flexibility to create your important proposal the way you want, then you need to put the magic wand of innovation to it, right from the start, because you want to make the short list, which gives you the opportunity to orally present your information later, or win the deal right away. That especially applies to unsolicited proposals, where you as a seller are trying to convince your potential buyer to clearly understand and appreciate their specific need and urgency to do business with you in some capacity.

This chapter focuses on creative proposal packaging — probably unlike anything you've seen before — and provides tips on presentation handouts as well. Although we don't cover proposal content in detail (see *Selling For Dummies* by Tom Hopkins), we do outline guidelines that you can apply to all proposals.

Creating Stunning Proposals

A *business proposal* is a written document or a multimedia file (such as in Apple's iBook app) you give to a prospective customer to obtain a sale for your products and/or services. It can be as simple as a one-page summary that briefly outlines what you will do, how much you will charge, and when you will complete the job. Other proposals dealing with mergers, strategic alliances, and especially large-scale, long-term complex projects (such as huge engineering or massive construction projects) can be several hundred pages and contain diagrams, charts, illustrations, tables, drawings, and photos to describe and explain how your company intends to meet the extensive stringent technical, cost, operating, materials, and scheduling requirements of the project and all the partners who will work on it.

In many situations, a buyer sends out a request for proposal (RFP) to numerous vendors, and after evaluating the documents, selects two or three as the short list. These vendors are then asked to give an oral presentation (usually by two or more presenters) to explain why their offering is the best for the prospective customer. The goals, obviously, are to develop a superb proposal, followed by giving the winning presentation.

The proposals we show you in the following pages are typically designed for unsolicited situations or situations where you have the flexibility to design and write your proposal as you see fit as long as you adequately address all the detailed requirements the potential client asks for.

The photos of proposals you see on the following pages take time and money to make compared to traditional proposals. If you don't need to use all that creative firepower and can close a deal without it, do it. However, for those big or important situations where you want to super impress your prospective clients — at the expense of your competitors — then give them some innovative shock and awe to clinch the deal.

Several of the proposals on the following pages are cleverly symbolic and metaphoric. Rather than give you proposal designs (in these fictitious scenarios) to copy, we want to inspire you and demonstrate the broad and unlimited imaginative possibilities you have — if you leap outside your thinking box.

Use these quick tips for an effective proposal:

✔ Make it relatively simple, easy, and interesting to read and view.

✔ Have a compelling, concise one-to-two page executive summary.

✔ Put all the focus on the client and her needs and requirements.

✔ Make sure the project objectives are clear and detailed.

✔ Describe and justify why your overall value proposition is the best. (A *value proposition* is the unique set of characteristics, features, and cost benefits your products, services, and company offers that differentiate it from your competitors.)

✔ Highlight and repeat your most important ideas, solutions, and benefits.

✔ Explain how your proposal is different and superior to all likely options.

✔ Show how results are quantified and success is highly probable.

✔ Describe how implementation will be relatively smooth, easy, and rewarding.

✔ Justify how any risk-to-gain ratio is more than acceptable.

✔ Describe the collaboration of all your team members and support groups.

✔ Highlight the competent qualifications of your project personnel.

✔ Include a detailed schedule of all activities.

Taking the competition to lunch

A sales executive from IdeaCatcher (a toy design company) wants to do business with a toy manufacturer, FunTyme, that values creative ideas. In a previous conversation, FunTyme's owner and founder told the sales executive "If you help me eat my competitor's lunch, you've got the deal!" The IdeaCatcher sales rep wants to show her company's innovative approach in ways that strongly demonstrate how they can boost FunTyme's sales and give them a big competitive lead.

At a meeting with four of the company's executives, including the owner, the IdeaCatcher's sales rep gives each person a personalized lunchbox with an illustration of a superhero on both sides. She tells the decision makers that the lunchbox holds a concise, complete executive summary proposal with all the key information they need to make a decision as shown in Figure 16-1. The lunchbox and its contents symbolize (subtly and subconsciously) ideas connected to the superhero archetype:

✔ Power and invincibility for FunTyme (the customer).

✔ Strength against competitors.

✔ Righteousness for the FunTyme cause.

Figure 16-1:
The package contains sweet money and the executive proposal.

Photograph courtesy of Ray Anthony

When the executives open their lunch boxes, surprises continue. Inside the lunch box are three 100 GRAND candy bars and a small booklet that summarizes the proposal information. The candy symbolizes tasty revenues and profits the customer will make as a result of their relationship with IdeaCatcher. Sweet! Underneath the candy bars, they find the executive summary proposal (Figure 16-2), which was specifically designed to fit within the small metal lunchbox. The title of the executive summary says it all:

"We'll Help You to Eat Your Competitor's Lunch"

Figure 16-2:
The small, yet complete, 20-page executive summary proposal.

Photograph courtesy of Ray Anthony

The strong, visceral metaphor was intended to immediately capture the attention, interest, and imagination of the decision makers — and it certainly did. The cover was laminated and trimmed using a ruler and X-ACTO knife. The font was selected to give a fun, cartoon feel to the cover. A white plastic comb bound it. The first page of the Executive Summary (in Figure 16-3) is simple, but strong. It sets a positive, expectant tone for the messages that follow with the enticing words "Opportunities" and "Possibilities." The next page is the ingenious summary of the Lunch Menu of intended benefits and projected results from working with IdeaCatcher. This was a relatively simple, easy, and inexpensive proposal that makes competitive ones look unexciting, uninviting, and downright boring.

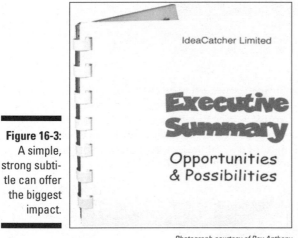

Figure 16-3:
A simple, strong subtitle can offer the biggest impact.

Photograph courtesy of Ray Anthony

Igniting profits for your customer

Imaginex Worldwide Consulting wants to snatch a nice deal with MagTech Inc. They decide to present an eye-popping 18-page proposal that addresses all of MagTech's requirements. An oversized matchbook represents the theme revolving around firing up profits for the customer.

Throughout this proposal, everything focuses on the benefits for MagTech. The theme begins with the bold, attention-grabbing title of the proposal, "Starting a Fire of Blazing Profits" and the subtitle, "A Creative Strategy to Significantly Boost MagTech's Competitive Position" as shown in Figure 16-4.

Figure 16-4:
Use a play
on words for
outstanding
proposals.

Photograph courtesy of Ray Anthony

Our graphic designer, Leonard Broussard, created the flaming cover with
dollar signs rising in the fire and printed it out on a tabloid-size glossy stock.
He glued black paper stock to the underside of the cover sheet using double-
sided adhesive. The large, industrial staple came from a big cardboard box.
The back view, as shown in Figure 16-5, includes a realistic-looking match
strike plate made out of confetti paper glued to the cover.

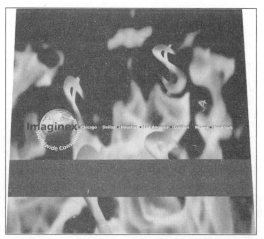

Figure 16-5:
Realism and
attention
to detail
convey
the atten-
tion your
team would
devote to
the client.

Photograph courtesy of Ray Anthony

This proposal has many small touches throughout that reinforce the main theme
and mimic the characteristics of a real matchbook. Attention to detail and realism
make a big difference in the overall visual and psychological impact of the proposal. For example, as shown in Figure 16-6, when the reader opens the proposal
as she would open a matchbook, she sees: "Open Cover to Strike Profits" in place
of the typical matchbook cover's, "Open cover to strike matches."

Photograph courtesy of Ray Anthony

These clever additions illustrate more than just creativity. They subtly communicate to your client that your account team is meticulous and motivated
by even the smallest details to ensure the success of your joint, team-based
projects. When a person opens the matchbook, as in Figure 16-7, she sees
matchsticks. Broussard found simulated-wood paper that he cut to size
to form the sticks of the matches. He used ⅛-inch-thick white foam for the
match tips. He cut a slit on the side of each tip (using an X-ACTO knife) and
positioned the white foam tips over each matchstick.

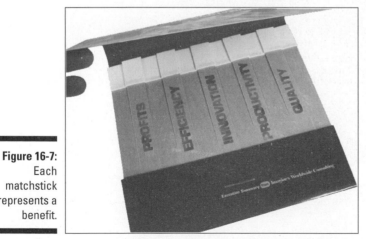

Photograph courtesy of Ray Anthony

The terms on the matchsticks represent the benefits the client receives
from working with Imaginex. The five words were created (with burn marks)
in Adobe Photoshop, printed on inkjet transfer paper in reverse type, and
ironed onto each matchstick. The removable proposal document is shown

in Figures 16-8 and 16-9. A real wooden fireplace match (coated at the tip to prevent accidental ignition) is used at the top of the booklet to decorate and further support the title theme of Striking Up Competitive Strategies, which is outlined on the inside of the proposal. The five main sections of the proposal, which match the benefits on the matches, are listed at the bottom.

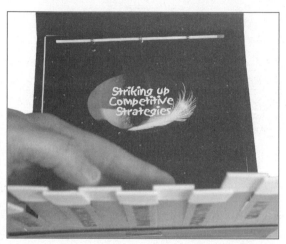

Figure 16-8:
Lifting the matches reveals the proposal.

Photograph courtesy of Ray Anthony

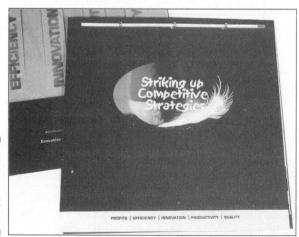

Figure 16-9:
The theme is carried throughout the proposal

Photograph courtesy of Ray Anthony

The proposal contains five tabbed sections, as shown in Figure 16-10, that expand upon the key benefits displayed on the matches. Each tab has an attention-grabbing key benefit statement written on it. For example, the first tab reads: Revenue Growth Between 35–40 Percent Over Five Year Period. These tabs reinforce the key points of the proposal.

Figure 16-10:
Each tab has a compelling benefit statement.

Photograph courtesy of Ray Anthony

Amazing-looking proposals cannot take the place of well-written, targeted content and valuable illustrations. You need both.

Revving up market share and profits

The sales vice president of Innovision Engineering wants to win over Acme Global Incorporated, an auto parts manufacturer and supplier, for a lucrative, long-term design, development, and manufacturing contract. Innovision develops two benefit-focused, attention-grabbing themes that drive the packaging and design of their spectacular proposal (see Figure 16-11):

Figure 16-11:
The proposal package mimics the industry.

Photograph courtesy of Ray Anthony

The proposal title and subtitle, *Powerful Engine of Growth* and *Supercharging Profitability,* set the persuasive tone. Around the metal bellyband of the proposal can (see Figure 16-12) are four simple descriptive terms, each beginning with the letter *S,* that characterize the solution Innovision proposes for Acme Global:

✔ **Stamina,** which the Innovision team has to ensure project success

✔ **Strength** of the solution for both the short and long term

✔ **Stability** of the partnership between Innovision and Acme

✔ **Significance** of this project on Acme's financial record

Figure 16-12:
Words on the bellyband reinforce the benefits.

Photograph courtesy of Ray Anthony

The sales VP found out that the key decision maker in the account loves to ride his Harley Davidson motorcycle. A detailed, die-cast model Harley engine (3½ inches high, bought in a toy store) as shown in Figure 16-13 was attached to the metal top of the proposal can with epoxy glue. Designer Leonard Broussard created the top and bottom of the proposal package by purchasing a chrome breather for an automobile air filter. For the bellyband (the part that encircles the metal can), he bought thin flashing metal at a building supplies store. He printed the graphic on glossy paper and glued it to the pre-cut metal sheet using double-sided adhesive sheets bought in an art supply store. The band was rolled to fit and the ends were glued together. Then, the bottom of the bellyband's edge was glued to the round bottom piece with epoxy. The design creates a sense of excitement, curiosity, and suspense for what's under the hood?

Figure 16-13:
Toy and modeling stores provide great sources for creative proposals.

Photograph courtesy of Ray Anthony

Removing the cover (see Figure 16-14) reveals four small die-cast race cars representing the four major characteristics of Innovision's solution for Acme — 1. Stamina; 2. Strength; 3. Stability; and. 4. Significance — that will drive Acme's success.

Figure 16-14:
Carrying the theme through the packaging and proposal reinforces the message.

Photograph courtesy of Ray Anthony

Each of the miniature cars is attached to the bottom round metal part by small pieces of Velcro. When the consultants from Innovision present the proposal, they thoroughly explain the important symbolism and specific meaning of all its elements to ensure understanding and appreciation of the messages.

The actual proposal document (see Figure 16-15) combines unconventional materials with attractive design elements resulting in a visual knockout. The front and back pieces are perforated steel. The leather spine was bought in a fabric store and then bound to the document using metal fasteners. The combination of metal sheets, leather, and steel fasteners gave the proposal (and its inside information) the rugged look of strength, power, and solidity befitting a durable, long-lasting engine-of-growth theme.

Figure 16-15:
The materials represent the strength and power of the proposal.

Photograph courtesy of Ray Anthony

Make sure all your proposals, handouts, and other giveaway materials and content are consistent in terms of creative design, branding, and signature.

The title and subtitle are printed over an image of a Harley engine on cover stock paper. Broussard came up with the gear concept (as in an engine transmission), which represents the two companies moving ahead with speed. Each gear represents a section of the proposal:

- Gear 1: Strength of the solution
- Gear 2: Stamina of the Innovision team
- Gear 3: Stability of the partnership
- Gear 4: Significance of this project

The designer printed the tabbed pages on glossy paper and mounted each on a thick stock using a double-sided adhesive paper. He then cut the rounded edges with an X-ACTO knife, as shown in Figure 16-16.

Few clients will ever experience this degree of creativity; the overall visual impact of the proposal packaging is stunning.

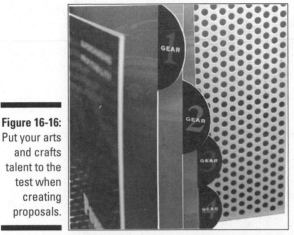

Figure 16-16:
Put your arts and crafts talent to the test when creating proposals.

Photograph courtesy of Ray Anthony

Painting a vision for bigger market share and profits

TRD Corporation does advanced materials research and development (R&D). Its CEO is changing the company's direction and focus to develop new, exciting products and markets. She seeks an outside firm to help communicate that change process along with the new vision and goals to her employees and industry. Fast Lane Communications is one of several firms to respond to a Request for Proposal (RFP) from TRD. The Fast Lane account team presents a blank metal gallon can (size of a typical can of paint) and a thick artist's brush to represent their theme, Painting Your Future, and they use a rich color design to symbolize the bright future for TRD as a result of working with Fast Lane. The "Can Concept" printed below the proposal title, as shown in Figure 16-17, refers to both the metal can and the can-do aspect of Fast Lane's solutions to exceed TRD's stated goals.

The covering on the can was printed on glossy paper. The can was sprayed with mounting adhesive and the paper was carefully positioned to fit around the can. Inside was a neatly rolled-up proposal, a miniature artist's color palette, a flash drive with client video testimonials, and multimedia stories of successful programs done by Fast Lane. "Color the deal done," the decision maker said after experiencing Fast Lane's impressive proposal and innovative presentation.

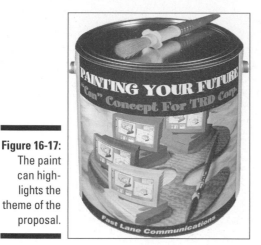

Figure 16-17:
The paint can highlights the theme of the proposal.

Photograph courtesy of Ray Anthony

Creating proposal cans and boxes

You don't have to spend lots of time and money developing imaginative designs for your innovative proposal packaging. On Amazon.com, in arts and crafts, hobby, art supplies, and novelty stores such as Michaels, Hobby Lobby, and Hallmark, you can purchase items (many theme-based) like those shown in Figure 16-18 and print a customized proposal to place inside or otherwise attach to your proposal package. The Container Store is a good source for all kinds of paper, metal, plastic, and glass boxes and containers to develop into ingenious proposal packaging.

Figure 16-18:
Look for metaphors that work with your proposal's theme or the potential client's product.

Photograph courtesy of Ray Anthony

You don't have to spend lots of time and money to differentiate yourself from competitors who write and design proposals in predictable, conventional, and dull ways — you do need to be creative.

Research your audience well in order to write and design a proposal specific to their needs, wants, and management style. Some prefer straight information in a traditional three-ring binder or spiral-bound booklet that contains just the plain facts without frills or fancy stuff.

Checking out other examples

There is no speed limit on the highway of creativity. Some unconventional proposal designs don't need a lot of explanation. Figures 16-19 and 16-20 show a proposal for a beach-themed sales conference for a major company using a real wood model surfboard. The designer, Vyto Petrauskas, has created numerous radically cool proposal designs for other big clients that helped to win large deals.

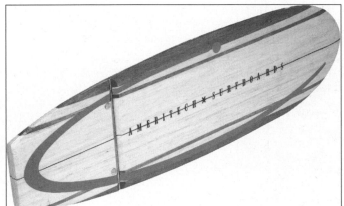

Figure 16-19: Look for proposal props that tie in to the project theme.

Photograph courtesy of Ray Anthony

Figure 16-21 displays a proposal from a video production company to a large client. The film-themed decorations, as shown in Figure 16-22, were purchased from Hobby Lobby and glued onto the cover to give it a 3-D look.

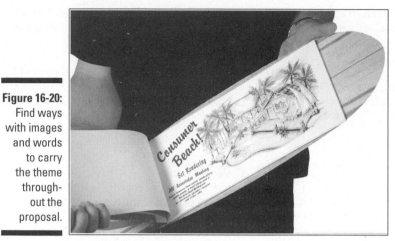

Photograph courtesy of Ray Anthony

Figure 16-20:
Find ways with images and words to carry the theme throughout the proposal.

Figure 16-21:
The 3-D approach works well for the film industry.

Photograph courtesy of Ray Anthony

Finally, a construction company (see Chapter 11 for the detailed scenario and other photos) wanted to go overboard to win a significant lakefront development deal where their bid was the highest. Combined with a spectacular innovative presentation, they handed out a surprise offer in this proposal as an incentive they hoped the customer could not refuse. (It worked!) The 14-page proposal shown in Figures 16-23 and 16-24 uses Plexiglas, parts from an Erector Set, metal hinges, and a detailed die-cast, scale model of a piece of construction equipment. They handed this proposal book out inside a model dump truck.

Figure 16-22: Keep your eye out for miniature objects that can add dimension to your proposals.

Photograph courtesy of Ray Anthony

Figure 16-23: Mixed materials were used for a proposal from a construction company.

Photograph courtesy of Ray Anthony

Figure 16-24:
The construction theme continues in the written proposal.

Photograph courtesy of Ray Anthony

Adding multimedia

Apple's iBook app is one of many that allows you to create a multimedia proposal with text, sound, narration, 3-D, and 2-D animation in the event you want to show the detailed operation of products, animated flow charts that show implantation and milestones, and so much more. In addition, you can create an authored DVD or flash drive with sections such as

- Text that describes and explains your proposal
- Video from your senior executives giving their commitment statements
- Demonstrations of your product
- Brochures and specification sheets and any other information that helps the decision makers choose your proposal.

To see some examples of multimedia proposals, check out these links: http://imvideobrochure.com and http://www.videoplusprint.com/43-inch.

Giving Out Effective Presentation Handouts

Presentations should focus on a crisp overview, key points, main messages, and critical information, which means they aren't always the most effective format for communicating dense information or large quantities of data.

Handouts, or leave behinds, allow you to provide detailed information that you can't effectively put on a slide, such as complicated flowcharts, diagrams, tables, or illustrations that would otherwise show poorly on a monitor or projection screen. Handouts also let your audience review and digest the information you presented and compare it to other proposals they're considering.

Innovative presentations deserve to have matching, well-designed, and valuable handouts that complement and enhance your spoken presentation. Although not every presentation needs handouts, it's often a good idea to give the audience a one-to-two page executive summary of all your important points to motivate your audience to accept your call to action.

Prepare your handouts in plenty of time and don't scrimp on quality.

Usually financial, technical, engineering, scientific-related, or other complex presentations benefit most from handouts that contain more comprehensive, in-depth information, especially if you're giving a working presentation that requires discussion and feedback either during or after the meeting in order to make an informed decision. Sales presentations that have product specification sheets, contractual information, and detailed brochures along with DVDs, flash drives, or links to videos can help a potential buyer make a decision.

If you're in doubt as to whether handouts are necessary, consider the following advantages:

- ✔ Your presentation can be lean in terms of detailed data you can appropriately place in your handout. No need to dump data on your audience and rush through your talk.

- ✔ People appreciate an attractive, useful handout that makes a presentation memorable.

- ✔ Knowing that specific information is available in handouts, the audience can focus their full attention on you instead of on taking notes.

- ✔ Handouts provide a source for repeated reference and decision making.

- ✔ You don't have to sweat forgetting some details in your talk because your handout will cover it.

- ✔ Attractive, imaginatively-designed handouts enhance your professionalism and credibility.

Make your handouts consistent with the graphic design, level of creativity, story line, information style, and branding or theme of your oral presentation.

Designing and using handouts

Keep these points in mind when planning and creating your handouts and use them appropriately:

- ✔ Determine the number of handouts (including DVDs, props, gifts, prototypes and others) you need and always bring an extra ten percent for unexpected attendees or those who want to take extras back to others in their organization.

- ✔ Consider which information, illustrations, diagrams, videos, and animations, as well as the level of detail and focus the audience needs, wants, and will use to make decisions or commitments or respond positively to your call to action.

- ✔ Don't crowd printed handouts with small text and busy charts or diagrams; white space and a studied layout encourage reading and viewing.

- ✔ Laminate handout pages that will have repeated reference and heavy use after your presentation.

- ✔ Consider dividing a handout into meaningful and easy-to-reference tabbed sections such as: Summary, Priority Information, Further Reading, Illustrations, Diagrams, Photos and Charts, and Appendix.

- ✔ Make your handout independent, self-evident, and easily understood by anyone who didn't attend your presentation.

- ✔ Make handouts available after your presentation, unless the audience needs to refer to them during your presentation. Distributing handouts before your presentation tempts some to look at them — or leave before you finish — even if you're compelling and captivating.

- ✔ Do the eco thing and put a variety of handouts, documents, videos, illustrations, charts, or animations on your website instead of giving copies of everything at your presentation.

- ✔ Put contact information on your handouts.

 For training sessions, public seminars or workshops, or even paid keynote speeches, a small, useful gift or fun giveaway adds meaning to your presentation and highlights your brand or theme. See Office Playground (www. officeplayground.com), 4imprint (www.4imprint.com), Branders (www.branders.com), and Crestline (www.crestline.com) for examples and ideas.

Adding originality, punch, and creativity to your handouts

Be creative in the design and packaging of your handouts. For the cover, choose the typeface, words, and images with the same consideration you use for visuals that accompany your presentations. Instead of always using letter-size (8½-x-11 inches) paper in portrait (vertical) format, consider legal size (8½-x-14 inches) paper in landscape (horizontal) format with a two-column layout and relevant sidebars, illustrations, photos, cartoons, or other design elements that lend eye appeal, interest, and value, and break up the text.

Print in color or high-quality black-and-white on well-chosen paper stock — you may be surprised at how the paper's weight and finish changes the impact and style of your proposal and handouts. For special, important presentations, such as trying to close a big deal or otherwise impress the audience, use your imagination and think about hiring a professional graphic designer — investing in such services often pays off in the end.

Chapter 17

Going Beyond Bullets on Slides

*A*n innovative presentation combines a well-planned, audience-focused message with compelling language and materials such as slides, props, and demonstrations that support the message. However, when the supporting material overwhelms the spoken material, it becomes a distraction rather than a support.

Consider the theater: Well-spoken monologues with few visual props can be more engaging, even thrilling, than grand productions with acrobats, musical scores, and colorful costumes and sets. The actors' skills in delivering their lines — the message — matters more than the supporting visuals. In other words, no amount of fancy staging can make up for a poorly written and executed script, and sometimes that fancy staging can even be the cause of a flop. Likewise, a simple, well-spoken presentation can have more impact than an over-produced event.

You must seek the proper balance between message and material. Throughout this book we present — pardon the pun — many ideas for building props and using special effects that complement your message and reinforce the solutions you offer to your audience. In this chapter and the next, we turn our focus to technology. Here we discuss slide design software and introduce you to apps that organize slides in ways that differ from PowerPoint, which you're probably familiar with. Many of them work on both Windows and Mac platforms and have iOS and Android counterparts so you can interact with your presentation from a computer or a portable device such as a tablet or even a smartphone.

We assume you use a computer to create and project your presentation. When we talk about *slides,* we intend those electronic visuals that replaced 35 millimeter slides many years ago.

In this chapter, we briefly explain the differences between linear and nonlinear presentations and consider the circumstances in which you might choose one over the other, and then we discuss the various apps themselves. To save you some time, we sifted and sorted through the apps in the Apple App Store (www.apple.com/itunes) and Microsoft's Windows Store (http://windows.microsoft.com/en-us/windows-8/apps) and here we recommend those that we found stable and easy to use and that are also in good standing with tech reviewers and the general public — people like you who make presentations.

Thinking in a Nonlinear Way

For years, constrained by production time and costs and the available technology, presentations consisted of slides projected on a screen, one at a time, one after another — just writing that makes us yawn; we hope you didn't fall asleep reading it! If you wanted to interact with your slides — circle a figure to emphasize a point, for example — you might have used transparencies and an overhead projector instead of slides. Changing the order of your slides at the last minute was clumsy at best, a disaster at worst.

The advent of computer-based slide projection changed the game. Usually, a simple click and drag changes the order of your slides. But what if you want to change the order during the presentation to respond immediately to a question or concern? Instead of saying, "I'll address that point in about ten minutes," you can switch gears and say, "Given your immediate problem with leaks, let me show you our leak-proof gaskets and towards the end of my presentation I'll review our spigots and spouts."

There are times when a request for more, or different, information is inappropriate, and you should continue with your planned presentation. Having the option is great; using it is your call.

Today, because slides are virtual and not physical, most linear and nonlinear apps let you change the order. The visuals between the two differ:

✔ **Linear:** Apps such as PowerPoint and Keynote mimic traditional slide design and layout, creating *decks* — a sequence of slides — and incorporating features like *links,* which are text or graphics that, when clicked, take you to a different location within the deck. You can easily change the order of your slides before you begin your presentation but once you start, you must click through a slide to skip over it or open the slide browser to move to a different spot, which is difficult to pull off smoothly.

✔ **Nonlinear:** Apps such as Prezi and iPresent fall into the nonlinear category. Think of Prezi as a giant white board that you zoom in and out of, moving from one area to another. For example, clicking the sketch in the lower left corner may take you to the upper middle zone and when you zoom out, you see both areas. iPresent groups similar decks together, and you can jump between them to meet the needs of your audience. You can have a deck for each product line and a price list within each deck plus a deck of price lists.

Preparing for every possible situation

The beauty of nonlinear presentations is that you're ready for any situation. In a conference setting, if the speaker before you runs over, quickly jot down the most salient points of your presentation (so you have a rough outline of your revised-on-the-spot presentation) and then jump from one topic to the next without skipping slides or fumbling with the slide browser as you would have to do in a linear presentation.

As we mention in other chapters, when creating your presentation, plan to end at least five minutes earlier than the allotted time. This practice not only earns you points with your audience, it also saves you from scrambling to cut out parts of your presentation at the last minute.

Responding to specific requests

In both linear and nonlinear presentations, you can prepare specific information in the form of charts, videos, or diagrams that support an anecdote. If, during the course of your presentation or the Q & A (question and answer) time, an audience member asks for more details or something that's related but wasn't specifically covered in your presentation, with a simple click, you can open the visual that explains or responds to the question.

We can think of two scenarios that work particularly well with nonlinear presentations — you can probably come up with others:

✔ **Speaking on a stage in front of a group in a theater-style setting** (something like a TED talk): More than likely members of the audience have smartphones and tablets with them and as soon as their attention wanders, out come the devices. As you look out at your audience, you see a faint glow on their faces. You can hope they're taking notes but more than likely they're checking e-mail or tweeting about how bored they are. With a nonlinear presentation, the screen displays interesting, interactive images and words — even short videos — instead of lines of text in a box.

✔ **Introducing your product to a small (6-to-8 person) group:** If you're presenting your products and solutions to a potential client, you can begin your presentation by showing a visual that lists your products in the order you plan to discuss them. For example, "I'd like to introduce you to our different lines of pipe. I usually describe our unique manufacturing process that avoids creating heavy metal deposits, then I discuss the various sizes available in copper, aluminum, and steel, and lastly I talk about our custom options. However, if there's an issue that's forefront in your mind, I can address that first." At which point, your listeners can say "We invited you because we already know about your manufacturing process. We need 10,000 L-shaped copper pieces in ¾-inch diameter. Can you make those and how much will they cost?"

We can't emphasize enough the importance of practice and rehearsal. If you know your topic inside and out, even if you memorized your presentation, you'll be able to respond quickly and efficiently to any situation.

Choosing the Best App for You

When you begin developing your presentation, you consider your audience and how your product, service, or message solves their problem. You consider tactics to use and language or props that will keep your audience's attention. You also decide which medium to use to present your case. Different situations often call for different app solutions. Even if you use traditional slides created in PowerPoint — which may be the best option — you can add a few innovative, non-traditional techniques.

Working online or offline

The almost omnipresent Internet makes keeping your presentation online a viable option. If you work as part of a team, each member accesses the same presentation, reducing the risk of misinforming potential clients. And, changes can be made in the home office, and then all team members have the latest version.

We spotted a presentations software trend that we're keeping our eyes on. Several beta sites for online presentation software have popped up on the Internet. With each, you create an account and create your presentation in the online app, then save your presentation to the app-related server. The advantage is that you can access your presentation from any device or computer with an Internet connection; the disadvantage is that you must have an Internet connection to create, edit, and view your presentation. The free versions usually have the company's watermark or logo somewhere on the screen; paid versions tend to eliminate the company advertising.

Online presentation sites we found include

- ✓ **emaze** (`www.emaze.com`) offers templates with text and graphic place-holders that you replace with your own information. The online emaze software then animates your presentation. (This is beta software at the time of writing.)

- ✓ **PowToon** (`www.powtoon.com`) makes animated videos for up to five minutes duration, probably not enough for your presentation but great for a link within a presentation or to post on a website or kiosk. (This is beta software at the time of writing.)

- ✓ **Slides** (`http://slid.es`) offers templates, themes, and transitions to create slide decks, but you don't have to install any software. With the paid version, you can download your presentation to play it offline.

- ✓ **Swipe** (`http://beta.swipe.to`) lets you drag and drop just about any kind of image, video, or text file and share it on any device. You can also write your presentation in Markdown, a text formatting syntax that Swipe uses to convert your commands into a colorful presentation.

Incorporating existing materials

If you've been working at the same company or presenting in the same field for several years or more, chances are you use the same slides as a starting point and then build on them — there's no sense rebuilding the wheel, right? Well . . . in some cases, yes. Apps such as SlideShark and Presentation Note take your existing presentation and transform it, adding styles and functions in the process, and then let you project your presentation from your iPad.

Reviewing available app options

With dozens of apps to choose from, keep the answers to the following questions in mind as you decide which app best meets your presentation needs:

- ✓ What device or operating system do you plan to use: Mac, Windows, iPad, Android tablet, or a combination?

- ✓ Will you share your presentation with others, and if so, will they use devices with the same operating system as yours?

✔ What kind of presenter's tools are helpful for you? Options include timers that show time elapsed for both the presentation and current slide, a touch screen or mouse-controlled laser pointer, a highlighter or pen that writes on your virtual slide, and a white board option that appears in place of your slide so you can draw explanations.

✔ Will your message come across stronger in a slide presentation, perhaps in conjunction with physical props and a video, or as a white board presentation that moves from one corner to another and then reveals the whole picture?

✔ Will your audience respond best to a traditional slide presentation or would a free-flowing, nonlinear presentation better keep their attention?

✔ Do you want to give the general public access to your presentation on websites other than your own?

Another question is whether your presentation will be viewed without a presenter, for example on a website or a kiosk in your office lobby.

PowerPoint and Keynote, although traditional slide design apps, have added a lot of flexibility and modernity with each new release. Nonetheless, in the next sections we present some other choices for presentation apps.

We talk about the hardware requirements and options of presentations in Chapter 18, but we indicate the device and operating system the app supports next to the name of each app.

You may notice that we don't mention PowerPoint, the stalwart standby for presentation preparation on both Windows and Mac computers. Many of the apps discussed here let you import PowerPoint files so you don't have to start from scratch — although sometimes that's the best thing to do.

Prezi (Mac, Windows XP, Vista, 7, or 8 Classic, iPad)

www.prezi.com (Free to $159/year depending on services)

There's nothing linear about Prezi, in fact, it takes a little while to get used to making a Prezi presentation. If traditional presentations are like putting a train on the track, one car hooked up and pulling another along, Prezi presentations are like making a painting — a cloud here, a tree over there, a river flowing through the woods — and you step back to see the whole complete picture. And the farther you step back, the more of the picture you see.

Unless you spring for the Pro version, you work online. The desktop version offers an easy way to create this interactive, mind-map style presentation, whereas the iPad version is limited to using text and photos.

The best way to take full advantage of Prezi is to create presentations on your computer and then access them through the cloud service. Like many of the other cloud-based presentation services, you have to create an account, or you can use your Facebook username and password if you prefer.

The free version allows you to create presentations stored on Prezi's server and available to the general public. The fee-based levels let you use Prezi's cloud service and maintain your presentations private or shared only with those to whom you give access.

In the desktop version, you choose a template that's a metaphor for your presentation, then choose a color and typeface theme from the theme chooser. Frame by frame you build your presentation. The frames link from one to the next although you move left, right, up, down, or zigzag depending on how those frames are arranged on the workspace. Zoom in or out to see details or a bird's-eye view of the whole. For example, you can move from one idea to another in a circle and then zoom out to see all the linked parts. You can also import PowerPoint slides. You can conduct a meeting in real-time with up to ten remote sites looking at the same presentation.

Aside from the original, freeform design, one of the biggest advantages of Prezi is the number of training and learning resources available on the website. You can even sign up for a webinar to learn how to use Prezi.

Doceri (iPad, Mac)

doceri.com (Free; Desktop version, free trial. $30 single site license. Stylus and watermark replacement available for purchase.)

We're impressed with Doceri's fun, creative user interface. We can imagine this as a great resource in a classroom setting — either educational or corporate. You can build an interactive presentation ahead of time or, because Doceri is so simple to use, your iPad or computer becomes an electronic blackboard (or white- or greenboard if you prefer) and you write on the board as you talk, illustrating your point or writing questions and comments from the audience, while facing them. Doceri isn't limited to text — you can also build graphs and charts and incorporate photos.

The proprietary timeline tool lets you move back and forth in the presentation by sliding your finger along the timeline. Instead of tapping or clicking Undo 15 times or erasing, simply drag the slider back to the point where you want to start over. The timeline tool makes creating screencasts much easier than traditional screencast apps. First, create your presentation and then record your voiceover separately. Move the timeline tool to the point where you want to insert the voiceover, and if you make a mistake, re-record pieces one at a time rather than starting from the beginning, which is much easier than using a traditional audio-video editor.

You can also share your presentation or screencast as a file or upload to YouTube. For example, if there were exercises or homework problems during your presentation or workshop, students can download them on their computers or iPads or watch the presentation on YouTube at home and work on them.

With Doceri Desktop you display your presentation on your computer screen (or projection screen if your computer is attached to a projection system) while managing it from your iPad. Doceri also reads PowerPoint and Keynote presentations, and you can write on top of them with Doceri's different pen tools. If you have a classroom setup with a computer at each desk, put Doceri Desktop on each one and your students or participants see your presentation on the screen, while you see the presentation along with the presentation tools on your iPad or computer.

There's a one-time site license fee associated with Doceri Desktop (after the initial trial period) but if you find yourself using Doceri, Doceri Desktop is probably a good addition to the package.

Keynote (Mac, iPad, iPhone; Windows on iCloud.com)

www.apple.com ($9.99 for iOS, $19.99 for Macs [free with Macs or iOS devices purchased after October 2013])

Keynote, Apple's answer to Microsoft's PowerPoint, offers strong presentation creation and editing tools, and some spiffy templates to give you a head start. (You can also purchase templates from third-party developers to give you a plethora of options.) The simplicity of adding charts, graphs, and animation belies the sophisticated results you can obtain. Keynote can also import most PowerPoint presentations with little or no loss of functionality. And, of course, you can create an Apple-style presentation with just a few words on a solid background — no bullets, no frames, no gradations.

You can start with a Keynote template and then modify it to create your own master slides and templates. By taking some time at the beginning, this feature lets you design custom templates that you then use for all your presentations, creating a cohesive identity for your products and services. With Keynote's sharing capabilities, your whole team can access the templates or prepared presentations so your customers receive a consistent message.

If you use both Windows and a Mac, you can access and edit your Keynote presentations at iCloud.com from Windows. You can also share your Keynote presentation with others by providing a link to it on iCloud.com or saving it as a movie and uploading it to YouTube. Add a voiceover to create a self-running presentation for your website or kiosk.

An honorable mention goes to Sparkol VideoScribe (www.sparkol.com). Although not a standalone presentation app, VideoScribe helps you create animated drawing videos — sometimes called *whiteboard animation* or *fast drawing* — even if you don't know how to draw. Download the free app for a seven-day trial. Choose from the font, image, and music libraries to create an instructional video that adds spark to your presentation or website.

SlideShark (iPad, iPhone)

www.slideshark.com (Free with fee-based upgrade options)

If you create your presentations in PowerPoint on your computer but then want to show the presentation directly on your iPad or projected from it, or if you share your presentations with a staff of people, SlideShark is a good choice. The free version offers 50 MB (megabytes) of storage, which increases each time a friend you recommend signs up, or you can purchase a gigabyte of storage for $8 per month. The team version offers five gigabytes of storage for $12.50 per user per month. Whichever offer you choose, you must set up a username and password because your presentations pass through the secure SlideShark server when being up- and downloaded from one device to another.

After creating an account, you upload your presentation to the secure SlideShark server. SlideShark converts your PowerPoint file to a SlideShark format which you then download to your iPad. If you store your presentations on a cloud service such as Dropbox, Google Docs, Box, Syncplicity, or SkyDrive, you can download those presentations into SlideShark on your iPad from within the app. You can also save a PowerPoint presentation to SlideShark from an e-mail, which means others can send presentations to you.

From the SlideShark app, simply Download and then tap Play. Swiping left and right moves back and forth between slides, while swiping up or down displays and hides the whole set of slides when viewing your slideshow in full-screen mode.

SlideShark offers several presenter's view options, which you can choose from when your iPad is, or isn't, connected to a projector. You can view your notes, all the slides in your presentation, and a nifty feature that we really like are two timers: one that shows the overall elapsed time of the presentation and one that shows how long the current slide has been open. Being able to use these tools when your iPad isn't connected to a projector is handy for practicing your presentation. A built-in laser pointer appears when you press and hold on the screen, although we find this feature a bit clumsy because the red laser dot is directly below your finger so you can't see it on your iPad screen and just have to trust that it's there.

SlideShark lets you share a link to your presentation so it can be watched on-demand online. Built-in analytics track who's watching and where. Much like tracking website hits or blog peaks, SlideShark's analytics help you measure your client base and give you insight into the effectiveness of your presentation.

The team version of SlideShark is a good option if you have multiple people giving the same presentation. Each member has a personal folder while an administrator manages shared content. Again, built-in analytics show which presentations are being used most.

SlideShark also maintains hyperlinks embedded in your PowerPoint presentations. Websites, including links to YouTube video, open in Safari and a simple navigation tool takes you back to the presentation. Hyperlinks can also reference documents stored in any of the supported cloud storage services so your linear PowerPoint presentation can respond to nonlinear requests.

iPresent (iPad)

`www.ipresent.com` (Free one-month trial, $21 to $30 per month/per user subscriptions)

iPresent takes sales presentation software to a new level. It combines output from traditional presentation media such as PowerPoint slides, PDF files, and video, and lets you create gesture-driven menus on an iPad to navigate seamlessly between them. This way, you get the best of both worlds — professionally designed interfaces that make it really easy to tell a story, combined with a custom look achieved in just a few minutes.

iPresent encourages you to break up your content into many different areas, any of which you can navigate to quickly and easily. The presenter engages the audience, especially in smaller meetings, and the audience can ask questions, seek clarification, and drill into details on an interesting point. You customize your presentation so that you talk about a specific variant in more detail depending on the questions the audience raises. iPresent holds a collection of information from which you pick and choose appropriately, leaving your audience with specific, relevant information. Each presentation, while starting from a common point of departure, evolves into a personalized interaction between presenter and audience, resulting in an informed and satisfied audience.

After you set up your account, you can begin building your presentation. iPresent refers to the visuals that accompany your presentation as a Content Set and the Content Set comprises resources, which are the document, slide, spreadsheet, graphic, audio, and video files. iPresent offers menu templates in several different styles: carousel, dock, and scrolling tiles among them. You choose a menu design that correlates with your business message and then add your logo, color scheme, and background image. The carousel menu works best for about six headings, while others, such as the tile menu, provide space for larger quantities.

In a nutshell, first you upload resources (your media files) or a URL to your iPresent account, you then build the Content Set using one of the menu templates, and lastly link resources to the menu items.

You, or members of your sales team, download iPresent to your iPad and then log in to the corporate account. The content sets appear and you tap it to download. Once the content set is on your iPad, you can view it directly on the iPad screen or connect your iPad to a projection system.

Presentation Note (iPad)

www.doxout.com (Free [lite version] or $4.99 [full version])

We like Presentation Note because you don't have to create a username and password since your files, although processed by Presentation Note, are stored locally. You can transfer PowerPoint or PDF files through various cloud services, and icons on the Presentation Note home screen automatically connect the app to your preferred cloud service. Or, as long as your computer and your iPad are on the same network, you can log in to the Presentation Note server from your browser and upload files directly from your computer, then download them directly to your iPad. The icon-based user interface is simple and easy to use.

Presentation Note assumes you'll connect your iPad to a projection system so the presentation controls — which include a slide counter, timer, laser, and slide advance/back buttons — reside at the top of the screen at all times. A white board option lets you explain something from your iPad rather than awkwardly moving between a physical white board or flip chart.

We appreciate the enhanced laser pointer options: Your finger can be a dot or tail, which are active only while your finger is on the screen, or you can use your finger to underline things or draw arrows or circles that remain on the screen until you move to the next slide. The ability to use your iPhone as a remote control with the free Presentation Note Remote app is a handy addition.

If you use your iPhone as a remote control with this app or any other, make sure you test it well as some users have reported unstable Bluetooth connections between the iPhone and iPad.

If you're new to making presentations from your iPad and don't want to spend a lot of money nor create a user account, Presentation Note is a good place to begin.

Perspective (iPad)

`http://pixxa.com/perspective` (Free app, fee-based publishing)

Perspective turns your data into a story by adding color and animation to your charts and graphs. You can build your presentation, which Perspective calls your *story,* directly on your iPad.

The user interface is clean and takes full advantage of iPad technology; rather than trying to re-create how things are done on a computer, Perspective's tools are original yet intuitive. To create your story, tap the Add button and then select a scene that fits the information you want to share. To add graphics or images, Perspective accesses Photos on your iPad or you can conduct an image search. The editing options are straightforward, allowing you to change the layout and alignment of the elements on each scene. You can integrate existing data from Excel, CSV, or PDF files and add a voiceover so viewers can listen to your story even when you can't be there to tell it.

Great stories come with a price but if you consider that you're buying graphic design and animation, it costs less than hiring a designer. You can purchase one style graph at a time for $9.99 or subscribe to the Pro edition for $49.99 per year, which we think is a steal considering the possibilities.

Slide Deck (Windows 8)

`http://dwcares.com/slide-deck-app` (Free)

Slide Deck's simplicity is its strength. Although it includes only nine templates, the colors and layouts help you create contemporary, effective presentations that can be shared across all your Windows devices. You can present directly from Slide Deck with touch-screen commands.

Presentation Next (Windows 8)

`www.presentationnext.net` (Free trial, $19.99)

With Presentation Next you can create either linear or nonlinear presentations, which can be viewed on multiple platforms including Mac, Linux, iOS, and Android. If you choose to create a linear presentation, you can use one of the included templates or design your own. Included clip art and images liven nonlinear presentations, or you can draw images with Presentation Next's drawing tools. You can also create charts in Presentation Next. You can insert your own images or clip art and apply filters and effects to them. If you use only one presentation app for your Windows 8 device, Presentation Next offers many options.

Chapter 18

Selecting and Setting Up Hardware

*H*ardware with the latest technology is an important component for giving your innovative presentation. The right equipment, used effectively and creatively, gives your presentation a decided edge over others.

In this chapter, we take you through different scenarios, from the simplest one-on-one presentation to complex and advanced auditorium keynote speeches, and discuss the equipment and hardware options that best meet the needs of each. We mention a few product names but for the most part (because new products come on the market so quickly), we explain the options you need to consider so you can make informed buying or renting decisions.

Determining the Best Equipment Setup for the Situation

In its simplest form, your voice and body are all you need to make a presentation, but certain accessories can enhance your presentation.

If you make infrequent presentations, renting equipment may be the best solution for you. Renting gives you access to the newest models and you don't have to worry about maintenance. On the other hand, if you make your living making presentations — whether you're a motivational speaker or hold client meetings in your onsite conference room — consider investing in the best equipment your budget allows so you can create a dependable setup that you're familiar with. The following sections describe seven common presentation scenarios and tools useful in each situation.

Presenting one-on-one

When you present to one person, you have the opportunity to be conversational and dedicate your presentation to the specific needs and requests of your one-person audience. Nonetheless, your visuals should be easy to see. When presenting in your office, project your visuals on a large monitor in a small meeting room if possible. If your meeting is in a café or another office, you can display the visuals on a tablet or laptop.

We like Apple's iPad Air with Retina display, which offers crisp, clear colors and images. If your budget permits, a pico (sometimes called micro or pocket) projector connected to your laptop or tablet or smartphone projects the image on a screen; a smooth, blank wall; or even the surface of a closed airplane tray table.

Many variables come into play when choosing a projector. You want to consider the number of lumens, which impact the brightness of your images. For a basic slide presentation, 50 lumens is the absolute minimum but if you have video, you want at least 200. A pico projector is smaller and lighter than a pocket projector and uses LED (light-emitting diode) or laser light, which means you don't have to replace the lamp, however, it has fewer lumens — anywhere from 15 to 85 lumens in a pico projector and from 100 to 500 for a pocket projector. Keep in mind that the farther you project an image from these tiny projectors, the more washed out and dim the image appears. These projectors have very limited use for up-close viewing only.

Many pico projectors, in addition to connecting to tablets and smartphones, have built-in memory or capability to read USB flash drives so you don't have to bring a laptop with you. Because of the higher lumens, pocket projectors have lamps that must be replaced and fans to keep the projector cool, so you want to consider the noise level of the fan as well. You should also consider the resolution and aspect and contrast ratios when making your choice.

We use www.projectorcentral.com to compare projectors. In addition to product reviews, you can find used projectors from third-party sellers on this site.

When choosing a portable projector to use in a medium-size room that accommodates 20 to 50 people, look for much higher lumens, at least 2,000, if not more. For larger venues with 100 to 300 people, a projector with at least 4,500 lumens is recommended. Screen size determines the number of lumens needed to create a good image: The larger the screen the higher the lumens number should be. In addition, buy or rent a projector with a resolution that matches the resolution of the image you're projecting. The higher the resolution, the crisper and sharper your text and images. The typical projector resolutions in pixels — with their designations:

- XGA: 1024x768
- SXGA: 1280x1024
- WXGA: 1280x768
- UXGA: 1600x1200
- 2K (HD): 2048x1080
- 4K (Ultra HD): 4096x3072

Consider using a projector with a zoom lens to help create the right size image at various distances, and look at projectors with ultra short throw lenses that enable you to project large images even in a small room.

Presenting to a small group in your conference room

After you invest in setting up a small projection system in a conference room, you find many opportunities to use it. Aside from client and project staff meetings, you can plan team-building and social events such as PlayStation competitions or movie lunch hour. Having your own state-of-the-art projection system also provides a fabulous location for rehearsing presentations that you eventually give on- or off-site.

Consider installing some or all of the following equipment in your conference room, choosing models that best fit the room size. Multi-functional items can be a good way to get the most for your investment.

- **Projector and screen:** Consider tabletop or ceiling mount. In either case, you want to place the projector in the best position for projecting to the screen and create an easily accessible location, or a mobile lectern, where you can connect a desktop computer, laptop, or tablet.

- ✔ **Large-screen monitor:** With a large screen (50 to 80 inches), you can eliminate the projector and connect your laptop or tablet directly to the monitor with a wired or wi-fi connection.

  If a great display is critical to your client presentations, you may want to install a video wall, a 3-D-enabled monitor, or a 4K monitor.

- ✔ **Interactive whiteboard:** After writing on the whiteboard, you can scan the information and send it to a computer as an electronic file or print it from the whiteboard or to a networked printer. An alternative is to connect a tablet to the projection system and use it as your electronic whiteboard. Many tablet apps offer this option. You can then save and distribute notes to meeting attendees.

- ✔ **Speakers for audio playback:** Although most projectors and computers have built-in speakers, the volume and broadcast quality is limited. You can consider installing a home theater-style audio setup or a portable Bluetooth speaker such as Philips Fidelio P9.

Bluetooth and wi-fi are two wireless connectivity technologies that link devices, for example a portable speaker to your computer. Bluetooth has a shorter range than wi-fi and although some devices have built-in capabilities for both, others have only one. Bluetooth is often easier to set up but the limited range can make it a less favorable choice. Wi-fi, on the other hand, can be a bit more complicated to set up because of compatibility issues but offers better fidelity and a greater distance between devices.

- ✔ **Microphone:** In a small conference room that can host 12 to 16 people at a conference table, your regular speaking volume is probably loud enough for everyone to hear, but in a larger room, a microphone may be one of the wisest investments you make. Depending on the type of presentations you plan to make, you may want to add a podium speakers can stand behind.

- ✔ **Video capture for video conferences or demonstrations:** If you work with offsite clients and colleagues, video conferences really can be the next best thing to being there. The webcam on your computer or tablet may be enough for you and one other person, but a video camera with built-in speakers such as Logitech's Conference Cam lets people on the other end see the whole group in your conference room.

  The better the lighting, the clearer your broadcast image, so do what you can to keep the room well-lit.

- ✔ **Flip chart:** Sometimes pen and paper provides the simplest solution to brainstorming or demonstrating a point.

Presenting to a small group in their conference room

When you go to another location to make a presentation, find out ahead of time what type of equipment they have and whether it meets the requirements for your presentation. Most companies have some sort of projector and screen, but bring the necessary cables to connect your laptop or tablet. You should also put a copy of your presentation on a flash drive or external hard drive in case you have no choice but to use their computer.

A great alternative is to use an online presentation site such as SlideShark (see Chapter 17 for details) and then from any computer with an Internet connection, you can sign in to your account and project your presentation.

Presenting at a training session

Given the sales numbers for handheld devices such as smartphones and tablets, it's highly likely that attendees at a training session will have, and bring, such a device. You can use this to your advantage by incorporating surveys, interactive activities, and quizzes into your training presentations. Before the event, remind attendees to bring their tablets and/or smartphones and if you'll be using a particular interactive app, provide a link to download an app like FeedbackFruits (`https://secure.feedbackfruits.com`) ahead of time.

If you run frequent training sessions, we recommend the Wireless Interactive Presentation Gateway from wePresent (`www.wepresentus.com`). The unit broadcasts a wi-fi signal that allows connections from up to 64 users at once with 4 of them able to present simultaneously in up to full 1080p high-definition resolution. The Gateway supports Windows, Mac, iOS, and Android computers and devices. The Sidepad feature allows the presenter to control the projecting computer via remote desktop using the touch screen input capabilities of an iPad, iPhone, or Android tablet or phone. The unit can also be setup to be its own wireless access point and is equipped with full WPA2-PSK security standards and full Enterprise Level Encryption for those with security concerns. Two models are available, the WiPG-1000 and the WiPG-1500, which has an integrated, interactive whiteboard/touch-screen display and the ability to completely customize the splash screen that shows when you start the device with your personal or professional branding.

Presenting at a conference or as part of a panel

When you're invited to speak at a conference or participate in a panel session, the meeting planner usually tells you how to provide your presentation materials ahead of time, such as on a flash drive the night before or uploaded to a remote storage site. To avoid technical difficulties, each speaker's presentation is copied onto a main computer connected to the projection system. A dedicated audio/visual technician makes sure the files work properly, and you need only show up at your designated time and click the Play button to begin your show.

If you have special effects you want to include, such as a video or interactive activity, talk to the planner well ahead of time to find out whether your technical requirements can be accommodated. Sometimes you can bring your own laptop but usually planners don't like this option because connecting and disconnecting computers between presentations wastes time — not to mention the high risk of technical difficulties.

Often, an abstract of your talk will be published in the conference guide and the visuals themselves may be distributed online or on a DVD to attendees after the event is finished.

Presenting a keynote speech

If you're invited to make a keynote speech, you probably have some flexibility to ask for special equipment. Simple, compelling, impactful visuals should reinforce your words and message. However, for a truly memorable speech, you can create a multi-screen extravaganza that keeps the audience looking from one screen to another while listening raptly to your words.

Presenting at a webinar or online meeting

Although these are two different types of encounters, both use similar equipment: a computer or handheld device with a good webcam and audio input and output. You also need the appropriate app and an account with the associated service. Find out more about both of these presentation types in Chapter 19.

Check out Sweetwater (www.sweetwater.com) for an excellent catalog of extensive sound equipment, apps, and audio products. B&H Photo (www.bhphotovideo.com) offers one of the world's most complete sources for everything to fulfill your audio, video, photographic, computer, smartphone, and tablet-related needs including accessories. Both these superb websites have highly knowledgeable experts to assist you.

Keeping Your Devices Presentation Ready

When you have an upcoming meeting or conference, you have time to prepare your message and the accompanying visuals and rehearse what you plan to say. Nonetheless, last-minute and chance meetings happen. Your boss may call or send you an e-mail at 4 p.m. Monday asking you to present the latest product development schematics to a potential investor at 10 a.m. Tuesday. Take a few deep breaths, make a pot of coffee, and keep the material you prepare simple and to the point.

Or maybe you're on the train to work or waiting in the dentist's office working on your laptop or tablet and the person next to you takes a sideways glance, and says "What are you working on?" Or, as you take your seat on a plane, your seatmate introduces herself and through polite small talk you find that she's been looking for a solution you can offer. With an opening such as "If you're interested, I can show you what I'm talking about," you then open a presentation or PDF document that shows your product or a case study.

Because these are impromptu situations, ask permission before going into a full-blown, or even half-blown, presentation; your seatmate may just want to chill, catch up on her own work, or watch the latest movie. On the other hand, if the person is amenable, take the opportunity to ask questions and have an informal conversation that can give you insight to an industry or profession that interests you.

If the situation lends itself, personal projectors connect to laptops and smart devices and create an instant presentation atmosphere. (See the preceding section, "Determining the Best Equipment Setup for the Situation.")

To prepare for unplanned or on-demand presentation opportunities, keep the following in mind:

- Check your equipment now and then, especially if you use battery-powered devices such as a microphone or remote control (obviously, you won't be using those when talking to your seatmate on an airplane). Remove the batteries from seldom-used devices to avoid corrosion.

- Create a folder on your laptop or a remote storage site such as Dropbox, or use an account on a visual social network such as Pinterest, to place images or videos that capture your latest developments — but remember to clean out older images as they become outdated.

- If you maintain an active, up-to-date website, the images, videos, or articles there often support your impromptu presentation.

Using State-of-the-Art Projection Equipment

Important presentations, such as product launches, initial public offerings (IPOs), and international tradeshows, and large seminars with hundreds of people attending require impressive visuals. Here we tell you about some of the amazing projection systems available to make a mind-blowing, mesmerizing, and unforgettable experience:

- **Display wall system:** Christie MicroTiles (`www.christiedigital.co.uk/`) let you create the screen size you need with multiple locking tiles that combine DLP (digital light processing) and LED technologies. Christie also makes LCD (liquid-crystal display) flat panels that combine to make a wall display. Consider contacting these other firms for ideas for stunning, large-format display solutions that will amaze your audience:

  - Barco (`www.barco.com`)
  - Impact Video (`www.impactav.com`)
  - NEC (`www.necdisplay.com`)
  - Planar (`www.planar.com`)
  - Cinemassive (`www.cinemassive.com`)

- **Multi-screen mix:** With the Roland VR-50HD Multi-Format AV mixer (`www.rolandsystemsgroup.com`) you can switch between four different video sources, record your event, and even stream to the Internet.

  LearnSpace from Pixelture (`www.pixelture.com`), which is an online presentation tool, and KeyShowX from KeyWebX (`http://keywebx.com`), a Keynote and PowerPoint enhancement app for the Mac, and Watchout from Dataton, a multi-screen presentation app for Windows (`www.dataton.com/watchout`), facilitate showing different visuals on multiple screens.

- **3-D:** Joy's 3DLive (`www.joys.com`) offers custom and off-the-shelf solutions for huge (30 to 60 feet) screens that combine live, video, and still media for a truly multi-media event.

Speaking of 3-D, if you use an HD or UHD monitor with 3-D capability in your conference room, you can create a 3-D presentation and supply attendees with 3-D glasses to enjoy the show. We'd love to see a presentation that combines 3-D with augmented reality to transport the attendees to a new place or experience that conveys how your product or service would change their lives.

No matter how fabulous your show is, your words need to be even more so.

Connecting to a Projector or Monitor

As we discuss in Chapter 17, many presentation apps have Mac and Windows versions along with iOS and Android versions, although many also support only one type of device or platform. The situations that you may encounter are as follows:

- Presentation on laptop connected to projector or large-screen monitor, controlled by tablet or smartphone

- Presentation on tablet connected to projector or large-screen monitor, controlled from tablet

- Presentation on tablet connected to projector or large-screen monitor, controlled from smartphone

- Presentation on smartphone connected to projector or large-screen monitor, controlled from smartphone

In any of these setups, you need the proper cable to connect your computer or device to the projector or large-screen monitor and sometimes you need both an adapter and a cable. The variables are many but in generic terms you need to know the following:

- **Type of projector or monitor port:** DVI, HDMI, VGA, or composite

- **Type of computer or device port:** DVI, Mini-DVI, HDMI, Mini-Display Port (Mac), or Thunderbolt (Mac)

Armed with this information, you can purchase the correct cables and necessary adapters to connect your device and projector.

Some projectors, monitors, computers, and devices are wi-fi enabled. If both components of your projection setup are, you need only log in to the local wi-fi network from both, and then connect the two. Wi-fi can be slower than a direct cable connection, and if you find that's the case, you may want to connect your computer or device to the projector or monitor with a cable and then control the computer or device with a cordless (wi-fi or Bluetooth) remote control.

If your monitor isn't wi-fi enabled or you want to broadcast your presentation to multiple computers, the AIRTAME HDMI dongle (http://airtame.com) may solve your problems. This new product adds wi-fi capability to your monitors or projection systems when you plug the dongle into an HDMI port.

Controlling the show from your tablet or smartphone

In order to use your tablet or smartphone as a remote control, you must install an app that works with the presentation app you use. Here are several that we found although others are available in the App Store (`https://itunes.apple.com/` or through the iTunes or App Store app) for iOS devices, Google Play (`https://play.google.com/store`) for Android devices, or the Apps+Games Store (`www.windowsphone.com/`) for Windows Phone apps.

> ✔ **i-Clickr PowerPoint Remote** (`www.senstic.com/`) Wi-fi remote control that supports iOS, Android, and Windows Phone and both Windows and Mac OS for PowerPoint and Keynote. (Free lite version; $9.99 for full version.)
>
> ✔ **Universal Presentations Remote** (`www.makaveli.eu`) Supports Android and works with any computer that has the free Any App Remote app installed (found on the same website). (Free.)
>
> ✔ **ShowDirector for PowerPoint** (`www.signalbeach.com/`) Supports Android and connects via Bluetooth or wi-fi to a Windows PC. (Free trial; $4.99 full version.)
>
> ✔ **Office Remote** (`http://research.microsoft.com/`) Controls all Office apps, including PowerPoint, from your Windows Phone. (Free.)

If you use SlideShark, you can install it on both your iPhone (or iPod touch) and iPad and use the smaller device as the remote control.

For other presentation apps such as Prezi or SlideRocket, your best option is to connect your computer or device to a projection system and then control the presentation from your computer or device.

Keep your eye on gesture control apps for both iOS and Android tablets that let you manipulate what's on screen with a wave of your hand or a nod of your head — all without touching it.

Bringing offsite guests online

Studies show that 20 minutes is the optimal length of time for a presentation as far as keeping the audience's attention. However, sometimes 20 minutes isn't enough time to say all you have to say or you've been given a longer amount of time to fill. In either case, when you hit the 20 minute mark, you should break up your presentation with a video, an activity, or a guest speaker.

With apps like Skype, FaceTime, Google Hangouts, and Tango you can call your special guest from your smartphone or tablet, which you connected to the projector or large-screen monitor, and conduct a live interview or listen to a brief presentation.

When a live call isn't an option, creating a video interview with the guest speaker and incorporating it into your presentation at the 20-minute mark works as an alternative. If you record an interview with the guest, you can even make it seem live by timing your questions to the responses.

Another type of fun guest is the remote man-on-the-street. Ahead of time, schedule phone calls with people (clients perhaps) around the country — or around the world, why not? — and ask for responses about your product announcement or something else relevant to your presentation.

Using your tablet as a teleprompter

Although we don't suggest reading your presentation from notes on the podium or, worse yet, from the slides you display, we do understand some presentations demand a teleprompter.

Looking natural while reading from a teleprompter is an art, so don't think having a teleprompter means you don't need to rehearse.

A neat way to set up a teleprompter is to download a teleprompter app to your iOS or Android tablet (sorry Windows Phone users but the one app available doesn't meet our standards), upload your speech, and then mount your tablet on a stand, like the iKlip (www.ikmultimedia.com/) which connects to a microphone stand.

A few of the teleprompter apps we like include:

- ✔ **Teleprompt+ for iPad** (www.bombingbrain.com) Allows you to control the teleprompter from your iPhone or use your Mac as a teleprompter. ($14.99.)

- ✔ **Best Prompter Pro** (http://ipad-software.smartphoneware.com/) This iPad app lets you record yourself so you can practice and playback. ($3.99.)

- ✔ **dv Prompter** (www.datavideo.info) Although actually a teleprompter scripting app which then works with the teleprompter devices sold by datavideo, you can also mount your Android device on an on- or off-camera rig. (Free.)

Chapter 19

Visiting the Future Today

In This Chapter

▶ Entering the fourth dimension

▶ Controlling the show with your hands

▶ Meeting remotely

▶ Presenting without being present

Innovative presentations combine imaginative approaches and ideas to communicate with your audience along with creative application of the latest technological developments. We present our take on preparing for and approaching the audience in the earlier chapters of this book. In Chapters 17 and 18 we discuss software and hardware, respectively. In this chapter, we introduce you to some technological advancements that you may not be familiar with or may know about but hadn't thought about how to dynamically apply to your presentations.

First we discuss three hot technology topics: augmented reality, gesture control, and 3-D printing. We explain how they work, give you some examples of incorporating them in presentations, and then point you in the direction of apps or creative types that can help you create them for your own presentations. Then we talk about virtual presentations, given through videoconferencing or webinars and recorded and played back on a website or kiosk.

Incorporating New Technology

New technologies can't save a mediocre presentation, but they can enhance a good presentation and maybe even ratchet up the audience response from good or great to WOW. The technologies we discuss here were pie-in-the-sky ideas just a few short years ago but now they're commonplace in certain circles, which means they'll be readily available for your presentations by the time this book comes out. These technologies, used properly for effect, are the stuff that helps make your presentation innovative to the max.

Augmenting reality

Augmented reality (AR) apps enhance what you see and show you more. AR apps insert virtual images in a real environment (so you can see what that new sofa looks like next to your existing armchairs) or give you more information about something you see, such as a video from the tourism board when you point your smartphone or tablet at an ad on the train into town. AR adds a digital dimension to static print — sometimes it's referred to as 4-D, in a nod to the conceptual fourth dimensional space.

One of the most common current uses of AR is in giving more information in the form of a video or 3-D image about something in a two-dimensional format. For example, after installing an augmented reality app on your iOS or Android smart device such as a phone or tablet, you can hold the device over a QR (Quick Response) code in an advertisement (those funny squares like the one in Figure 19-1), and the ad comes to life.

Figure 19-1:
Smart
devices
read QR
codes
to open
augmented
reality.

Illustration courtesy of Ray Anthony and Barbara Boyd

The AR triggers aren't limited to QR codes, however. Static images of just about any kind as well as locations can trigger an AR response. Pointing your device at a shoe ad at the bus stop may list addresses of nearby stores that sell the shoes, and moving your device over your feet shows you how the shoes would look on you. Scan a movie poster to see the trailer, or a street in an unfamiliar city to see the names of nearby eateries and shops superimposed on the buildings you see on your device's screen. You can project an image on your screen, and people in your audience can point their phones or tablets at this hot spot to activate AR.

In the not too distant future, AR apps will work with connected glasses such as Google Glass.

This type of AR app is known as an *AR browser,* which gives you options for applying augmented reality to your print advertising or brochures. With these apps, you scan a trigger image and then link a video, podcast, or an interactive 3-D image to the trigger. People with an AR browser app on their devices can then point the device at the trigger image and automatically see the augmented reality information (the video or 3-D design). For example, the logo of your event could be the trigger image and when someone points his device at the logo, a video opens in which you talk about the event and invite him to sign up.

The following augmented reality browser apps work with iOS or Android devices. The user apps are free to download from the AppStore or Google Play; fees for storing your AR content vary from company to company.

- ✔ **Aurasma (`www.aurasma.com`):** An HP Autonomy product, Aurasma calls the trigger images Auras, which you then link to a video, web page, or 3-D image. When someone opens the Aurasma app on his device and then points the device at the Aura, the video, web page, or 3-D image appears. The Aurasma cloud stores Auras so after one is saved, anytime that Aura is displayed as a print or online image, it can be scanned and viewed. This means you can create Auras and then use them in your presentation handouts, brochures, print advertising, or your website.

- ✔ **Junaio (`www.junaio.com`):** Junaio is the augmented reality browser for content created with metaio Creator (also available from the Junaio website). Like Aurasma, you create a trigger — usually a print image — upload a video, website, or 3-D image that connects to the trigger and then print your advertising or brochure.

- ✔ **Layar (`www.layar.com`):** With 35 million downloads, the Layar app seems to be the most popular AR browser, and the Layar Creator offers simplicity for the do-it-yourself version as well as custom solutions.

- ✔ **Ricoh Clickable Paper (`www.ricohclickablepaper.com`):** You create the hotspots, such as print ads, brochures, or catalogs — anything printed — and link them to the augmented reality media stored on the Clickable Paper cloud. Your (potential) customers download the Clickable Paper app to their devices and then scan the hotspots to see the AR media. You get analytic information from the Clickable Paper cloud about which hotspots are most effective.

If you're looking for someone to design an augmented reality solution for your company, rather than using existing images and one of the apps we mention, try DAQRI (`http://daqri.com`), Total Immersion (`www.t-immersion.com`), or Perfect Prototype (`www.perfectprototype.com`). The iCreate team (`www.icreate3d.com`) designs flythrough augmented reality images, which work well for real estate and development professionals. With a bit of imagination you can find many uses for augmented reality — and the uses will only increase as the technology advances.

Gesturing and gesticulating

Gesture recognition lets you control your presentation without touching a remote control or even the screen of your smartphone or tablet! Without getting too technical, your hand or body motion is detected by a camera and an action occurs. For example, wave-o-rama (http://www.nanocritical.com/wave-o-rama) is an iOS photo album app that moves from one photo to the next when you wave your hand in front of the iPad screen.

We see amazing possibilities for presentations with the Leap Motion Controller (www.leapmotion.com). For less than $100, you add gesture control to your Mac or Windows PC. You can paint, sculpt, turn pages, even rotate three-dimensional objects with your hands. Rather than holding a prototype in your hands, which makes it hard to see, you can show the image on the screen and rotate it with hand gestures, as if you were holding it. The audience sees the rotating figure but not your hands.

Imagine you want to talk about your company's state-of-the-art circuit board, which you want to convince a potential client to purchase to control a manufacturing device he's developing. Instead of holding up a circuit board, you bring up a 3-D model on the screen of your computer. The computer is connected to a projection system, and the Leap Motion Controller is connected to your computer. Using your hands, you rotate the virtual circuit board to show the thinness, conductive tracks and pads, and then virtually insert the circuit board into a 3-D image of the manufacturing device, showing how it takes up less room than the competitor's circuit board, which means more flexibility in the design of their new device.

Announcements of new gesture-control products arrive almost daily. There seems to be a particular trend for *wearables*, objects you put on such as clothes or jewelry that incorporate gesture control. Here are just a few of the latest products:

- ✔ The **Myo** gesture control armband (www.thalmic.com/en/myo), scheduled to ship in 2014 for $149, offers full control of your digital and remotely controlled devices.

- ✔ Put on a pair of **DrumPants** (www.drumpants.com) and then slap your knees to clang a cymbal or tap your toe to add a kick drum. Music aside, DrumPants can be used to control your slideshows, just tap your belly to bring up the next slide.

- ✔ Step aside smart watches, **Ring** from Logbar (http://logbar.jp/ring/) manages gesture control, takes your messages when you draw letters in the air, and connects to other devices to control them remotely.

✔ A beta product that could be interesting is **Mauz** (`http://mauzup.com`), an adapter that plugs into an iPhone and turns it into a gesture-controlled mouse that commands your computer.

✔ **Dizmo**, (`www.dizmo.com`) a combination of *digital gizmo*, turns touch-screen surfaces into infinite work boards. Digital objects, for example spreadsheet apps or appointments on a calendar app, appear on the surface and you write on, resize, and move them around. Dizmo would be an amazing addition to a traditional presentation or a team meeting.

Demonstrating prototypes

We admit the best use for a 3-D printer we've seen so far is the father who made an artificial hand for his son (from CBS Evening News and available at `www.youtube.com/watch?v=FGSo_I86_1Q`). When you finish drying your eyes, you can come back to the book.

3-D printers could put the gadget business out of business. Think of the possibilities for giveaways to accompany your presentation: product prototypes or even customized smart device covers generated the day of the event personalized with the name of each attendee. Consumer-grade 3-D printers range from $400 to around $3,000 and some manufacturers sell kits that you assemble yourself, which cost about half the price of an assembled model. As with any printer, you should consider your production needs and cartridge costs, as well as compatibility with your modeling system.

Taking Your Presentation Online

With increased travel costs and clashing schedules, you may have trouble reaching the presentation site or find that a key player in the decision-making process can't attend. Alternatively, you may want to distribute a recording of your presentation and reach a nationwide or international audience in different time zones. A simple solution exists for each of these scenarios: videoconferencing, webinars, and presentation-sharing websites.

We talk about videoconferencing and webinars together since the service providers we suggest offer both; presentation-sharing websites have their own section. We also give you tips for preparing visuals and conducting these types of presentations.

Meeting virtually

Often you give a presentation at an event, such as a conference or tradeshow, conveying information the audience will use to make a decision or take another action. At a meeting, instead of a mostly one-way presentation, everyone there discusses a topic with the objective of planning something or coming up with a solution to a problem with a client, partner, or your staff. You may still find yourself in the role of principal presenter or your role may shift to one of meeting facilitator, whether physically face-to-face seated in the same room or remotely located and viewing the other attendees on a screen.

When meeting attendees gather from remote locations and meet online, we call that a *virtual meeting,* also known as a *videoconference.* Essentially, each attendee uses the same app or signs in to the same URL from a tablet or computer, and participates in the meeting from the comfort of his own office, home, or hotel.

Specific companies manage videoconferences for a fee. You reserve a virtual meeting room, which attendees access from an app or a URL. You, and other attendees, can upload visuals such as a PDF or presentation to accompany the discussion, and most service providers offer the possibility of screen sharing and a virtual whiteboard so that more than one person can show something on his computer or write notes on the shared document or whiteboard.

In a *webinar,* or web-based seminar, you present to attendees who watch, listen, and ask questions — much like its literal counterpart. Most services offer a call-in option or a direct connection with a computer's or device's built-in mic and speaker. With a call-in webinar, attendees call a conference-enabled phone number while viewing the visuals on a browser and ask questions from the telephone. If attendees use mics and speakers built into their computers or devices, they can ask questions directly or via written chat. The presentation or video is streamed live, and the attendees can number in the thousands.

During a *webcast,* attendees watch and listen to the live, streaming presentation but don't interact with the speaker.

Webinars and videoconferencing can be cost effective when compared to traveling and renting a meeting or event space, especially if you're a small business. They can also be an effective way to do market research or have an initial meeting with a potential client without taking up too much of his time. Both are a great way to host press conferences, board meetings, and industry-specific events with a smaller, discreet audience.

The service providers listed in the next sections offer both videoconferencing and webinar services.

Cisco WebEx (www.webex.com)

iOS, Android, Windows Phone 8, Blackberry, and browser enabled (Free for attendees; purchase a host account to create a meeting.)

WebEx offers complete meeting services. You can schedule a meeting or create one on the go. Participants share a virtual whiteboard, can make live annotations on shared documents, and zoom visuals to get up close to details, as well as share the screens on their computers or devices. High definition in 720-pixel resolution is supported, making for crisp viewing. Participants can choose to focus on the presenter or the presentation and see all video participants in a carousel at the bottom of the screen. While in the meeting, you can start an instant chat with one participant or everyone. WebEx also offers training and webinar services.

GoToMeeting (www.gotomeeting.com)

iOS, Android, and browser enabled (Free for attendees; purchase a host account to create a meeting — one month free trial.)

Conduct meetings and webinars with up to six active video feeds, which means that in meeting mode, six of the participants can be seen at a time and in webinar mode, up to six presenters can participate from remote locations. You can have up to 1,000 attendees, which makes it a great tool for training. Meetings may be recorded and screens and documents can be shared, making for truly collaborative efforts.

ClickMeeting (www.clickmeeting.com and www.clickwebinar.com)

iOS, Android, Blackberry, and browser enabled (Free for attendees; purchase a host account to create a meeting — one month free trial.)

ClickMeeting makes videoconferences and webinars affordable for small and medium-sized businesses. Five different levels of service provide a solution for most videoconference and webinar needs. You can record your meeting or webinar and administer surveys or tests, making ClickMeeting a good training tool as well. The ClickMeeting Learning Center on their website stores many articles and tips for preparing and conducting your meetings.

MightyMeeting (www.mightymeeting.com)

iOS and Android enabled. (Free for attendees, various price levels for hosting after a free 14-day trial.)

The benefit of MightyMeeting is that it works for both in-person and remote participants in your meeting. It's quick to set up and easy to use. First, you want to upload your presentation to MightyMeeting, by either saving it as a PDF and e-mailing it to yourself, then opening the PDF in MightyMeeting or accessing your PowerPoint files, images, or PDFs from Box, Dropbox, or GoogleDrive. Let your participants know the assigned Room ID so they can join your meeting from their devices by entering the Room ID in the appropriate field in the app. You can also send invitations via e-mail from the MightyMeeting app, which provides a URL that gives invitees access to your meeting from a web browser.

If you use MightyMeeting with remote participants, it's a good idea to simultaneously conduct a conference call so you can have a conversation while everyone is looking at your presentation. All participants can add documents to the meeting from their devices as well as mark up the document being displayed. A blank whiteboard page is added to the end of each PDF file so you can add notes and you can also open a Sketchbook page to create a new document within MightyMeeting.

Sharing presentations

Most of the online presentation apps we discuss in Chapter 17 — SlideShark, SlideRocket, Prezi, Keynote — offer public and private sharing since your presentation is already stored in the service provider's cloud. Public presentations can be viewed by anyone, and the free version of online presentation services usually offer only public viewing. This can work to your advantage since you never know who might happen upon your presentation. However, as far as target marketing goes, it's casting a wide net. If you want to keep your presentation private and only use it yourself or give limited access to colleagues or clients, you may have to pay a monthly or yearly fee for this service.

If you maintain a website, you can store your recorded presentations, also known as *webcasts,* there. Ask your webmaster to create a public or private viewing area, and then share the link to your presentation.

We really like 9Slides (`http://9slides.com`) for sharing presentations because the screen is split into two. On one half, you record yourself making the presentation, and the other half displays your PowerPoint slides or PDF files. Viewers can access your presentation with the 9Slides app on an iOS or Windows mobile device or at the 9Slides website and watch you make your presentation.

Presenting remotely

Perhaps the hardest thing about presenting remotely — whether with active participants in a videoconference or webinar or in a recorded presentation — is not seeing your audience directly. (Studies show that not seeing you, the presenter, in person makes attending remote presentations difficult, too.) If creating compelling visuals and a speech that packs a punch is essential for in-person presentations, it's critically important for remote presentations. We do our best here to help you prepare for both kinds of virtual presentations.

Prepping your visuals and content

The visual impact and voice inflection of virtual presentations are perhaps more important than for in-person presentations. Your viewer may be reading text messages or packing a suitcase while absentmindedly watching your video online. Your visuals need to be so eye-catching, your words so stirring that the viewer stops and pays attention and really listens to what you have to say.

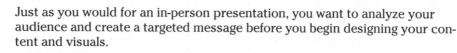

Just as you would for an in-person presentation, you want to analyze your audience and create a targeted message before you begin designing your content and visuals.

Whether you're a one-person show or a participant in an online event, allow time for your introduction and closing and question breaks in addition to your actual presentation. Interactive webinars usually run from 60 minutes for a marketing event to 90 minutes for an educational event. Videoconferences and webcasts or recorded presentations vary based on the focus; you may have just 15 minutes to present your case in videoconference with a decision maker. Recorded presentations can run the gamut from a 30-second video or a 6-minute vlog (video log) that's a sort of commercial for your product or service to a several-hour training session that's broken into separate chapters.

People pay attention and learn best in 20-minute chunks of time, so even if your presentation is longer than that, incorporate a break or a change of pace with a guest speaker, video, or activity at the 20-minute mark.

It goes without saying that your visuals should enhance what you're saying. A visual can be a phrase on a clean background, a graph, diagram, or image. Rather than show a list of bulleted facts and describe the impact, show an image of the impact and tell a story that describes the facts. Although a picture is worth a thousand words, when you absolutely must use words, choose a sans serif font, such as Arial or Helvetica, in 24 point or larger and leave a margin around the visual to allow for letterboxing.

To explain complex ideas, use *builds,* which visually show a chart, diagram, or other visual and add pieces of information as you talk about them. As the layers build, your audience is able to follow and understand the makeup and entirety of a visual or information chunk. Show the complete image with a recap at the end. You want the viewer to stay with you and your words, not jump ahead or fall behind trying to decipher your image. At the beginning, tell viewers you'll supply notes from your presentation so they don't have to worry about writing everything down.

Some viewers may watch your presentation on a small-screen device — all the more reason to keep visuals plain and simple.

During a videoconference, use interactivity to your advantage. Highlight specific parts of your visuals with onscreen pointers and overlays. When appropriate, ask for input and, if possible, let viewers point and highlight your slides or use a working document or virtual whiteboard. Prepare questions for your participants that can be used throughout your presentation or meeting.

Rehearse, rehearse, and rehearse again. When you present at a webinar or videoconference, you must speak fluidly and confidently to hold the viewers' attention.

Setting up your equipment

Choose a place where you will sit or stand with good lighting and a neutral background, such as white or cream walls, in a room that's quiet and free of distractions (no street noise coming through closed windows or people walking by). Wear clothes with simple, solid colors — webcams can have difficulty focusing on patterns — and sit or stand about an arm's length from the camera.

When you host or present at a videoconference or webinar, you want to have the following equipment:

- A webcam (on your computer or mobile device)
- A broadband Internet connection
- A computer or mobile device that has a meeting app or link and the visuals you plan to show
- A microphone and speaker, which may be freestanding, a headset, or built into your computer

Most webinar and videoconference service providers offer some technical support — take advantage of this feature to conduct smooth, glitch-free meetings and events.

If you're creating a recorded presentation (as opposed to recording a presentation at an event), you want to create as real a setting as possible, even with a few people in the audience, and use the best recording equipment you have available. In this case, record in a format that you can edit so you can record multiple takes and create an interesting, interactive presentation.

Part V
Tailoring the Message

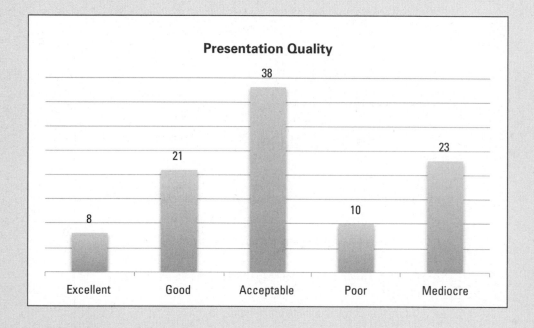

Visit www.dummies.com/extras/innovativepresentations for an article about using the assertion-evidence structure in your presentations.

In this part . . .

✔ Make a sales presentation by offering benefits and results.

✔ Learn to analyze and address the audience's needs.

✔ Discover what drives executive decision-makers.

✔ Create a focused presentation that communicates to executives.

✔ Develop a brief, concise message to describe yourself or your product.

✔ Understand how to build a presentation team.

✔ Define team member responsibilities and roles.

✔ Create and deliver a successful team presentation.

Chapter 20

Giving an Opportunities, Results, and Benefits Presentation

*A*lmost 40 years ago, in 1975 to be exact, Frank Watts developed the concept and method of solution selling. In the 15 or so years that followed, Mike Bosworth and Keith Eades perfected it. Prior to solution selling, people sold their products and services without strongly communicating how their offering uniquely solved a problem or need. So, an old-time computer salesperson sold hardware, while an enlightened solution-selling computer professional sold improved order entry, inventory control, and accounting functions that could be done better, faster, and cheaper.

The problem with solution selling lies in its name — it implies that a problem exists. Chances are, your targeted client is a successful company and a successful company doesn't think of itself as having problems, although every single organization has its share of various problems or "challenges." However, successful companies usually want to do better and be more successful. So, rather than talk about a solution-selling presentation, we want you to use the *opportunities, results, and benefits* (OR&B) presentation. Selling opportunities involve alerting a potential client to a situation, that if grabbed and capitalized upon would greatly benefit them in ways they want.

To be successful, you want to present the benefits and results a potential client will realize if she purchases your product or service, partners with you, or agrees to the investment you want her to make. As we repeat throughout this book, your presentation must focus on the audience, and an OR&B presentation is no different.

For example, if you're a dentist whose patient asks for a whitening treatment, you may show a before-and-after rendering on a computer with an image of the patient so she can see just how she'll look with pearlier whites. You present the result you offer, rather than selling a whitening treatment. If the person is going on a job interview, you explain that whitening her teeth is an opportunity to look more youthful, professional, and be at her best appearance. In this manner, you focus on the patient's situation and offer a beneficial result. The value of that result is the price you ask, so more than selling, it's an exchange of value for value.

We cover overall audience analysis in Chapter 4; in this chapter we narrow our focus to clients who may be patients (as in the dentist scenario), students for a seminar you offer, or other companies who purchase your products or services. We discuss interpreting each situation and then showcase how to develop your presentation around the results and benefits you offer. We also include a sidebar that examines a presentation format — the infomercial — and point out what you can learn and copy from it.

Focusing on Your Client's Needs and Wants

We refer to potential clients, but the decision makers on the listening end of your presentation can be anyone to whom you offer your services, products, or ideas in exchange for money or another type of value such as a knowledge-sharing joint venture or an exchange of services. The audience may even be your manager or executive team from whom you want a larger investment or more manpower for a project you propose.

Regardless of who's sitting across the table from you, by focusing on her situation, needs, and desires, your OR&B presentation will be personal and specific — and who doesn't respond well to a little personal attention?

Ours is not a sales book; we assume you have collected customer leads through various channels and have obtained an appointment to meet with your potential client.

Interpreting needs analysis and interviews

Your first step in understanding the potential client's situation is to visit her website. The design and tone of the website gives you insight as to whether you're dealing with a formal, traditional company, a hip startup, or somewhere in-between. Read between the lines as if you were an undercover detective. Read the bios of the execs, especially if you'll be meeting with them, so you can see what their experience and outside interests are.

Continue your detective work on social networking sites such as LinkedIn and Facebook to understand the client's presence there, if any. Conduct a general online search using your favorite search engine to see what the trade and general publications have to say about the company. Be sure to sift rumors from fact when possible.

Take advantage of the analytics available from your website service provider to determine the pages most often clicked through, which is a helpful indication of the types of information people want to know about your company.

Talk to the contact you made the appointment with and ask as many questions as possible about the client's situation before your actual presentation meeting. You want to understand the potential client's situation from various angles, such as:

- ✔ **Individual versus department:** Will your product or service benefit an individual or improve the entire department or company?

- ✔ **Contributor versus manager:** Does your product or service affect a contributor-level employee, who usually deals with problems, or a management- or executive-level person, who usually thinks about planning and expansion?

- ✔ **Local or national:** If you're meeting with a local representative of a national company, can she take your product or service to the next level, putting her in a good light and benefitting the company as a whole?

- ✔ **Well-known or secret:** Is the situation you're addressing known to the general public or is it secret information, such as an upcoming product launch or merger?

- ✔ **Past, present, or future:** Has the situation been ongoing or occurred in the past and how would your product or service change the future?

If a company is in trouble, savvy, informed decision makers or buyers have likely already analyzed the problem and defined a solution and, what's more, researched you and your competitors before you step in the room, which makes comparing offers a purely financial proposition of fulfilling a request for proposal (RFP). Don't wait until a company calls you; if you hear of a difficult situation that your product or service can assist with, don't be shy about approaching the company.

Begin your presentation with a brief overview of your understanding of the client's situation, but be sure to ask questions to confirm that understanding. Sometimes you go to a meeting with little knowledge of the potential client's situation, and need to use this initial meeting as an opportunity to learn about the client. It may not be the opportunity to garner a sale but you can, nonetheless, demonstrate your ability to provide results and benefits.

When Barbara worked as the marketing director for a graphic design company, part of her job was identifying and meeting with potential clients and showing the firm's portfolio. When presenting to small companies, the meeting often focused on a specific upcoming design project, and Barbara showed and discussed pieces developed for similar projects and gathered enough information to develop a proposal. When presenting to large corporations, the first meeting was often just to review the portfolio. Barbara would ask about the company's design and production cycles for marketing campaigns or annual reports and then contact the person again when those timed opportunities arose. Although the fees of Barbara's design firm were often higher than the competition, the design of the pieces often resulted in better brand recognition and return on investment for the client, which justified the higher fees.

Covering key priorities in order

Business is dynamic, and even when things are going great, decision makers are making plans for future growth, expansion, or even positioning the company to be sold at a high price. They want to create opportunities or take advantage of ones in front of them. When you give your OR&B presentation, consider the company situation from different points of view, which could be from a different time perspective or a different person's perspective (company versus customer or company versus department), and then present a prioritized scheme for implementing your product or service.

For example, say you provide a customer service software package and in talking to a friend hear about how slow the response times are at XYZ Company. You contact the customer care manager at XYZ Company, explain how you heard about her and tell her that you might be able to offer better results and benefits in how XYZ services its customers. You set up a meeting and do some research before your meeting, only to find that many customers of the XYZ Company have had problems with XYZ's product. Depending on your point of view, the situation is different:

- **Customer** experiences products that require a call to customer service plus customer service that's delayed.

- **Customer service rep** sees work overload and not having a large enough department.

- **Customer service manager** blames a faulty product.

Your software package may alleviate some of the short-term stress in the customer service department, which gives priority to responding to customers in a timely fashion. You can address this priority, which is near and dear to the customer care manager who is your contact. In the long term, however, (albeit out of your field) the priority for the company should be to make a more stable product. If XYZ Company fixes the product, which can take time, without addressing the customer service component, by the time the product is repaired, the reputation of the company will be so far gone that people won't buy the new product.

An interesting, stimulating question to ask your potential client is "If money were no object, what would you do?" or "If you were capable of anything, what would you do?"

Giving Your OR&B Presentation

Like any presentation, you want to talk about the current situation (or problem) and the results and benefits that your product or service can bring. During your presentation, you interweave these two positions — present and future — with the other components of an OR&B presentation, which looks something like this:

- ✓ **Executive summary:** Speak to the high-level concerns of your audience, addressing both the present situation and where your product or service will take them. If things are going well for the potential client, compliment her and explain how things could be even better. If, instead, there are specific problems, acknowledge them and then describe how the situation would be rectified with your product or service.

- ✓ **Current situation:** Go into the details of the potential client's situation. She knows what her situation is, but this is an opportunity for you to demonstrate your comprehension of the facts and express empathy for her position. Give ample space for the audience to add details to what you already know or confirm what you say.

- ✓ **Proposal:** Talk about the specific results and benefits that the potential client will perceive if your offer is accepted. For example, if you offer a social media management service, the result could be reaching 5,000 qualified followers in two-months' time and the benefit is greater brand recognition. Use examples from other clients in the same industry or in a company of similar size to testify to the efficacy of your product or service.

✔ **Financial proof:** All businesses, from a sole proprietorship to a Fortune 50 corporation, non-profit or publicly traded, have their financial situation at the top of the list of decision-making criteria for a new purchase or partnership. You need to give evidence of the value and return on investment (ROI) that your product or service generates. Sometimes it's a purely monetary value, other times, especially in cost-center operations (as opposed to profit-center operations) such as human resources or facilities, the value shows up in employee satisfaction or environmental impact.

Do your research before the meeting. If the company you're approaching is public, you can access their annual report and look at historical data to create an analysis that supports your understanding of the situation then apply your results to that data. Otherwise check with industry associations, the Bureau of Labor Statistics, and other governing bodies that do research. Search the web to see if an independent research firm has reports or information that help you build your case.

✔ **Conclusion:** Although everyone in the room knows you're there to acquire a client, partner, or funding, you must state a specific call to action. Statements like "Are we in agreement that . . ." or "I'd like to sign a contract with you today" or "When will you present this to the executive decision makers?" Clearly state your next action as well.

Choose the media that works for your field and group size — a traditional slide show often isn't the best way to highlight your solution. Rather than projecting your visuals, showing them on a laptop screen or a tablet propped on a stand can be more effective. (We talk about various presentation methods in the chapters in Part IV.)

Listing options

In the peaks of your presentation, when you describe the future results the client can receive, you may find you have several scenarios based on the level of buy-in she agrees to. In these cases, you can use the Law of Repetition: Cite the current situation, then outline the results and benefits of the first option; cite the current situation again with slightly different wording, and then describe the results and benefits of the second option, and so on. (We discuss the Law of Repetition in Chapter 12.)

You can use the same visual for the current situation or use several to demonstrate different aspects, and then use a separate visual for each option you offer.

You must highlight the results and benefits for the potential client, not necessarily the features of your product or service. When creating and reviewing your visuals, ask yourself if the visual focuses on the potential client or on you — the correct answer is the potential client.

But wait, there's more: The power of infomercials

Infomercials, those 28½-minute commercials that annoy yet compel millions of people to purchase a Slice-O-Matic or Swivel Sweeper, make their presentations fast-paced, real, entertaining, and interesting and rely on the power of persuasion. They grab your attention and hypnotically convince you that your life will be incomplete without the Slice-O-Matic and as such you're compelled to buy it in four easy payments.

Kidding aside, you can apply the infomercial method to your OR&B presentation. We've saved you hours of watching and analyzing infomercials — not to mention saving you from buying all those items you didn't even know you needed — by listing the techniques they use, like this tried and true formula:

1. Identify a problem people have — even one they didn't know they had — and make it personal, such as "Is that mold in your grout taking your breath away?"

2. Describe the problem's pain points. For example, "Mold is one of the most common causes of asthma and allergies, and you inhale it every time you take a shower."

3. Show an ideal, quick, easy, and relatively inexpensive solution, like "Mold-X eliminates the spores that cause mold to grow and leaves an invisible film that prohibits regrowth."

4. Be ready to respond to probable objections.

5. Prove all the claims you make. With our simulated Mold-X example, having a chemist cite studies that attest to the ingredients that attack the mold along with testimonials of people who clean with Mold-X would support the case.

6. Make buying easy and attractive by offering a toll-free, 24-hour phone number and access to time-limited or quantity discounts, free shipping, bonus products, and/or a payment plan.

Here are a few more tips:

✔ Follow the 10-minute rule and use repetition: The entire formula is repeated three times in the almost 30-minute duration. Words and testimonials vary each time but the message remains the same. This addresses the average viewer's attention span and catches channel surfers.

✔ Speak with enthusiasm. Use empathy when describing the problem and describe the product dynamically.

✔ Show convincing, slightly exaggerated demonstrations and testimonials with seemingly real people getting the benefits of the product. Diverse people relate how diverse problems were solved with the product. The viewer will identify with at least one of the testimonials.

✔ Repeat the name of the product throughout and frequently mention how to buy it, adding a limited-time offer to create a compelling call to action: buy now.

Comparing to competitors

Truth be told, we don't like mentioning competitors' names during our presentations — why give the other guy free advertising? Nonetheless, you must be aware of your competition and be ready to respond to questions from your potential client about how your product or service is different than the competition's. If the potential client already has a service or product from another provider, you must be prepared to address why a change should be made.

Businesses often associate change with risk and sometimes the fear of change outweighs the potential benefit. You must give overwhelming, convincing evidence that the value of your product or service far outweighs the potential risk involved.

Chapter 21

Presenting to Executives and Decision Makers for Surefire Wins

In This Chapter

▶ Surveying the decision makers

▶ Impressing the big guys

▶ Structuring your presentation

▶ Designing content your audience needs

Giving an impressive presentation to executives is a path to career advancement or to growing your business. These opportunities provide a terrific forum for you to display your innovative and visionary thinking, your refined communication skills, and your leadership traits all at once. By following the advice in this chapter and constantly honing your high-level presentation skills, you can become a consummate executive presenter in a relatively short period of time.

Successful presenting to business executives or other high-level corporate decision makers and organization or association leaders — in government, military, academia, or science fields, for example — requires a different approach than you take when talking to lower-level staff or operations professionals.

Stakes and visibility are high. Giving an important talk in a boardroom, even for otherwise intrepid business presenters, can be a daunting and anxiety-ridden exercise, unless you plan well and deliver your presentation in a way most top-level people need and want. In this chapter we give you some valuable, tested, and proven tips and insights to ace this type of presentation and help reduce any jitters you may experience.

Surveying the Decision Makers

It was Charles Kettering, the inventor and head of research for General Motors who noted, "My interest is in the future because I am going to spend the rest of my life there." Executives echo that sentiment. They are responsible for creating a better, brighter future for their organizations. They are tasked with doing strategic planning and large-scale change and innovation to help their corporations grow and prosper. They are the generals and architects of their companies.

As such, executives are interested in the big picture of how their organization can be more effective, more profitable, more competitive. They're not interested in the details of day-to-day operations. Many a first-time presenter to CEOs, presidents, and executive vice presidents has made the mistake of trying to impress these VIPs with her wealth of knowledge about a topic by inundating them with tons of data and including endless details. Don't let this be you. Give high-level executives and leaders only the summary pieces of critical data and concepts they need in order to make an informed decision.

Good leaders focus on the future and keep in mind the challenges they have to deal with as well as the potential, exciting opportunities they must consider exploiting. Their work schedules are jam-packed, and they have to make high-stakes, sometimes risky decisions often with little time to properly weigh their options.

Although many leaders rely on intuition and experience, they also look for solid information that readily facilitates timely, good decisions. However well paid *C-level executives* (CEO, COO, CFO, CTO, and so on) are, they feel constant, unrelenting pressure to perform well and deliver results. If, through your presentation, you gain their trust, you win their appreciation and admiration, too. As such, they are likely to give you more business, responsibility, or job advancements in the future.

How do corporate executives and top leaders from the military, government, and other organizations act during presentations, and what do they expect from a presenter? Various research studies and general consensus from other presentation trainers and coaches indicate that executives become impatient and lose attention quickly during a presentation that doesn't address their areas of interest and priorities. They have a tendency to interrupt a presenter to ask meaningful questions rather than wait till the presentation is concluded.

Time is a precious commodity for top decision makers, and they won't tolerate rambling or stumbling that are signs of winging it, improvising, and otherwise being unprepared.

Various studies about the personality profiles of top executives in decision-making positions concur that most are either the Director personality or Thinker types (as in Chapter 4). These are forceful, authoritative, strong-willed, and strong-minded people who readily accept challenges, take action, and get quick results. In general, they are all about making a difference, and leaving their organizations better than when they came in. They are systematic thinkers and planners and sticklers for accuracy and competence. They like a crisp, no-fluff presentation (with no loose ends) that gives them just enough of the right information for them to consider your proposal, sale, program, or recommendation.

Ray did a comprehensive 25-question research study in which he asked more than 200 senior, C-level people from 14 companies to rate presentations given to them. Some important findings that came from the study include:

✔ A majority of executives (63 percent) said 30 minutes was the ideal length of time for a presentation given to them with only 4 percent saying 60 minutes was best.

✔ Almost 9 out of 10 executives said good visuals were either very important or important to the effectiveness of a presentation. However, almost 60 percent rated the quality of visuals used by presenters as being of moderate or poor quality!

✔ All (100 percent) of the executives agreed with the following statement: "A well-prepared and nicely executed introduction and conclusion is important (23 percent) or extremely important (77 percent) in a presentation."

✔ About 8 out of 10 executives agreed with this statement, "I enjoy listening to speakers who are organized but nevertheless informal, relaxed, and conversational in their delivery." Only 5 percent said "I prefer listening to a speaker who is formal and essentially conservative in his or her style of personality." Executives indicated they also appreciate meaningful, relevant humor that breaks the tedium of typical presentations, and creativity such as metaphors, interesting examples, impacting visuals, and video specifically targeted to explain and make the topic more enjoyable and the presentation more compelling.

✔ Almost 6 out of 10 executives surveyed said that they generally depend upon intuition even though they examine the facts involved. They agreed that "very often in the face of facts, a gut decision is usually the right one."

✔ When asked what areas were important for a speaker to demonstrate during an executive presentation, respondents to the survey listed these as critical:

  • Knowledge of topic (98 percent rated it as very important, 2 percent as important)

  • Ability to be concise, yet thorough, complete, and accurate (79 percent rated it very important, 19 percent as important)

  • Enthusiasm and energy (72 percent rated it very important, 21 percent as important)

  • Fluency and clarity of communication (71 percent rated it very important, 29 percent as important)

✔ One of the most shocking was the answer to this question: "Looking back on presentations that you were a member of, how would you rate the overall quality of those presentations?" The responses from the survey:

Excellent: 8 percent

Good: 21 percent

Acceptable: 38 percent

Mediocre: 23 percent

Poor: 10 percent

This means that only about one of three presentations were seen as being good or excellent, and the majority (seven of ten) were viewed as just okay or worse.

Structuring Your Presentation

When you make a presentation to executives, you want them to rate the quality of your presentation as excellent, not acceptable, and by no means mediocre. By following the guidelines and suggestions we explain here, you increase your chances of giving a winning presentation to power brokers of any kind.

Key to any presentation is knowing your audience. Do your homework about the executives attending your session. Your presentation is all about them and their priorities, concerns, preferences, needs, and wants — not about you. Try to check with their assistants, lieutenants, or others who have presented to them to find out the best approach and content to use with that group.

Keeping it simple

As intelligent and prepared as executives are — or perhaps because of it — they don't tend to make assumptions or jump to conclusions, so don't expect them to connect the dots with your information. The more simple, obvious, clear, and direct you make your presentation, the better your chances of having them appreciate it. Use diagrams, illustrations, and graphics where you can to illustrate your concepts or proposed solutions and distribute handouts, a flash drive, or website address where they can review more detailed information after the presentation. The ideal balance is to make your presentation succinct, but rich in focused content.

Edit your presentation as you would a written document:

- ✔ Strip out adverbs.
- ✔ Keep clichés and common phrases to a minimum.
- ✔ Prefer the active tense over passive verbs and tenses.
- ✔ Use words or images that show rather than tell.
- ✔ Give each sentence/slide the TMI (Too Much Information) test: As you look at the slide, take the time to ask yourself, does it point to the conclusion or is it just a neat anecdote? If it's an interesting, relevant anecdote that points to the conclusion, by all means, leave it as part of your presentation.

Opening with a strong introduction

Your critical window of opportunity for making a favorable impression and grabbing your audience's interest is short. You must begin strong and sure and communicate benefits immediately. Address their concerns in about one minute. Demonstrate right away that you are a concise and effective communicator. Set expectations, let them know that you know what they want and tell them what you want, and then summarize — up front — as in this example:

> "Today I am highlighting a major opportunity for us in advanced manufacturing technologies that will provide five strategic benefits for our company. One: a return on investment that exceeds our hurdle rate by 65 percent and current gross margins by 45 percent; Two: an overall reduction of 45 percent in total manufacturing costs; Three: the numerous tangible and intangible advantages of bringing our manufacturing back to our country; Four: three vital ways we gain an impressive competitive advantage; and Five: the ability to do all these things in the next 18 months. I will cover the major highlights of each benefit and give you a handout with the details and supporting data to verify and prove our projections. If you are as convinced as we are about the efficacy of this uniquely engineered solution, I will ask for your specific support and funding to bring about these achievable financial returns. Let's start with a big-picture overview of the technology involved and how it translates into a financial bonanza for us."

Focusing on the big picture

Executives focus one-to-three years out and constantly review strategies and tactics to boost revenues, profits, competitiveness, and market share. Show how your high-level presentation topic will directly connect with and help fulfill their vision, mission, goals, and grand strategies for a better future.

Explain how the specifics of your recommendations address an urgent business requirement, will give an excellent return on investment, and positively benefit the organization's bottom line.

Showing and telling

Any time you can use photos, video, or animation to show your points better than you can describe or explain them in words, use them. Visual elements aid understanding. In addition, demonstrating a prototype, finished product, or service can dramatically reinforce what you're saying. Emphasize and highlight your key points to have them stand out.

Projecting confidence and flexibility

Although it may seem difficult, especially if you're new to presenting to decision makers, try your best to come across in a natural, relaxed, and confident way.

You know your topic better than anyone in the audience, and you need to project that expertise without any hint of arrogance. If you come across as someone who is an optimistic, realistic, can-do leader who gets results, your presentation is sure to be successful. You want to display an appropriate amount of energy, passion, and enthusiasm without overdoing it.

Expect executives to pose questions at any time and ask you to jump back to a slide that interested them. You may also have to fast-forward through your slides and otherwise be able to quickly and randomly move around your visuals. If someone asks a question, even though you have that information either on a slide or as a prepared remark later on, go ahead and answer the question right away — if you can do so effectively — rather than telling someone that you will discuss that later on. Doing an articulate job of extemporaneously answering questions enhances your credibility on the spot.

It's a good idea to engineer your slides with hyperlinks that navigate to hidden slides with extra detail or supporting data including videos, diagrams, and illustrations that quicken understanding and acceptance of your points.

Being a master of your topic

To establish utmost credibility, know your information completely and be able to give in-depth facts, statistics, and other data without referring to your slides or notes. Being articulate and organized in your communication without employing slides as a crutch testifies to your knowledge of the situation, the problem, and the proposed solution. Anticipate tough questions and have a strategy and answer at the ready to handle them with grace and poise.

Telling a compelling story

Executives often trust their intuition more than they do sterile data. A brief, interesting, relevant story that highlights or supports your key points can be invaluable, especially if you can tell the story with video that includes examples, metaphors, testimonials, quotations, or embedded facts and statistics that illuminate and support your presentation's focus. A good story with a strong moral at the end is memorable and impactful, both intellectually and emotionally. Tom Peters said, "The best leaders . . . almost without exception and at every level are master users of stories and symbols."

Describing implications and situations

When you're giving facts, statistics, or examples, or telling brief stories, indicate what that data shows and proves — such as definite trends, solid relationships, accurate projections/forecasts, causes and effects, consequences, and undeniable conclusions. Indicate likely risks, probabilities, options/alternatives, and tradeoffs to help executives accurately assess your recommendation.

Planning time wisely

Unlike a conference where you have about ten minutes for a question-and-answer session (Q & A), a presentation to executives demands ample time for questions. Plan to give the same amount of time to your presentation and the Q &A. If you have 30 minutes allotted for your presentation, for example, then plan on giving a 15-minute presentation and leave 15 minutes to answer questions. The Q & A is a way of engaging your group and encouraging feedback about your topic. Always plan to end on schedule or even a bit early — never run over! Your audience will appreciate that you understand the value of their time.

Rehearsing your lines

If millions (or billions) of dollars depend upon your presentation, your preparation and rehearsal time should be extensive. When we coach our clients on career-affecting presentations, we recommend they plan, prepare, and rehearse anywhere from 20 to 50 times the length of the presentation. So, if you have an hour allotted for your presentation, invest at least 20 hours and probably more on rehearsing, especially if it's a team presentation.

Ray had an international accounting firm client bidding on a huge deal worth more than $50 million. Together, Ray and the client team spent almost three days rehearsing for a 30-minute presentation. That dedicated preparation and practice resulted in winning the deal in spite of a ferocious competitor that was favored before the presentation.

Considering Content

This section of the chapter gives you some guidelines about the types of content and information decision makers require when evaluating projects, programs, capital acquisitions, or other business-related purchases or organizational changes. Even if you're not presenting to higher-level groups, understanding the questions they may want answered helps you with practically any business or even technical presentation.

Most strategic presentations should last no longer than 30 minutes. Even though you provide summary information — almost like an oral rendition of a brief, well-written magazine article — you need to be prepared to get into specifics and details on any aspect of your talk. Structuring your presentation to be effective and efficient, thorough, precise, and yet concise, in such a limited time period becomes all the more important. Your presentation content should follow these seven general steps:

1. **Review the problem or opportunity.**

2. **Summarize your proposed solution or way of capitalizing upon the opportunity.**

3. **Outline the goals, benefits, and strategies of your proposed approach.**

4. **Discuss potential options, drawbacks, risks, and limitations regarding it.**

5. **Present the overall cost and returns on (short- and long-term) investment.**

6. **List the resources and implementation needed.**

7. **Justify moving ahead on it now.**

Discussing additional details

Executives are most impressed with presenters who are thoroughly versed in their topic and eminently prepared to discuss any aspect of it. That's why smart presenters always have extra visuals and specific information — in reserve — to bring out and cover when questions or concerns from the group pop up.

Whether it is a proposed solution, program, project, opportunity, organizational change, or innovation of some type, make the facts and numbers come alive and be ready to discuss more detailed items.

Coming up with solutions to problems

Your job, when presenting to executive decision makers at your own or another company, is to offer solutions — in the form of specific ideas, plans, products, services, or other proposals — that help the company meet its goals.

Here we share a list of questions to guide your thought process to arrive at the solution you want to present. Take the time to write out the answers, perhaps with your business partner or team, and you'll begin to see the solution take shape. The resulting solution is what you'll present to the decision makers.

- ✔ What specific evidence indicates the importance of the problem or opportunity facing the group?

- ✔ What are the main issues (in priority order) revolving around it?

- ✔ When did the problem or opportunity first present itself and what has been its prior history in whatever form?

- ✔ Does the problem or opportunity require quick, decisive action? What will happen if nothing is done?

- ✔ What areas, operations, departments, and people in the organization are impacted by the problem or opportunity now and to what extent? What will the future impact likely be? Where would its effect be most felt and by whom?

- ✔ What has been done to date (if anything) and what were the results?

- ✔ What are the key goals and objectives of the solution or program?

- ✔ What changes will be brought about by the solution or opportunity and when will they occur?

- ✔ What has been the experience (if any) of other organizations implementing this type of solution or taking advantage of this form of opportunity?

- ✔ What are the determining critical success factors for solving the problem or capitalizing upon the opportunity?

- ✔ What are the possible negatives from best-case to worst-case — drawbacks, disruptions, temporary setbacks, inconveniences, limitations, special requirements, and risks — that may impact current systems, processes, procedures, and methods?

- ✔ What internal organizational issues, politics, or cultural aspects may impede implementing the solution or going forward with this opportunity?

- ✔ What are the alternatives to dealing with this solution or opportunity?

- ✔ What is the process, timeframe, and strategy to implement the solution or opportunity?

- ✔ What internal and external resources, personnel, and activities are required for success?

- ✔ How simple or complex will the implementation and ongoing operation be? What continuous maintenance is required?

- ✔ How will operational effectiveness, efficiency, quality, and productivity be impacted?

- ✔ What milestones and measurements will gauge the progress and completion of the program?

- ✔ What progress reports are planned and when are they developed and given to whom?

- ✔ What preventive measures, contingency plans, or other safeguards are built in to deal with potential problems, setbacks, and challenges?

- ✔ Is it possible to test the solution or take advantage of part of the opportunity in a relatively fast, quick, easy, and inexpensive way?

- ✔ What is the breakdown of implementation costs? What costs are there to sustain the solution or opportunity?

- ✔ What short-and long-term cost savings and other financial returns, such as ratios, averages, return on investment, and payback, (best-to-worst case) can be expected?

Be ready to provide evidence of the various financial outcomes by inputting data that shows options. Thinking about these questions prepares you for "what if" questions from your target presentation group. Understanding the interrelationships with various factors and data helps decision makers make informed decisions.

Chapter 22

Condensing Your Pitch: The Elevator-Ride Approach

*O*ne of the questions you'll be asked most often in your lifetime is "What do you do?" You hear it when you meet someone new at a party, when you run into an old classmate in the airport, even when you see a long-lost cousin at a family reunion — and these are just informal situations. At organized networking events, tradeshows, benefits, and job fairs, it's one of the first questions you hear.

Do you stumble and mumble a response out of the side of your mouth along the lines of "I'm a, um, manager for a, er, plumbing supplies company." Or do you smile and respond, "I help forgetful people keep their floors and ceilings dry — my company designs and sells overflow valves so if you leave the faucet open when the phone rings, the kitchen doesn't flood. Has that ever happened to you?"

Although only one to two minutes long, this type of introduction, or *elevator pitch* as it's called, should compel your listener to say, "Tell me more." According to an article in the Harvard Business Review about giving an elevator pitch, the average New York City elevator ride lasts 118 seconds. In that brief time, you creatively explain what you do by describing the solution you offer and who you offer it to. When the listener responds with interest, you can then ask questions to determine if there's an opportunity to do business.

In this chapter, we explain the concept and content of an elevator pitch, and then take you through guided steps to creating your own. We also show you how to tweak your elevator pitch to meet the needs of different circumstances. Throughout, we give you examples to spur your imagination.

Making the Most of Your Sound Bite

Your elevator pitch is a sound bite from your longer, introductory presentation. A *sound bite* is a concise statement extracted from a television or radio interview used to publicize the television or radio show containing the interview.

Much like your full-blown presentations, your elevator pitch should be about the person or company your product or service helps, not about you and your company directly. You want to find a balance between telling enough in plain language to solicit interest without giving so much detail that you confuse or bore your listener. After you hear an invitation in the form of a "Tell me more," response, you can go in to more detail. But even then, you want to keep the exchange conversational. Ask the person you're speaking with questions — she may want to give her elevator pitch to you, too — to see where the conversation leads. When the elevator stops, virtually or literally, offer your business card and state a call to action, such as "It was nice to meet you. I'm looking to expand my client base; do you use a service like mine or know someone who does? Give me a call if you do."

During an elevator pitch, you want to introduce yourself, your company, and your product or service — not close a sale.

Describing what you do

Creating an elevator pitch isn't a matter of telling everything about you and your business in the shortest time possible, speaking rapidly without breathing. You craft an elevator pitch that effectively communicates what you do in as few carefully chosen words as possible.

Start by jotting down the answer to the following questions and then use your responses to hone your message:

- **What** do you do? The answer encompasses you personally as well as your company.
- **What** benefit does your product or service provide?
- **Who** do you do it for or with?
- **When** did you begin or when did a significant event occur?
- **Where** do you do it?
- **Why** should the listener care?
- **How** are you different?

The following is a sample elevator pitch:

> "We're a presentation consulting and development firm unlike any other. We work with all sorts of clients in all industries to help them close more and bigger deals by developing incredibly compelling innovative presentations that will beat — hands down — even their strongest, toughest competitors. Over the last three years we helped our clients close an extra $450 million in deals that they admit they would have likely lost had they not used our services. These clients, like yourself, can expect from us an unheard of return on investment of roughly between 300 to over 2,000 percent! We invented and engineered a radically new and special communication model that combines creativity and technology to give you presentations that are light-years ahead of traditional PowerPoint ones. We can do the same for your company, whether we do it on-site or virtually to any location around the world. Can I call you to briefly discuss specifically how we can boost your deal-closings ratio?"

Developing a concise, compelling pitch

With your answers in hand, start to compose your pitch. You can begin with your name and describe the benefit your product, service, or company brings to its customers — this is called the *value proposition*. Think creatively. For example, if you're a baker, rather than say "I make cakes for people," say "I sweeten people's lives." If your company is designing jet-propelled rockets, rather than "We design rockets" say "We send people to the moon." Use an opening phrase that surprises, or even shocks, the listener.

Your elevator pitch should induce your listener to invite you to "Tell me more" not shut you down with a "So what."

Follow up with a bit about who your customers are and specify what you do for them. For example, for the baker who wants a corporate catering contract, after "I sweeten people's lives" add "by delivering scrumptious birthday cakes to corporate clients."

At this point, if your time is almost up, you can say, "Let me give you my card. I have a special promotion for first-time events."

You can also add a few details from the other questions you answered before getting to your call to action, such as, "My bakery's right downtown, near Union Square." Location is appropriate for the baker because a company might like to know the caterer won't be held up in traffic. For another business, location may not matter, so you can talk about the number of clients that use your product or service.

Your elevator pitch changes based on the amount of time you have — the ride from the ground to the fourth floor is shorter than that to the thirtieth floor — and you have to quickly adjust your message to fit the few seconds you have. For example, with less time, say 15 seconds, you answer only the What, Who, and Why questions from the list in the preceding section, something like this:

> "Hi, I'm Sara and my company, Redwood Music, helps people concentrate while doing tasks that require focus. On our website, people listen to music specially written to calm the part of the brain that normally distracts the part that's working. Would a service like that help your customers?"

With more time, you can add a little more information:

> "Hi, I'm Sara. My company, Redwood Music, helps people concentrate while doing tasks that require focus. On our website, you can listen to music specially written to calm the part of the brain that normally distracts the part that's working. Writers and programmers make up a good portion of our listeners. I'm looking for parallel companies that want to reach that audience. Here's my card in case you or someone you know might want to consider advertising with us."

Depending on who's standing in front of you, not to mention your position and personal style, you might want to use a different style of delivery. For example, you can tell a story like this:

> "You know when you're trying to write a press release but you write two words and then check Facebook, write another two words and then get up to get a cup of coffee, change the first two words you wrote and then check your e-mail? (Listener nods and grimaces, identifying with the story.) My company, Redwood Music, helps people focus on the task at hand."

At which point, the listener might say, "Really? How? Tell me more," and you give more details, perhaps telling the story of how the composers and neurologists work together or highlighting how the music taps into a specific part of the brain.

You can also use a question to begin your elevator pitch. Try a rhetorical question and go directly into the answer or ask a genuine question to get an idea of the level of information that would benefit the listener. Consider something like this:

> "Are you easily distracted while working on a task that requires focus? Who isn't, right? Redwood Music, where I'm the ad sales manager, puts music online that helps you concentrate."

The listener says something like "No way, how's that work? Where can I sign up?" and you have your invitation to tell her more about your company and job and make your request as appropriate.

Make your elevator pitch about the listener and her problem (or the type and problem of client you seek). Every word you speak should be about what concerns the potential client — even though it's about you.

Testing your pitch

After you hone and winnow your elevator pitch, you want to test it. First, edit your pitch so that someone who isn't in your industry can understand it. Do the following:

- ✔ Replace passive verbs (is, are) with active verbs (creates, provides).
- ✔ Eliminate adverbs (mostly words ending in -ly).
- ✔ Replace jargon with common words.

    Jargon can confuse your listener, who may be embarrassed to ask questions or wrongly assume she knows what you mean.

After you refine your pitch, test it on people you know will give you honest, helpfully critical feedback. Ask them to

- ✔ Identify words they don't understand so that you can replace them with simpler words, describe the terms, or eliminate them.
- ✔ Tell you what they remember so you can see if the message you want to convey is the one that comes across.

Refine and test your pitch again until your listeners understand it and the message they remember is the one you want to communicate.

Minding Your Business

After you develop your pitch, distribute it to whomever in your company may need to use it. People who deal with the public frequently, such as the receptionist or customer relations representative, should understand and be able to clearly state what your company does and be able to direct the listener to the right department for the next step.

Upper management and executive staff members should use similar elevator pitches, and their positions give them the freedom to make adjustments according to their experience and level of command.

Customizing your pitch

Although what you and your company do remains the same, the way you talk about it changes slightly depending on the situation. For example, if you go to an association meeting or a cross-industry meet up, it's a networking opportunity. You may meet people in your industry or you may meet people who know people in your industry, so you want to put the networking spin on your elevator pitch. If, instead, you have a potential client in front of you, you want to be more specific about your product or service and how it could help them.

You can use one of the different styles of elevator pitch or adjust the call to action at the end, as in these examples:

- ✔ **Networking:** "I'm looking to meet people who want to increase their social media reach."

- ✔ **Potential client:** "I'd really like the opportunity to show you some of our samples, can I call you to make an appointment?"

- ✔ **Fundraising:** "I want to bring a smile to orphans' faces and am looking for people to donate toys."

Using your elevator pitch in other circumstances

Just as elevator pitches aren't limited to elevators, they also aren't limited to sales pitches. The same strategy for developing an elevator pitch for your business applies when you want to talk about yourself or a project or idea you have.

When you want to change jobs, create an elevator pitch about yourself, your experience, and how you can help the type of company you want to work for. Keep in mind that other candidates will be doing the same thing and have similar experience so look for the trait or experience that distinguishes you from the crowd.

The more elevator pitches you create, the better you become at crafting a clear, concise, effective message. If you have a project or idea to propose to your colleagues, managers, or company executives, craft an elevator pitch both to better define your idea but also to be ready to present it in an unexpected encounter.

Now that you spent the time developing your elevator pitch, use it as the tagline for your social networking profile, the signature block on your e-mail, or a 30-second introductory video for your website.

Chapter 23

Presenting as an Impressive Team

*L*arge-scale, complex deals for sophisticated projects costing hundreds of millions — or billions — of dollars demand team solutions. Whether presenting to potential clients or corporate decision makers, meetings about big systems or infrastructure projects and programs in multifaceted industries such as aerospace, construction, engineering, and high tech often require a team presentation. In these situations, the team comprises numerous experts speaking about their technical, scientific, engineering, financial, logistical, and project management knowledge.

At its simplest, a team presentation translates into a single presentation with several participants: There is one plan and one person in charge. Nonetheless, these types of presentations, which may last several hours in total, necessitate the participation of specialists who communicate information relative to their area of expertise.

Team presentations can be dazzling displays of collective expertise, impressive communication, and top-notch professionalism. Although presentations with three or more presenters have the potential to be exciting, energetic, and compelling, they are also more difficult to execute well compared to a single or dual presenter forum because they require careful planning, coordination, and orchestration. Preparation for such a presentation can take weeks or sometimes months.

In this chapter, we define a quality team presentation, with examples, and then take you through the steps of choosing team members, assigning roles, rehearsing, and giving an innovative, winning presentation.

Team presentations aren't limited to mega-deals. Sales, advertising, or public-relations teams, as well as many other types of business and technical teams, often give joint talks. For example, a sales team of four people gives a presentation about their new product. The team leader kicks it off with a strong introduction, another person discusses the features, capabilities, technical aspects, and benefits of the offering, the third member covers pricing and return on investment, and the fourth talks about implementation and contractual terms and conditions. Finally, the team leader concludes with a compelling summary and a sales close or other call to action.

Defining a Quality Team Presentation

A great team presentation that demonstrates a variety of knowledge and skill and shows commanding leadership will win over an audience immediately compared to average (acceptable) presentations by other teams.

For example, say a company wants to construct an ultramodern, showcase headquarters using the latest energy-saving technologies, materials, and construction techniques. They request presentations from three leading architectural firms. The team presentations mirror the working style and ethic of each firm (who if chosen, will be critical parts of the design and development team). The thinking, personalities, and cooperation shine through the team presentation dynamics. The presentations give the audience a trial run with the teams and indicate how the presenting company will work with the purchasing company. The audience wants to feel the team will be easy to work with and can deliver on their promises. If they cannot plan and deliver a unified, well-assembled, smooth presentation, how can a customer trust them to work on a project that requires even more comprehensive teamwork from the various areas in the company? This rule applies to projects and sales of any size.

Investors love to experience teams that demonstrate firsthand how the dynamic entrepreneurial CEO is in charge and can lead smart, talented people to grow their firm. John Briggs, the author of *Fire in the Crucible: Understanding the Process of Creative Genius* said, ". . .collaboration is one of the best kept secrets in creativity." With the right team working in the right ways, that collaborative creativity during the presentation will make all the difference that matters.

It was basketball great Michael Jordan who said, "Talent wins games, but teamwork and intelligence wins championships." You can compare a team presentation to playing sports or doing any number of activities that require people to work together in a seamless, flawless fashion — for example, an orchestra performing a symphony. Each musician plays a single instrument and specific bars and measures, but all are playing in a synchronized, integrated, and harmonious way. The audience not only listens joyously and perhaps with wonder, but feels the performance as well.

Think of your outline as the sheet music of your presentation. The interaction between the various components of a presentation is perfectly timed and well-rehearsed. A championship team presentation has one resounding sound comprised of those vital, compelling messages and supporting information like perfect notes that strike the right tone with an anticipating audience. The team leader — a talented maestro or band leader — plans, coordinates, communicates, and keeps everyone on track, on tempo, on target. Consider how every slightest movement and action of a racing car pit crew is choreographed for maximum speed, effectiveness, and efficiency. Champions of all kinds aim for that level of superb teamwork and dedication to win.

We worked with an extraordinary high-level engineer who led dozens of team presentations resulting in almost a billion dollars in international deals for his automated manufacturing and robotic equipment company. His philosophy and strategy are telling. He said, "We always focus on what we deem the Art of Disruption in our team presentations. We structure and deliver them in the most innovative ways using video, multimedia animation, impressive prototypes, models, and live demonstrations. We have continuously improved our presentation styles so they are supremely polished and smooth, but always conversational, sincere, and natural in ways that we can connect emotionally, not just intellectually, with our buyers. By our having superb team presentations, packed with compelling technical and financial information, we disrupt any thoughts that a potential customer might have about not buying from us. And, we certainly disrupt the presentations of our competitors by our unmatched team communication, genuine enthusiasm to deliver exceptional results for our customers, our confidence, and our professional excellence!"

We couldn't define a quality team presentation better ourselves!

Making the Team

A successful team presentation has a strong, action-oriented leader. Within the company, the leader may have the title of project manager, sales account manager, owner, or executive responsible for a strategic change or innovation. Although the presentation team leader may choose to delegate some of the execution of specific tasks, he takes responsibility for many or all of the following jobs:

- **Selecting well-suited team members:** Typically team members are subject-matter experts who present effectively, or who can at least be coached or trained to present well.

- **Defining desirable goals:** Often the goal is inherent in the presentation or audience type, although an obvious goal of wanting to win a new client can be further defined by the scope, such as the monetary value of the new business.

- **Planning practical strategies:** Strategies are not set in stone, but open for discussion and enhancement with the rest of the team.

- **Managing the creation of materials:** Overseeing the design and production of content, handouts, and visual materials.

- **Setting deadlines:** Keeps presentation preparation on schedule and takes swift, decisive corrective action when needed to keep things on track.

- **Managing team members:** A presentation leader facilitates, motivates, evaluates, and coaches team members during the team rehearsals, as well as during the preparation leading to the rehearsals.

The strong, creative team leader, like a good quarterback, calls the plays ahead of the meeting and takes the lead at the start and throughout the actual presentation. The leader gives each member of the presentation team a detailed overview of the situation; identifies the major decision makers, their needs, wants, priorities, and preferences; directs members what to focus on during the presentation and what to avoid saying and doing; anticipates the potential competitors; foresees likely obstacles or resistance posed by some in the group; and does anything else that helps each member best craft their part of the overall presentation. A good team leader motivates and manages the team before, during, and after the presentation.

Although a C-level executive (CEO, COO, CFO, CTO, and so on) may be present at the meeting to make firm commitments and assure the audience of the organization's full support, the team leader presides over the presentation and runs the show as emcee, moderator, host, and the central — though not exclusive — focal point with whom the audience communicates. During the formal question-and-answer session (Q & A), the team leader stands up to either answer questions or direct them to the person who can answer them. The clients or audience should get a clear sense of who is in charge of the process.

It was the lovable double-talking curmudgeon Casey Stengel, former baseball manager, who aptly said, "Gettin' good players is easy. Gettin' 'em to play together is the hard part." The Old Perfessor, as he was known, spoke from experience. Garnering cooperation from team members who share common traits (successful, experienced, smart, creative, and likely [or rightly] opinionated) might not be easy, but the guidelines in the following sections can help you facilitate the process and demonstrate your competent leadership.

Passing the baton

The team leader should typically kick off the presentation with a riveting introduction and an enticing call to action. He can also introduce team members. At the start, the leader can say something like, "On my right is Sally G., our Operations Planning Manager, who will talk about our current process and why it is not meeting our goals. Next to her is Marcus J., our Innovation

Development Manager, who will give you an overview of our proposed new process and the beneficial innovations it will bring to our company. Next to him is. . . ." The team leader, as emcee, can re-introduce the co-presenters as they step up to present with something like, "I've already quickly introduced Marcus who will discuss our new process. I think you will be impressed with the innovations he will cover. In the three years he has worked with us, Marcus has implemented over 18 breakthrough improvements that saved our company almost $50 million. Marcus . . ."

The introductions you make at the beginning of the meeting and before each presenter speaks should be brief, yet give three key pieces of information:

- ✔ The presenter's name, which confirms the personal connection between the leader and the presenter and begins to create a personal connection with the audience
- ✔ The presenter's title, or a brief mention of his responsibilities, which testifies to the expertise he brings to the presentation
- ✔ The part of the presentation the person will be giving

Another way of making a transition from one presenter to the next is to have each presenter introduce the next speaker along with a topic transition such as, "As you have seen during my presentation, our current process is wholly inadequate to deal with our competitor's improvements. I'd like to get Marcus up here to discuss how six vital benefits of our new, innovative process will enable us to now clobber our competitors. Marcus has a master's degree in process improvement and more than ten years of extensive experience in achieving significant results. Marcus . . ."

The team decides how best to handle the transition introductions. Having the team leader make each introduction lends a formal tone to the presentation as a whole, while having each member introduce the next speaker makes the presentation more conversational.

Here is an example of a two-way transition and buildup:

> Marcus does a quick summary, "I've discussed how our new process design will not only dramatically boost productivity and efficiency, but quality as well and give us a competitive edge for years to come." He introduces the next speaker with a benefit-related buildup, "Now Gerald will cover what it will take to properly implement our new process. I think you will be quite pleased with the ease and cost to do it. Gerald . . ."

> Gerald transitions with, "Thank you, Marcus. As Marcus has covered, it is clear we can get definite substantial strategic enhancements in productivity, efficiency, and quality. No doubt! But what will it take? Will it disrupt our present operations? Will it involve a lot of time and money? Will our departments resist this change? And what are the real returns on our investment. The answers are . . . No, No, No and a very worthwhile return — over 36 percent — on our short- and long-term investment! Let me explain . . . ."

The mutual summarizing and transitional buildup of important information between speakers creates a seamless and transparent story that your audience follows. There are different ways to hand off to each other and have a smooth transition between topics. These skills must be practiced in your rehearsals until they become second nature to you.

Smooth, effective transitions and buildups can impress an audience, although they probably won't be noticed unless they're done poorly. The right type of repetition and summarizing help reinforce key points and emphasize vital facts or statistics that help achieve your presentation goals. You leave the audience with the impression that they've seen a cohesive, professional presentation.

Sitting on the bench

During every moment of the presentation, non-speaking team members support the speaker. All team members should focus on the speaker, even if they've heard that part dozens of times before. If people in the audience see some team members tuning out, looking bored, or worse yet, texting or reading e-mail, that sends a negative message to the group and draws attention away from the presenter.

If you absolutely must respond to an urgent call, discreetly excuse yourself at an opportune moment, ideally after you've presented your part.

Steady eye contact, smiling, nodding in support of key points, and laughing when the presenter delivers an amusing comment shows that team members appreciate each other and are interested in hearing the information — as if for the first time. What's more, if you're asked to respond to an audience question generated from something said by a presenter or asked a question by the speaker, you'll know what was said last. Likewise, the presenter should occasionally look directly at the other team members while presenting as if he was talking just to them. And if a member of the team is having difficulty answering a question from someone, the other team member(s) should jump in to help out. Teamwork is all about assisting and encouraging each other!

If you have trouble paying attention to something you've heard a dozen times, try taking notes while listening to your colleagues' presentations, which can help you stay focused on the words being said.

The other thing team members who are not presenting (especially the team leader) should do is subtly and casually observe the faces of attendees to see how they're reacting to information in the presentation. Do any seem confused, skeptical, frustrated or, perhaps enamored? During the Q & A, a team member can jump in and probe to clarify, confirm, or find out what concerns audience members have. You can also use the opportunity to reinforce positive feelings people indicated by their facial expressions or subtle comments.

What do you do if a presenting team member says something incorrect or makes a commitment that was not agreed upon in the planning and rehearsal sessions? Instead of jumping in to abruptly interrupt right after the gaffe, wait until your colleague pauses and say something like, "I need to clarify something that was just said" or "As account manager, let me modify what David mentioned about a term and condition." The presenter who misspoke should not show impatience or irritation to an important, needed comment interjected by the team leader or other member wanting to help.

Team members need to be very careful about their reactions to their fellow speakers while they're presenting or responding to a comment from the audience. We've seen situations when a presenter was answering a question from the group and his teammates' body language made it evident that they were not happy with his reply. Avoid rolling your eyes, suddenly crossing your arms defensively, sighing, and grimacing. Be very careful of your body language while sitting on the sideline. Remember, showing good camaraderie and being a consummate team player is vital to success.

Avoiding common mistakes

We've been on both sides of the podium, so to speak (pardon the pun), and as much as we can explain how things should be done to give a successful, team presentation, we thought we should point out some things you shouldn't do. In keeping with a positive spirit, we also point out the positive, thing-to-do counter action. Table 23-1 summarizes our advice.

Table 23-1	The Dos and Don'ts of Team Presentations
Avoid	*Do*
Stealing someone else's lines.	Repeat someone else's line for emphasis, citing the original speaker's name (as Marcus said . . .).
Bringing more people than necessary.	Evaluate the role of each team member and eliminate overlap.
Dictating and forcing your opinions on others.	Express you own opinion firmly once and listen openly to the other side — if opinions should even be expressed about the matter at hand.

(continued)

Table 23-1 *(continued)*

Avoid	*Do*
Frequently interrupting to add comments.	Take note of the comments you'd like to add and share them when the speaker has finished. Each speaker could ask if colleagues have anything to add before handing off to the next speaker.
Not adequately participating in planning meetings.	Decline taking on more responsibility than you have time for. Speak up if you aren't participating because there's a personality conflict.
Going in and out of the room while the presentation is live.	Leave the room only for an emergency.
Talking too softly and having low energy.	Before the meeting, take a brisk walk, do some deep breathing exercises, touch your toes to encourage your blood to circulate to your brain.
Delegating your presentation development to others.	Ask for help if you need it, otherwise, knuckle down and make the presentation your own.
Doing something other than watching the presenter.	Take notes to help channel your attention.
Refusing to rehearse, especially the dress rehearsal.	Remember this is a business presentation, not improv at open mic night.
Becoming annoyed at audience questions or comments	Consider them an opportunity to add insight and explanations about the presentation
Disagreeing with each other in front of audience.	Make necessary corrections politely, otherwise, make a note and discuss the problem with team members back at the office.
Trying to wing it or make up an answer you don't know.	Ask if another team member can address a question you don't know the answer to. If not, take a note and promise to follow up with an informed response.
Being inconsistent with information or commitments.	Make team agreements and review materials and data before the presentation.
"Studying" your notes right before you present. (It makes it look as if you're not fully prepared.)	Rehearse, rehearse, and then rehearse again, and use a presentation app that shows the presenter notes on your computer screen or tablet.

Rehearsing Your Lines

The higher the number of moving parts and the more presenters present, the more complicated the presentation and challenging its goals. So, team rehearsals are not just desirable, they are critical, indispensible, absolutely, positively necessary! Rehearsals provide an opportunity to fine-tune the overall content, strategy, and visuals, and polish everyone's presentation skills resulting in a seamless presentation given by a cohesive, unified team. Rehearsals also show each team member how the whole presentation comes about and how their parts fit in to contribute to the desired outcomes.

Planning your rehearsals

You probably have several planning meetings leading up to rehearsals. The initial meeting(s) focus on the overall presentation goals and content development. The team, guided by the team leader, decides who will present which information then individual members work on creating their parts of the presentation. Ideally, each person rehearses his own part and gets the visuals and handouts he uses as ready as possible before everyone presents together. Rehearsals begin after individual presentations are created.

Use Skype or other live video programs if people are in other parts of the world and cannot meet for the initial round of rehearsals. But all members should physically be together one or two days before the big meeting to rehearse live on the spot several times.

Expect the first two or three rehearsals to be choppy and rough. Performances will improve and smooth out with each subsequent go-through. After each rehearsal, the team leader and others should give constructive feedback to each team member in a specific, positive, and encouraging way. Itemized evaluation sheets filled out during each person's practice help focus comments and feedback on presentation content and skills. The evaluation sheets can guide the feedback discussion and the speaker can refer to it when practicing alone. (Head to www.dummies.com/cheatsheet/innovativepresentations for a sample evaluation form.) For very important presentations, consider hiring and using an experienced professional presentation trainer/coach to lead the improvement effort.

We recommend videotaping after the second or third rehearsal to give people a chance to improve by seeing themselves on playback. Time each person's part. Play back the video immediately to enable people to see what to do differently at the next go-around. Depending upon the team's skills and the strategic nature of the presentation, as a general rule, have five to ten rehearsals until the team nails the last two or three in a row.

Finalizing the presentation with a dress rehearsal

Plan for a final dress rehearsal a day or morning before the big event. On the day of the meeting arrive early (even two hours early or the night before) to check out the room, set up equipment, position handouts and visuals/displays, and rearrange the seating if necessary and possible. Then relax before the group comes in so you can calmly meet and greet people as they arrive.

Consider bringing your own equipment such as a projector you know how to set up and use. Always ask for backup equipment if it's critical to your presentation.

Follow these suggestions for getting your rehearsals just right and ready:

- ✔ Focus on achieving smooth introductions of the team and seamless transitions and handoffs between team members.

- ✔ Invite an internal group to serve as an audience for the final two or three rehearsals. Give them a list of questions — including tough ones — to ask of the presenters and elicit their overall feedback on the performance. The team should develop a complete list of anticipated questions the audience might ask, including simple and difficult ones.

- ✔ Make sure each person concisely and subtly reinforces the key points that previous speakers made to ensure the audience absorbs and appreciates the message. Fix any inconsistencies or other aspects that would adversely affect the quality of the event.

- ✔ Practice fielding questions. The account or project manager, as team leader, acts as the moderator handling questions. The team leader practices either answering key questions or deciding which team member is best qualified to answer. In addition, the team should practice answering objections or other forms of possible negative or hostile comments. Consider all potential responses from the audience.

- ✔ Assign someone to keep a close eye on time in both rehearsals and the actual presentation. A good idea is to use a monitor (small television or computer screen) in front of the presenter that shows the time remaining for his part.

- ✔ If a C-level (CEO, COO, CFO) is attending the presentation as part of the team, he should attend at least one rehearsal (if not more) and be thoroughly briefed on critical points to stress, agreed-upon commitments, and anything else that might otherwise cause surprises or problems. You want to ensure compatibility and uniformity.

- ✔ Try to present in conditions as realistic as possible using the equipment you expect to use and in a room similar to that you will be in during the presentation. Try to visit, or get a photo, of the room you will be in to plan your room setup and become familiar with the layout.

✔ Develop an attention-getting, dynamic introduction that sets the tone and anticipation for the rest of the presentation. The team leader should also practice a strong summary of key points of the entire presentation along with a call to action for the audience.

✔ Consider assigning each person a backup/alternate presenter in the event there is an unavoidable no-show for one of the presenters. During rehearsals, have those team members competently perform the presentation originally assigned to someone else.

Famous football coach Vince Lombardi said, "Practice doesn't make perfect. Perfect practice makes perfect."

Planning for Ultimate Success

Most lawyers fervently believe that a case is won or lost before they ever enter a courtroom because it is the research, analysis, preparation, and strategies that firmly set the wheels in motion for a decisive win. The same is true with important team presentations. The more critical the presentation and consequences of it are, the more extensive the time and effort you dedicate to getting ready. Preparation can't begin soon enough, and waiting only increases risks of all kinds. Begin by carefully selecting a team that will work effectively together. Follow these guidelines to help ace your planning and preparation.

Giving background information

The team leader should inform team members about all aspects relevant to giving a winning presentation, including an audience description, the situation they're likely to encounter, the goals and strategy for the presentation, what to focus on, and what to do and not do. Write a common document that summarizes this important information and refer to it when someone goes off on a tangent or strays from the task and goals at hand.

Creating a strong outline

The team leader should draft a proposed outline (some call it a *straw man* or *skeleton outline*) as the starting point for planning the entire presentation. Then, brainstorm with the team to get their ideas and recommendations for improvement and their agreement.

A good outline shows logical flow, continuity, consistency, and transitions of each part playing into the whole. Shorten or omit parts of the outline deemed unnecessary. Provide enough content to present your case and cover all the points; use examples to support your case without digressing to gratuitous anecdotes. Do the topics support and complement each other? Do they lead to the presentation goals? Check for overlap, contradiction, and possible ambiguity.

Focusing on priorities

Whether you call it a core message, main point, or winning theme, have the team agree on what it is so they can repeat it during their portion of the presentation and otherwise appropriately reinforce and highlight it for the audience. Likewise, the facts, statistics, and metaphors that act as vital supporting points and reminders throughout the session should emphasize your key points.

Implementing a timeline

Together with the team leader, all members should put together and agree upon a detailed, realistic implementation plan and timeline of activities to finish, and then make firm commitments to meet the milestones. The team leader should send out reminders to each person for upcoming milestones, and address and help any team member struggling with a deadline before he falls too far behind.

Determine the total time allocated for the presentation, and then with the team decide which portions require more or less time based upon the perceived priority of the topics.

For example, say you have a total time of an hour and a half (90 minutes) and four presenters. You can start by saying that each one has about 15 minutes (even though later it's decided some may get some 10 minutes and others 20 or so). Assume you give 10 minutes for the presentation introduction and conclusion (which is generous) and 30 minutes for the formal Q & A at the end.

Always aim to finish your presentation 20 to 30 percent quicker than the time you are given. Consider the following mishaps that eat into your allotted time:

- ✔ The customer starts late, but asks your team to finish at the stated time.
- ✔ The computer or projection system crashes.
- ✔ You get many more questions than expected during each portion of the multi-part presentation.
- ✔ The main decision makers want to focus on just one aspect of the presentation.
- ✔ Key people in the audience must suddenly leave for ten minutes or more.

Even if you allocate roughly 15 minutes per presenter, ask each to adequately finish his part in 10 minutes with 5 minutes devoted to answering questions or having discussions with those in the audience.

Presentations should not be designed to fill every minute available on the agenda. Plan for flexibility and adaptability. This time-based strategy will help you enormously. If you finish early, while achieving your objectives, the group will love it.

Preparing for the worst

The previous section touched on several what-ifs from the audience. There are numerous other Murphy's Law scenarios for which you should have contingency options, such as equipment malfunctions or breakdowns, or an unexpectedly absent presenter. Assign someone to deal with malfunctioning equipment while another team member sets up a backup piece of critical equipment. Create a backup plan for a team member's unexpected delay or absence on presentation day. Some team leaders ask each member to not only perfect their own presentation but get to know another assigned one as a kind of understudy ready to jump in. Think through anything that might negatively affect your presentation and come up with some viable work-throughs.

Creating support materials

Assign one person (usually a graphic designer) to merge files together to create handouts, slides, and other visuals that have the same format, color coding, design elements, fonts, and themes, templates, and layouts. Spell-check and look for inconsistencies. You don't want your visuals looking like a patchwork cavalierly strung together at the last minute.

Years ago while working with a graphic design firm, we learned a tip for finding typos and other spelling or grammatical errors: Read your copy upside down, which forces you to read slowly and really see something you saw already dozens of times. Flip the printed copy around, as if you wanted someone on the other side of your desk to read it, and then start reading from the beginning. Of course, if you're editing on a computer, you have to rotate the screen or stand on your head.

Part VI

The Part of Tens

Enjoy an additional Part of Tens chapter online at www.dummies.com/extras/ innovativepresentations.

In this part . . .

✔ Discover ten characteristics of innovative presenters.

✔ Put the Laws of Communication Impact to good use.

Chapter 24

Ten Traits of Innovative Presenters

*T*hroughout this book, we give you strategies and tactics to create and deliver the most effective, innovative presentations you can. In this feel-good chapter we describe the positive traits that transcendent presenters exhibit and give you tips for accessing them in yourself when you give presentations. We list them in alphabetical order because one isn't more important than another. You may (probably will) find that several traits are an inherent part of your character and personality but that you need to develop others.

Coherence

Whether you know a little bit about a lot of topics or everything about one or two topics, you probably have too much information for your presentation. When preparing the outline and content, test each point and sentence to be sure it's necessary and adds value. An anecdote about your singing goldfish may be entertaining, but unless you need an example about unexpected talents, it probably doesn't fit in your presentation.

After you have whittled out the interesting-but-unnecessary tidbits from your presentation, consider the order in which you present your visuals and accompanying spoken words. Is there a logical progression?

Nancy Duarte, author of *Slide:ology,* analyzed dozens of great speeches from the Gettysburg Address to those given by Martin Luther King, Jr. and Steve Jobs and developed a chart that represents the composition and flow of all great speeches. In each memorable speech, the speaker states the current situation and the future situation — what will happen if the action the speaker proposes takes place — and moves back and forth between these two points of view throughout the speech. The speech progresses from the present state to a climactic conclusion. This format, which is applicable to most types of presentations, not only makes your presentation coherent, but also compelling and memorable.

Curiosity

A curious mind never suffers boredom. Keeping an open, eager-to-learn attitude toward the subject you're speaking about and the audience you're talking to leads to rich content that satisfies the audience's needs. Think of curiosity as the opposite of assuming — anytime you think you know a fact, let out your inner Curious George, and check the fact to confirm it — you may find a new aspect that deserves a mention.

Likewise, don't assume you know your audience, find out what problems they need solutions to, what their interests are, what benefits they seek. Talk to people you know in similar situations, or if it's possible, speak to select audience members themselves before giving your presentation and ask about their expectations, their doubts, and what it would take to agree to your call to action.

Enthusiasm

Charismatic speakers share a trait: enthusiasm. The audience mimics your behavior, so if you're enthusiastic about your topic, they will be too. When developing your presentation, look for the part that excites you, the part you want to share with the world, the part you're proud of — and don't be shy about sharing your enthusiasm.

Enthusiasm isn't a turn of phrase to trick people, like a huckster selling snake oil. Enthusiasm is that tingling sensation you get when you know your idea or solution can make a difference, no matter how big or small. Share that, and your audience will hang on every word.

Generosity

When you go to a concert and feel the presence of the performer on the stage, almost as if she's singing to you personally, you're feeling the generosity of the performer. Don't be stingy with your attention when you present. When you give your presentation you don't have to be anywhere or think of anything else in that short time. Focus on your audience, say what you have to say, and then actively listen in silence to their questions or comments before responding. Even if someone asks an uncomfortable question, respond sincerely and directly. When you acknowledge your audience, they perceive your generosity.

Don't answer a question with a statement you want to make but that doesn't respond to the question. (We describe how to handle questions of all types in Chapter 13.)

Honesty

Benjamin Franklin said, "Honesty is the best policy." We say "Honesty is the best policy for presentations." Don't promise things you can't deliver or a deadline you can't meet, and don't be afraid to say "I don't know" or "I hadn't thought of that question."

Prepare a response for those times when you don't have an answer ready for the question or comment posed, such as "I don't know, but I'll find out." If you're presenting as part of a team, identify team members who can answer different types of questions and defer to the appropriate person, such as "Steve Smith, our research director, can address that better than I can."

Humility

Humility liberates you. If you've done your best to prepare an engaging, informative, solution-providing presentation, the comments, questions, or even someone leaving the room aren't about you. Maybe the irate questioner got rear-ended on her way to the meeting or her boyfriend — who has the same tie you're wearing — left her the night before.

What's more, give credit where credit's due: Acknowledge those who assisted you and the sources of facts and figures that you present.

Innovative

It goes without saying that you should be innovative. While developing your messages and designing your visuals, squeeze your creative juices and look for places to present your points in a new or different way.

Keep in mind the adage "everything old is new again." Referring to presentations and advertising from 50 years ago — pre-PowerPoint — can point you in the right direction.

Preparedness

To borrow from the Boy Scouts, always be prepared in all aspects of your presentation. Be prepared for:

- ✔ **Questions:** Think about what your audience might ask and practice answering the potential questions when rehearsing. If the question seems of particular importance, put the answer directly in your presentation.

- ✔ **Audience needs:** Consider your audience's point of view and the call to action you want them to respond to, whether you want them to purchase your product or service, fund your startup, or donate to your charity. Figure out what you need to provide to obtain their agreement.

- ✔ **Technical difficulties:** Test your equipment a day or two before your presentation and keep back-up supplies in your office or take them with you if you're presenting offsite. Carry extra batteries plus power and extension cords, a copy of your visuals on an external drive, and a cellular modem if you need an Internet connection.

Punctuality

Show up for your meeting or conference ahead of time and plan to speak for at least five minutes less than your scheduled time. If time permits, finish your proposed visuals a week to ten days before your presentation, and make any necessary changes during rehearsals. Plan to have your final visuals ready a couple days before the scheduled event.

Rehearsed

We can't stress enough the importance of practice and rehearsal. You want to practice your public speaking skills as often as possible, even outside of your business in speaking clubs such as Toastmasters or by volunteering to share your knowledge in local community events.

When you have to make a presentation to your staff, a client, or a conference with peers, begin planning as early as possible and leave plenty of time to rehearse. When you see a dynamic speaker make a presentation, you can be sure many hours and days of rehearsal took place before the actual event.

Chapter 25

Almost Ten Reminders from the Laws of Communication Impact

In This Chapter
▶ Getting your audience to take notice and pay attention
▶ Engaging your audience with visual stimuli and verbal cues

*I*n Chapters 9 through 12, we discuss the Laws of Communication Impact in depth. In this chapter, we put all the laws in one place for quick reference and review of the most salient points.

Law of Primacy

Remember two important facts about the beginning of your presentation: It sets the tone for the rest of your speech, and — along with the ending — it's what the audience will remember.

With this in mind, start your presentation with a compelling statement, fact, or brief story told with enthusiasm and impact. You want to grab your audience's attention because even if you lose them for a little while in the middle (it happens), they'll be affected by your opening words.

Law of Emphasis and Intensity

You want to maintain your audience's attention for as long as possible. Follow your presentation introduction with a statement or series of statements that elicit emotion. You want to keep up the high energy that kicks off your presentation. The statements you make reinforce and provide evidence for the story or anecdote you use to begin your presentation. The way you communicate those statements highlights — or emphasizes — its importance. Use your voice, images, and/or video to add intensity to the statement at hand.

Law of Exercise and Engagement

You engage your audience through eye contact and comments that appeal to their personal, professional, or emotional interest. Now that you have a rapt audience, you want to invite them to participate, which can be as simple as prompting them to ask — or answer — questions or a more complex activity that requires them to use their smartphone or tablet to interact with the presentation or a physical exercise that gets them up and moving. The level and type of exercise or activity depends on the character of both your presentation and the audience, as well as the length of time and size of the group.

These tactics also work well when your audience's attention begins to lull.

Law of Interest

If you performed due diligence of audience analysis, you know what interests them. You know their worries and fears, their hopes and desires, as well as their current state of affairs. Each piece of information gives you a point of entry for addressing their interests, and when you address their interests, an audience sits up and pays attention. Introduce your statements with a few words about how what you're about to say relates to their interests.

Law of Effect

When you reach the point of your presentation where you state your call to action, using the Law of Effect is, well, effective. Describe the current state of the situation, and then describe the improved state — people will experience — that will come as a result of your offered solution. Clearly state the benefit (effect) the audience will receive if they agree to your call to action (cause).

Law of Recency

You probably know the phrase "save the best for last," and that's the idea behind this law. Because people remember what they saw and heard most recently, you want to make your closing memorable. Conclude your presentation with a story or visual that touches the interests of your audience and sums up your offer or solution.

Law of Repetition

At the risk of repeating ourselves, repetition — when used judiciously — drives your point home. Look for as many different ways as possible to say the same thing. This tactic not only reinforces your message, but if someone misses or misunderstands something the first time you say it, he's likely to hear it or understand it the second or third time you say it with different words.

For emphasis, repeat a statement verbatim but change your volume, for example growing from a whisper almost to a shout or stress a different word in the sentence each time you repeat it.

Index

About the Authors

Ray Anthony is a national leading authority in advanced presentation engineering, training, consulting, and executive coaching and a dynamic keynote speaker. He founded and is president of the Anthony Innovation Group in The Woodlands, Texas. Ray's clients include numerous Fortune 500 companies, the CIA, NASA, and the military. An expert in business creativity and innovation, he has a passion for helping people use creativity in ways that will boost their careers, bring extra prosperity to their organizations, and enrich their lives.

Ray has written over 60 articles on numerous topics in leading publications and authored seven books on sales and presentation techniques and organizational change and innovation. His books include *Killer Presentations with Your iPad* (co-authored with Bob LeVitus), *Talking to the Top,* and *F-A-S-T FORWARD . . . AND STEP ON IT!.* Ray has been showcased in various magazines and newspapers as well as a guest on numerous radio and television programs.

Early in his career, Ray sold complex computer systems for Burroughs Corporation and Digital Equipment Corporation (DEC) to international banks and financial institutions in New York City. He holds a BS and MA in economics with a focus on national productivity improvement strategies.

Barbara Boyd writes mostly about technology and occasionally about food, gardens, and travel. She's the co-author, with Joe Hutsko, of the first, second, and third editions of *iPhone All-in-One For Dummies* and the third and fourth editions of *Macs All-in-One For Dummies*. She's also the author of *AARP iPad: Tech to Connect* and *iCloud and iTunes Match In A Day For Dummies.* She co-authored (with Christina Martinez) *The Complete Idiot's Guide to Pinterest Marketing.* Barbara was a contributor to *Killer Presentations with Your iPad,* written by Ray Anthony and Bob LeVitus.

Barbara worked at Apple from 1985 to 1990 as the first network administrator for the executive staff. She then took a position as an administrator in the Technical Product Support group. She learned about meeting facilitation and giving presentations during that time and produced quarterly offsite meetings. She went on to work as a conference and event manager and later as an associate publisher at IDG (International Data Group). Before leaving the San Francisco Bay area, she worked as the Marketing Director for a small graphic design firm. In 1998, she left the corporate world to study Italian, write, and teach.

Presently, Barbara stays busy writing, keeping up with technology, tending her garden and olive trees. She divides her time between city life in Rome and country life on an olive farm in Calabria, the toe of Italy's boot.

Dedication

Ray dedicates this book to: To all those courageous, bold, and daring innovators who want to change the world and make a difference in it with one big, crazy idea at a time.

Barbara dedicates this book to: My dear husband, Ugo de Paula, who gives more than 20 presentations a year and provided inspiration and insight.

Authors' Acknowledgments

This book, like any book, is a collaboration of a many-membered team. Thanks go to Stacy Kennedy at Wiley for commissioning this book and helping shape the contents and title. A big thank you to project editor, Tim Gallan, the quickest e-mail draw in the East — we never waited more than five seconds for a response to our questions, and to our sharp copy editor, Kathleen Dobie, who polished our book to a fine shine with her concise edits. A shout out to the anonymous people at Wiley who contributed to this book — not just editorial and composition, but legal, accounting, even the person who delivers the mail. Working with the Dummies professionals has been a joy! We wouldn't have written this book without the nudge from our fab literary agent, Carole Jelen, who deserves kudos for so easily getting our book contracts and whose representation creates a foundation for the success of each of our books. Warm thanks go to communications expert Bill Lampton, PhD, and designer Leonard Broussard for their contributions, and actors Lori Van Delien and Alfred Castillo, Jr., who did a great job modeling for the photos in the book.

Ray adds: There are so many people who directly or indirectly helped me write this book, and I thank you all. Special, deep thanks to my friend and colleague Charlie Lindahl, one of the most innovative people I know, who assists me with the critical technologies portion of presentations. Charlie is a marvelous researcher who finds sunken treasures of information. I appreciate the dedication of April Canik who promotes me and my presentation offerings to new clients. Finally, I thank Almighty God for giving me the talent to write such a book with my wonderful co-author Barbara Boyd.

Barbara adds: Many thanks to Ray Anthony for his contagious enthusiasm, mild-to-wild ideas, and skill at putting his vast presentation experience into words.

Publisher's Acknowledgments

Acquisitions Editor: Stacy Kennedy

Senior Project Editor: Tim Gallan

Copy Editor: Kathleen Dobie

Technical Editor: Steve Dailey

Project Coordinator: Lauren Buroker

Cover Image: ©BlendImages/Alamy

Math & Science

Algebra I For Dummies,
2nd Edition
978-0-470-55964-2

Anatomy and Physiology
For Dummies, 2nd Edition
978-0-470-92326-9

Astronomy For Dummies,
3rd Edition
978-1-118-37697-3

Biology For Dummies,
2nd Edition
978-0-470-59875-7

Chemistry For Dummies,
2nd Edition
978-1-118-00730-3

1001 Algebra II Practice
Problems For Dummies
978-1-118-44662-1

Microsoft Office

Excel 2013 For Dummies
978-1-118-51012-4

Office 2013 All-in-One
For Dummies
978-1-118-51636-2

PowerPoint 2013
For Dummies
978-1-118-50253-2

Word 2013 For Dummies
978-1-118-49123-2

Music

Blues Harmonica
For Dummies
978-1-118-25269-7

Guitar For Dummies,
3rd Edition
978-1-118-11554-1

iPod & iTunes
For Dummies, 10th Edition
978-1-118-50864-0

Programming

Beginning Programming
with C For Dummies
978-1-118-73763-7

Excel VBA Programming
For Dummies, 3rd Edition
978-1-118-49037-2

Java For Dummies,
6th Edition
978-1-118-40780-6

Religion & Inspiration

The Bible For Dummies
978-0-7645-5296-0

Buddhism For Dummies,
2nd Edition
978-1-118-02379-2

Catholicism For Dummies,
2nd Edition
978-1-118-07778-8

Self-Help & Relationships

Beating Sugar Addiction
For Dummies
978-1-118-54645-1

Meditation For Dummies,
3rd Edition
978-1-118-29144-3

Seniors

Laptops For Seniors
For Dummies, 3rd Edition
978-1-118-71105-7

Computers For Seniors
For Dummies, 3rd Edition
978-1-118-11553-4

iPad For Seniors
For Dummies, 6th Edition
978-1-118-72826-0

Social Security
For Dummies
978-1-118-20573-0

Smartphones & Tablets

Android Phones
For Dummies, 2nd Edition
978-1-118-72030-1

Nexus Tablets
For Dummies
978-1-118-77243-0

Samsung Galaxy S 4
For Dummies
978-1-118-64222-1

Samsung Galaxy Tabs
For Dummies
978-1-118-77294-2

Test Prep

ACT For Dummies,
5th Edition
978-1-118-01259-8

ASVAB For Dummies,
3rd Edition
978-0-470-63760-9

GRE For Dummies,
7th Edition
978-0-470-88921-3

Officer Candidate Tests
For Dummies
978-0-470-59876-4

Physician's Assistant Exam
For Dummies
978-1-118-11556-5

Series 7 Exam For Dummies
978-0-470-09932-2

Windows 8

Windows 8.1 All-in-One
For Dummies
978-1-118-82087-2

Windows 8.1 For Dummies
978-1-118-82121-3

Windows 8.1 For Dummies
Book + DVD Bundle
978-1-118-82107-7

Available in print and e-book formats.

Available wherever books are sold. **For more information or to order direct visit www.dummies.com**